METALLICA

METALLICA

THE $24.95 BOOK

Ben Apatoff

Guilford, Connecticut

An imprint of Globe Pequot, the trade division of
The Rowman & Littlefield Publishing Group, Inc.
4501 Forbes Blvd., Ste. 200
Lanham, MD 20706
www.rowman.com

Distributed by NATIONAL BOOK NETWORK

British Library Cataloguing in Publication Information Available

Library of Congress Cataloging-in-Publication Data

Names: Apatoff, Ben, author.
Title: Metallica : the $24.95 book / Ben Apatoff.
Description: Lanham : Backbeat Books, 2021. | Includes bibliographical references
    and index. | Summary: "Metallica: The $24.95 Book features an in-depth look at
    Metallica's cultural significance with chapters devoted to each member, each album,
    touring, fashion, books, film, influences, fandom, and more, exploring the band's
    ideologies along the way"— Provided by publisher.
Identifiers: LCCN 2021001788 (print) | LCCN 2021001789 (ebook) | ISBN
    9781493061341 (paperback) | ISBN 9781493061358 (epub)
Subjects: LCSH: Metallica (Musical group) | Rock musicians—United States—
    Biography. | Heavy metal (Music)—United States—History and criticism. |
    LCGFT: Biographies.
Classification: LCC ML421.M48 A63 2021 (print) | LCC ML421.M48 (ebook) |
    DDC 782.42166092/2—dc23
LC record available at https://lccn.loc.gov/2021001788
LC ebook record available at https://lccn.loc.gov/2021001789

For Kyle, who insisted I start wearing earplugs to metal shows.

CONTENTS

CONTENTS

FOREWORD

In 2017, a review of Metallica's tour stop in Denver, Colorado, described the sold-out show as feeling "like a rally concocted by Leni Riefenstahl in *Triumph of the Will*." The combination of thousands of enthusiastic fans cheering in unison, fiery pyrotechnics, trademark militaristic drumming, and what was described as violent imagery projected behind them, drew comparisons with how Germans in the 1930s were drawn to Adolf Hitler's rallies. The writer suggested that the atmosphere was akin to providing a soundtrack to a far-right Republican rally. This, he wrote, in addition to the provocative visuals and rabid fandom, was "wholly American, for better or for worse, in its power and in its rage."

The politicization from journalists and news pundits about heavy metal music and aesthetics is nothing new. For the most part, negative class and religious connotations lead non–metal fans (in this case, it was evident that the writer was *not* a fan) to make sweeping generalizations, not understanding that the power, and, yes, the rage, attracts a myriad of people who positively feed off the energy that Metallica has offered the world since 1981. As I'm writing this, the current contentious political and social climate has raised the question that is always on the minds of music fans of various music styles: Do politics have a "place" in music? And how do heavy metal fans react to political ideologies, images, and lyricism?

The discussion has been a decades-long and contentious one for two reasons. First, the use of "politics" as a descriptor is subjective as the definition shapeshifts from individual to individual. This is often applied to insinuate a negative connotation, or as a catchphrase to dismiss critiques about lyrical content or discriminatory behavior. It is also used to defend or dismiss the bad behavior of a band they admire by accusing the victim of being "political" if the situation involves a sexist, homophobic, or racist interaction. If, for instance, a metal band member decides to punch out a fan or verbally assault someone during a live performance because of a perceived slight, cries of "freedom of speech" or "metal is supposed to be dangerous" are common responses. Discussing relevant and current social, political, and cultural events has always existed within heavy metal, a genre that relies on culturally transgressive thoughts and ideas for meaning-making and musical relevance. The chronicling of historical events, such as civil or global conflicts, found within Slayer's "Angel of Death" is acceptable because Auschwitz happened in occupied Poland and seemingly has no relevance in contemporary culture (but actually, it still does). However, definitions of what is *now* considered "political," such as critiques of racism, anti-Semitism, and misogyny within the lyrical and visual content, are usually accompanied by varying and often troubling levels of cognitive dissonance. No one wants to talk about it, hence the often-vicious response when a band even hints of publicly sharing an opinion that isn't about the music and is in opposition to the general opinions of their fanbase.

Metallica is undeniably the most successful heavy metal band in the world. Outside of their longevity—a rarity these days—they have been able to transition from young, broke, sweaty youths who probably (and regularly) used to drink their body weight in beer and Jack Daniels, to adults that demonstrate a remarkable amount of resilience to grow and flourish despite deaths, addictions, infighting, and emotional uncertainties. Now regarded as a foundational band within mainstream popular music culture (which has led to some consternation from metal fans who want to keep the music underground), Metallica has been musically and financially prosperous and generally immune to long-lasting controversies that could have caused irreparable damage to their career. However, I argue that despite the naysayers who want to keep "real-life" issues out, the band *is* political, but in staunch opposition to the abovementioned concert review, their politics are founded on the fact that they defy the cultural stereotyping of the band's genre, and continue to explore, experiment, and develop their musical palate while they reinvent and rediscover parts of who they are.

Scholars and music nerds alike have dissected the meanings behind Metallica's lyricism, including critiques of conservative policies, organized religion, and an exploration of the problematic factors of existentialism, but it was "One" from . . . *And Justice for All* which made an impact on me and many listeners who might have otherwise dismissed the band. Vocalist James Hetfield embodies the protagonist on his deathbed; emotionally and physically vulnerable, unable to speak, and waiting/wishing to die. Accompanied by a stark, mostly black-and-white video that relies on clips from the 1971 antiwar film *Johnny Got His Gun* to provide a visual narrative that captures senseless violence and the consequences of war through the eyes of a vulnerable soldier, which defied metal's stereotypically hypermasculine tropes. And maybe that is the key here: A heavy metal band that wanted to challenge the genre while still keeping it heavy, and to explore toxic elements of masculinity by revealing themselves through thoughtful and nuanced interludes. As historical narratives are a common lyrical hook, the antiwar critique from a first-person perspective made an impact within a country where war veterans are still struggling for proper medical and mental health services. That single propelled them from a talented yet underground thrash metal band to becoming a global phenomenon, as these musical and, later, personal reflections (*St. Anger*, *Lulu*) both shocked old-school metal fans and attracted new ones by challenging the notion that showing vulnerability in heavy metal is taboo (outside of glam metal, that is).

The second reason Metallica is political is that their financial success threatens the fantasy bubble that all heavy metal musical genres are known for—creating a positive atmosphere for those who use the loudness, extremity, and depictions of emotional and physical power to escape from the realities of day-to-day life. They are political because their later albums, which reflected the maturity of the band by offering motivating lyricism that featured James Hetfield's admissions about his sobriety (check out *Death Magnetic*) were a 180 from the in-your-face, fearless *Kill 'Em All* and *Ride the Lightning*. Creating heavy music within a commercial, capitalist music industry threatens to water down the authenticity of any musical style, and while Metallica is not the only band to make a substantial living off their art, there were fears that they would turn into another Kiss, or a nostalgic concert draw whose musical relevance has diminished. While the logos of other bands, such as Slayer, Iron Maiden, Judas Priest, and Megadeth, have also appeared on T-shirts, hats, and other items now found in retail stores around the world (and bootlegged versions sold at flea markets and online), they do not compare to the Metallica marketing machine, as there is a powerful and iconic purity to the name *Metallica* that created an indelible imprint in our consciousness. Everyone has heard of them.

Despite this, the musical and cultural innovators that made the Bay Area thrash metal scene foundational to heavy metal history, and because of the cherished early demos and recordings made when the band was hungry—both literally and figuratively—the decision to explore business opportunities to expand their brand was met with skepticism. These decisions raised a number of questions in terms of legitimacy: Can Metallica still be "metal" while taking advantage of mainstream opportunities? Will the music change for the worse in order to capitalize on attracting more listeners? And what does it mean when band members take on individual, "non-metal" projects, such as creating a horror festival (Kirk Hammett), producing a documentary (Robert Trujillo), or acting roles (James Hetfield)? Do they automatically lose their street cred?

Despite critiques about "selling-out," Metallica as a global phenomenon has benefited heavy metal as a genre and culture, as they have brought relevance to music that has always been judged through the eyes of classism. People have started metal bands because they were inspired by their parents' Metallica albums, and the audiences at the sold-out concert stadiums are multigenerational. In the 1990s Black, brown, and Asian kids that might have not had access to the genre within their communities were turned onto the band through after-school cable video TV programs, such as VH1's *That Metal Show*, or *Headbangers Ball*, in which Metallica's self-titled 1991 album served as a gateway for many in discovering the genre. Heavy rotation on regular and satellite radio coupled with sharing CDs with their schoolyard friends allowed a culturally diverse generation to explore Metallica's music and memorize Hammett and Hetfield's guitar riffs for inspiration.

As mentioned earlier in this foreword, the current political climate has challenged the promotion of inclusivity of the genre. "True" fandom and legitimacy has devolved back to the archetype of an authentic "metalhead" as being a heterosexual white man, even though Metallica has always been culturally diverse. The participation of women and ethnocultural minorities as musicians is often treated with suspicion and contempt, and fans of color are often not perceived as "real" fans. Despite mainstream heavy metal bands creating a gateway to a new listener demographic, racial, religious, and cultural divisions magnified by populism and tribalism make attending shows—direct-to-fan ticket and merchandise sales are crucial, especially to independent, underground bands—more difficult, as some are reluctant to go to shows where they will be the minority. This is why concert reviews that use right-wing authoritarianism as a descriptor are so dangerous.

Challenging the long-held notion that heavy metal is only for a certain cultural demographic by making their music as widely accessible as possible is a political act in itself. Instead of representing America's power and rage in a negative light, Metallica's brand of politics breaks down walls that exclude, offering the music to people who utilize the aggression and energy to thrive. So yeah, Metallica is political. Heavy metal is political. And politics do have a place in heavy metal.

Laina Dawes is the author of What Are You Doing Here? A Black Woman's Life and Liberation in Heavy Metal *(Bazillion Points, 2012, 2020). She is also a music journalist and cultural critic who has written for several print and online publications, such as* The Wire, *The Deciblog,* Metal Edge, The Guardian, Toronto Star, *Invisible Oranges, Bandcamp, and many others. Originally from Toronto, Canada, she currently resides in New York City where she is completing a PhD in ethnomusicology at Columbia University.*

ACKNOWLEDGMENTS

"Roaring Hella Mega-Stylin' Cheers, Danke, Tak, Merci, Skol, Ta, Right on Bro Dudez, Fucken a rights baby man!!!" . . . . THANX TO:* My stone cold crazy friends and family, my hero Katherine Turman for her help and encouragement, Laina for writing a better fore-word than I could have imagined, John, Barbara, and Carol at Rowman & Littlefield, Robert and Bernadette at Backbeat Books, Brianna Westervelt and Emily Natsios, Rob and Frank at Metal Injection, Vince and Axl at MetalSucks, Letitia and the Morbid Anatomy Museum, Steve Thrasher, Sarah Anne Wharton, D. X. Ferris, Tim Ford, Lupe Lozano, Andrew Buonfiglio, Richard Contreras, Joe Berlinger, Adam Dubin, Michael Alago, Bryan Steele, Nick Monteleone, Sylvia, Eat, Katie and Detective Nerses, William Lent, John Sherman for his editorial brilliance, Gabri-elle Moss and Margaret Eby for their wisdom and writing inspiration, Saint Vitus, Hank's Saloon (RIP), Lucky 13 Saloon, the Brooklyn Public Library, James, Lars, Kirk, Cliff, Jason, Robert, and, of course, Metallica fans all over the world.

This book would not exist without Michelle Campagna, who was wear-ing my *Garage Days Re-Revisited* shirt when she said yes.

*Some of you recognized this quote from the *Master of Puppets* liner notes. But did you know it's also one of the first documented uses of the adverb "hella," sixteen years before it made its way to the *Oxford English Diction-ary*? Metallica, ever the trailblazers.

INTRODUCTION

"We're just questioning a few things, you know."

—Lars Ulrich

"I feel like maybe they're ahead of everybody in a way we can't imagine," party metal hero Andrew W. K. said of Metallica in a 2003 *Rolling Stone* interview. "They're on a page that hasn't even been printed yet. They're working on paper that hasn't been made from the tree that hasn't been cut down yet."

With that insight, Andrew may have best summed up why, after selling over 125 million albums worldwide, packing stadiums for decades, winning numerous awards, inductions, and other prestige, and receiving endless coverage in ink, video, and broadband, Metallica deserves another book. Their status as the biggest, most influential, most fought-over metal band seems permanent. The Black Album consistently outsells new releases and is now the highest-selling album of the SoundScan era. Musicians who weren't born when "One" crashed *Headbangers Ball* cite Metallica as their biggest influence. Metallica get by far the most metal coverage in mainstream publications, and their stories get the most hits on metal news sites, even on (especially on?) the sites that make the most fun of them. Their tours gross well into the hundreds of millions and their new albums always top the charts. They're the biggest gateway band for new metalheads, and the go-to metal band for people who don't like metal, like

Miles Davis for jazz or Johnny Cash for country. They're the only metal band your parents could name even if you didn't blare their songs or wear their shirts. They're the standard that upcoming metal bands are graded by. "The next Metallica" is as much of a discussion point among metalheads as "the next Dylan" is among rock fans.

As recently as 2016, Metallica's music was added to the National Recording Registry of the Library of Congress, for works that are "culturally, historically, or aesthetically significant," making them the first and thus far only metal band to be given this honor. That same year, Metallica's *Hardwired . . . to Self-Destruct* was the world's highest selling rock album. Metal news site MetalSucks found in 2018 that Metallica stories generated more traffic than any other metal band in the previous five years, beating out Slipknot, Slayer, Megadeth, and Ghost, covering an era in which Metallica released a total of one studio album. A 2019 *Pollstar* study named Metallica as the biggest touring band of all time, with nearly 22.1 million total tickets sold and $1.4 billion in revenue since 1982. They've performed in forty-eight countries and on all seven continents. Bands such as Apocalyptica and Beatallica, whom Metallica has respectively performed with and praised, have created successful careers just by playing Metallica songs. Rodrigo y Gabriela shot to worldwide fame in part on the strength of their acoustic Metallica covers, fulfilling the flamenco potential of "One," "Orion," and "Battery" (sometimes with guest bassist Robert Trujillo, who's been known to join them onstage).

At an age when most major artists start winding down, Metallica are breaking their own touring, revenue, and streaming records, and garnering more press. Despite their sometimes-contentious history with the internet, it's clear no amount of cyberspace can replace or overthrow Metallica. The principles of metal, punk, and hard rock have been drastically rewritten by this metalhead quartet who built a musical and cultural empire with their own rules.

Yet decades after smashing through the boundaries with the last song on a little-heard *Metal Massacre* compilation with pressings that misspelled their name ("Mettallica") and their then-bassist's name ("Ron McGouney") in 1982, Metallica stays ahead of their peers and followers. They pioneered the idea that American metal could exist, and more important that it could be awesome, tearing out of San Francisco at a time when

100 percent of the world's best metal acts were English. Their innovations, from dressing like their fans to serrated logos to covering punk songs, are now unshakable metal tropes. They so thoroughly changed the idea that punks and metalheads could get along that it's hard to believe they were ever enemies. Imagine CBGB horror punks White Zombie never getting their minds and music flipped by *Ride the Lightning*, or the Misfits' "Last Caress" going out of print on the *Beware* EP without Metallica's *The $5.98 E.P.—Garage Days Re-Revisited*.

Many of Metallica's career choices are baffling. They've built a career on curveballs, making decisions that would destroy lesser bands. Fans have been up in arms against Metallica's choices ever since they planted the acoustic "Fade to Black" onto the otherwise pulverizing *Ride the Lightning*. Who would've guessed they were on their way to cutting their hair, suing their fans, publicizing their group therapy, and teaming up with Lou Reed for one of the most derided (yet misunderstood) albums of the century? "Metallica actually did what other rock bands only aspire to do," wrote Chuck Klosterman in the *New York Times*. "By ignoring trends, it became immune to cultural change." Notice the pronoun is *it*, not *they*. Metallica are guys, individually, but Metallica is also a force.

Thus, Metallica marches on as if glam metal, grunge, alternative, grindcore, black metal, death metal, nu metal, metalcore, doom metal, djent, or any other trend never happened. Astonishingly, they've done so by bucking the very trends they set and perfected. Metallica brought thrash metal to the mainstream, and then abandoned it on the Black Album. They crossed over into superstardom with "Enter Sandman," then slowed into grooves on *Load*. They won back thrash purists with *Death Magnetic* and sent them running away with *Lulu*. "Who we are, ask forever," James bellows in "Through the Never," coming closer to elucidating his band than any number of rock critics. Metallica asks forever, examining itself, constantly changing as a result. Is this the same band that wrote *Master of Puppets? . . . And Justice for All? Hardwired . . . to Self-Destruct?* If not, how can those changes be reflected in the music?

Metallica does not give easy answers or questions. No search engine is sufficient for the biggest and most controversial metal band of all time. A curious fan can sift through endless encyclopedias, databases, comments sections, and fan pages without getting a better sense of which Metallica song was Kurt Cobain's favorite, or why the "Hero of the Day" demo is called "Mouldy," or why James yells "Pancakes!" in *Metallica Through the Never*. There are more websites cataloging Metallica's discography, tablature, lineups, and lyrics than I care to count, but Metallica raises questions that run deeper than those. Metallica-spiked debates show no sign of dying down. James Baldwin wrote, "The artist cannot and must not take anything for granted, but must drive to the heart of every answer and expose the question the answer hides." Metallica serves that purpose as well as any artists known to humanity.

Or, as Hetfield reflected on *Marc Maron*, "I have no answers. I've got a lot of questions. . . . When someone identifies with your question, it's better than them telling you the answer. I identify with that question, 'I don't know, let's find out together or let's just ponder it together.' That's a higher power showing up to me."

By exploring the questions Metallica raises, through music, film, artwork, and more, we come closer to seeing why Metallica stays the world's biggest metal band, and why their best music is still the best metal. They've given us more room for discussion and interpretation than any other metal artist, only getting more abstract and harder to pin down the more we know about them. Musically, lyrically, and artistically, they've stayed unpredictable, with mixed but never dull results. Long after their contemporaries started writing inferior versions of their early successes, Metallica is still capable of surprising us, four decades into their storied career. In *Metallica: The $24.95 Book*, we'll take an in-depth look at some of those surprises, searching for Metallica wherever they may roam, on a different page from the rest of us.

1

MISSING ONE
INSIDE OF ME

The Controversial Birth of Metallica

"We started to see he was on a road to killing, possibly, all of us."

—James Hetfield

The greatest metal band in history started with the most controversial event in any metal career. Metallica had a name, they had shows, and they even had a demo (*No Life 'Til Leather*, taking its name from Motörhead's *No Sleep 'Til Hammersmith*), but they weren't yet the classic lineup that started changing the world on their first record. Sure, Metallica's biggest controversy got nary a headline when it occurred in 1983, and events like Dimebag Darrell's murder or the Norwegian black metal church burnings are more notorious. But everyone with any sense agrees the murders and church burnings were tragedies. When we're talking controversy—something that sparks heated, endless debate and leaves us with unanswerable questions—nothing in metal history has caused more arguments than the lineup of Metallica's first record. Even Ozzy biting the heads off small animals, for all its insanity, offends and impresses all the right people.

On the morning of April 11, 1983, Metallica wakes up their lead guitarist Dave Mustaine. They're in New York after two city shows, weeks away from recording their first record and blowing a hole through the world's consciousness with *Kill 'Em All*. Mustaine, the son of an abusive household and a part-time pot dealer, has cowritten four of the songs that will make this record. His rock star power is already undeniable, from virtuosic guitar playing to prodigious songwriting and an unforgettable stage presence. At twenty-one he's the band's oldest, the first one who could legally get beer for his mates, and about to be first in a long line of authority figures Metallica will overthrow. His musical brilliance and thick, bright red hair will make him one of metal's most recognizable figures, as will the sharp tongue he's already displayed in his Metallica stage banter (sample Dave: "Hi fuckers! How many of you have a middle finger?"). Early live reviews have singled him out as the band's star, and he dominates their interviews. "I'd live and die for our music," he tells one reporter. Mustaine is destined for greatness, stardom, and infamy. But not with Metallica.

Rhythm guitarist James Hetfield and drummer Lars Ulrich have been secretly planning to give Mustaine the boot. While Dave sleeps in the U-Haul, James and Lars are playing tapes of other bands, listening for lead guitarists. They've already bought Dave's bus ticket for the four-day trek back to California. James has been designated to wake up Dave and tell him the news. At twenty, James has already replaced his father with himself and his family with his band. Now he has to replace his band's star. By later accounts, Dave is too tired, stunned, and hungover to protest when his bandmates break the news and drop him off at Port Authority for the long ride home. The entire dismissal takes about forty-five minutes.

Ten days earlier, Metallica had gotten their sound engineer, Mark Whitaker, to call up the guitarist of the band he managed, Exodus, to ask if he wanted to audition for Metallica. Guitarist Kirk Hammett, an avid *No Life 'Til Leather* fan, thought this was an April Fools' joke. In Exodus, he had opened for Metallica at the Old Waldorf in San Francisco, and his first meeting with Lars included the drummer stripping naked backstage in front of him (Kirk guessed it was "a European thing"). But Kirk was interested and scraped enough money together to fly to New York. He showed up for his 6 p.m. audition to find the band passed out ("How rock 'n' roll," thought Kirk). But when they woke up, he nailed "Seek & Destroy," complete with a solo, and James knew this band would be all right. On April 16, 1983, five days after Dave's firing, Metallica played their first show with Kirk Hammett, at Showplace in Dover, New Jersey. It's the last show where they'll play "The Mechanix," Dave's signature Metallica song, which over the next few weeks they'll work into "The Four Horsemen" with Kirk's solo, James' bridge, and new lyrics. Within a month, they're recording *Kill 'Em All* with Kirk.

There's no way of knowing this at the time, but Mustaine is on his way to forming Megadeth, for many years Metallica's greatest thrash metal rivals and the second highest-selling band in the classic "Big Four" (rounded out by Slayer and Anthrax). He'll release records every metalhead should own and play to huge audiences of dedicated fans. He'll be one of the most influential figures in metal, but he'll never escape Metallica's shadow. Early Megadeth records, conveniently alphabetized ahead of Metallica in record store "M" sections, came with a sticker advertising the appearance of a former Metallica guitarist. Nearly every Mustaine interview or Megadeth article brings up Metallica, even ones where he insists he doesn't want to talk about the other M-word. Mustaine's always entertaining, sometimes trustworthy autobiography, *Mustaine: A Heavy Metal Memoir*, starts with the sentence, "James Hetfield, who used to be one of my best friends, as close as a brother, once observed with some incredulity that I must have been born with a horseshoe up my ass." For years he could seldom play Megadeth's "Mechanix" live without first calling out the band most of his fans learned that progression from. In 1999, he was still wounded enough to tell reporters he named Megadeth's album *Risk* after something Lars Ulrich had said about him. (Dave: "He thinks I am talented but that I should take more risks, which I took as good advice.") On Megadeth's *Behind the Music* episode, Mustaine reveals that being kicked out of Metallica was worse for him than watching his father die. He has declared his Metallica grudge over and restarted it, cursed out and apologized to his former bandmates, loving Metallica and hating them. But he can't get them off his mind.

Mustaine's complaints about Metallica are the second most famous thing about him. Reading through decades of Mustaine interviews, one finds Dave insisting Metallica stole his song ideas, that Megadeth writes better music, that Metallica are only more popular because they sold out, that Metallica would have been bigger and better if they'd never fired him, that he slept with Kirk's girlfriend, that James ripped off his stage persona, that Megadeth is faster and heavier, that James really wanted to fire Lars, and worse, to anyone who will put a microphone in front of him. "I already smashed James in the mouth one time, and Lars is scared of his own shadow. . . . Kirk is a yes-man," Dave mouths off in an early interview, in which he also claims to have written most of *Kill 'Em All*. "I might as well still be in the band because they're still using my music." Dave's assertions that Metallica would be screwed when they ran out of his riffs turned out to be unfounded.

Metallica made the morally dubious decision to keep some of Mustaine's songwriting on *Kill 'Em All* and *Ride the Lightning* (and *Master of Puppets*, if you believe Dave, who insists the middle riff of "Leper Messiah" is worked from his "The Hills Run Red"). But by keeping some of Dave's riffs while ditching his lyrics and solos, Metallica showed razor focus on writing the best songs. Mustaine was an irrefutable talent, but at twenty-one he was a puerile lyricist. He'd get much better on *Peace Sells . . . But Who's Buying?*, but the lyrics to "Mechanix" and even the rest of Megadeth's ripping debut *Killing Is My Business . . . and Business Is Good!* (seen by many fans as a response to *Kill 'Em All*) didn't reach *Kill 'Em All* standards. "The Call of Ktulu," Metallica's last song with a Mustaine credit, was originally titled "When Hell Freezes Over" before Metallica started working themselves away from metal clichés like Hell and Satan. Dave's original "Jump in the Fire" lyrics, before James' rewrite, read like a cutup of *Penthouse* letters. But Dave's influence is undeniable. James even sings like Mustaine imitating Diamond Head's Sean Harris on early Metallica bootlegs, to the point where to this day demos of songs like "Jump in the Fire" are mislabeled with Mustaine vocals. In shows leading to *Kill 'Em All*, James mixed out Dave's lyrics before replacing them all on the album. Losing Dave meant James not only stepping into Dave's role, but becoming more James in the process.

Comparing Dave's Metallica songs to Megadeth, it's clear Dave grew into himself by leaving, too. "I don't really know that when Megadeth started that it was anything other than just pure revenge," Dave told VH1. For all the shit fans give Mustaine for getting kicked out of the world's biggest metal band (in *Some Kind of Monster* Dave says kids still yell "Metallica!" when they recognize him), he had the best possible response—form the second-biggest metal band. Could there be a *Peace Sells* if he weren't trying to out-thrash *Ride the Lightning*, a *Rust in Peace* if he weren't trying to outplay . . . *And Justice for All* (enlisting original *Justice* producer Mike Clink), or a *Countdown to Extinction* if he weren't trying to outsell the Black Album? However, James learned leading a band onstage because he had to after Mustaine left. The default singer was now the default performer. Megadeth perfected thrash on *Rust in Peace*, but Metallica had already perfected metal.

People love to argue to Metallica vs. Megadeth, and you can like them both, even if only one gets to be your favorite. But people also argue Metallica vs. AC/DC, or Metallica vs. Guns N' Roses, or Metallica vs. Nirvana. Nobody compares these bands to Megadeth, or anyone else in the Big Four, because with Metallica we're debating a metal band, but also a cultural icon. Megadeth changed metal, but never crossed over in the way Metallica has. For years, Dave has watched his Megadeth bandmates cite Metallica's influence in interviews (guitarist Marty Friedman: "I was just blown away [by Metallica]. I was shocked, I was happy, I was a bit jealous"), and even Dave's longtime first mate bassist Dave Ellefson sings their praises. "We owe everything to Metallica," Ellefson said in 2020. "Those guys broke down the doors for every one of us—Anthrax, Slayer. Bands today—Lamb of God, Pantera—none of this would have happened without Metallica. . . . The stuff that they're able to do and the size and the scope of which they were able to break those doors down, it changed all of our lives—as musicians, as fans, as everything."

Even among the Big Four, where Megadeth was sometimes seen as Metallica's top rival (the Rolling Stones to Metallica's Beatles is not a bad comparison), Megadeth seems further behind Metallica with the passage of time. At the fourteen Big Four shows that ran 2010–2011, putting Metallica, Megadeth, Anthrax, and Slayer together onstage for the first time, second billing went to Slayer. Slayer was too extreme to sell as many records as nineties Megadeth, but their stature increased with *Reign in Blood*'s growing influence, making them Metallica's more sinister top rival. Metallica vs. Megadeth these days is more like the Beatles vs. the Who (Slayer being the Stones and Anthrax the Kinks). The Metallica vs. Slayer as metal's Beatles vs. Stones argument was proposed as early as queercore heroes Pansy Division's 1996 song "Headbanger," in which the narrator picks up and bones a Guitar Center metalhead ("He turned on his CD player / Did I prefer Metallica or Slayer"). Inquisitive metalheads might wonder why the song's solo, credited to "Al Shatonia," sounds curiously like the work of one Kirk Lee Hammett.

An entire book could be dedicated to the unanswerable questions raised by Mustaine's firing. What would have happened if he'd stayed? Who's telling the truth about the incidents leading up to the firing? What would *Rust in Peace* sound like with James singing? How would the *Peace Sells* riffs sound on *Master of Puppets*? Is that "Hangar 18" arpeggio from "The Call of Ktulu"? Would Lars have eventually been fired instead of Dave? Would Exodus, with prodigious guitarist Kirk Hammett, have sneaked their way into the Big Four? What if the Beatles fired Pete Townshend instead of Pete Best? Is it better to reign in Megadeth than serve in Metallica?

More than rivaling Metallica, Mustaine inevitably adds to Metallica's legacy, the same way Dave Grohl's continued success enhances Nirvana's. The most famous thing Mustaine has done this century is appear in *Some Kind of Monster*, making a heartfelt case to Lars over his dismissal. Directors Joe Berlinger and Bruce Sinofsky filmed three hours with Dave and Lars on Dave's fortieth birthday on September 13, 2001. Just weeks earlier, Dave had released a supportive message about James' rehab, though it may have stung that James was given a second chance. "Am I happy being number two? No," Dave tells Lars. "Do I wish it was 1982 all over again, and you guys woke me up and said, 'Hey, Dave, you need to go to AA?' Yeah. I'd give anything for that chance." Dave asked the cameras to be turned off three times, and eventually wanted the scene removed, refusing to let the filmmakers use Megadeth's music in the final cut.

He's seemingly softened on Metallica since *Some Kind of Monster*, more at ease with his position in both Megadeth and Metallica's stories despite the occasional lashing out (he prevented an official, expanded *No Life 'Til Leather* release over legal issues in 2017). But no matter what his take is this week, Dave's year and a half in the life of Metallica follows him to even Megadeth's biggest stages. When Megadeth won their first Grammy after twelve nominations, the Academy celebrated by playing "Master of Puppets" while Megadeth walked up to accept their award. (Dave responded on Twitter, "Ah, you can't blame 'em for not being able to play Megadeth.") When Mustaine passes, all of his obituaries will mention his time in Metallica, probably in the lede. It's hard to see him having an equivalent presence in Metallica tributes.

NO LIFE 'TIL LEATHER

"As much as a problem as Dave was, he was still the most charismatic guy in Metallica," remembers band friend Ron Quintana. "He was way ahead of James at that time. He was the guy who would yell out between every song and get people involved and into the show." More important, he was a musical tornado, joining Metallica in February 1982 after one rehearsal. Metallica had formed the previous October, after seventeen-year-old Lars had placed weekly ads in *The Recycler*, the same LA classified that would introduce Slash to Izzy Stradlin and Eric Erlandson to Courtney Love. "Drummer looking for other metal musicians to play with. Tygers of Pan Tang, Diamond Head, and Iron Maiden." Lars had no patience for drum lessons, and started looking for guitarists to play with before he could keep time. People use this story to mock Lars' ability, but like many great artists he valued chemistry over proficiency. Over in Southeast LA, guitarists Hugh Tanner and James Hetfield looked for musicians every week and kept seeing the same guy.

"My ability on the drums at that time was basically zero. I think they were secretly laughing at me," Lars said of the first rehearsal. It was no secret. Lars' one-cymbal kit kept falling over, to the point where James and Hugh wondered if he'd ever drummed before. James remembered it resembling the kit Animal had on *The Muppet Show*. But Lars was taken with James and worked to get a second rehearsal. In VH1's Metallica episode of their *When __ Ruled the World* series (changed just once from its usual format to *When Metallica Rules the World*, because Metallica still rules), James smiles remembering his earliest days with Lars. "His drumming was not amazing, but he had this drive." Young James didn't plan on inviting Lars back. But how many other kids were you going to find in SoCal who listened to Motörhead?

Lars learned that Brian Slagel, a twenty-year-old Sears employee and the founder of indie record label Metal Blade, had borrowed $800 from his aunt to finance a Metal Blade sampler album called *Metal Massacre*. Lars told Slagel he had a band for the album, and called James to tell him he could get him a spot on *Metal Massacre*. Lars had drastically improved by his second rehearsal with James. *Metallica* was the title of an obscure English reference book on metal bands, hard to find in the United States, putting Metallica in the running with the Velvet Underground for the best band to name themselves after a forgotten book. James and Lars were hardly a band, but James had a song, "Hit the Lights," with his previous band Leather Charm, which he rewrote with Lars and recorded the night before the deadline for *Metal Massacre*. Lloyd Grant, a Jamaican lead guitarist, was found through a *Recycler* ad and brought in to solo. Lars borrowed $50 for the reel-to-reel transfer and handed in the tape. The resulting album, Metal Blade's first record, was a compilation featuring Pandemonium, Malice, a then unknown Ratt, and several other long-forgotten bands that strove to stand out in the dawn of American metal's breakthrough. As with most promo compilations, it's a pretty boring album that could barely qualify as a freebie—until a smattering of distortion introduces the last song.

Long before they had more worldly and introspective views, Metallica wrote about what they knew best—playing faster and louder than anyone else. James promises to kick some ass tonight in the first verse, which in hindsight is one of Metallica's biggest understatements. Metallica sounded like they might self-destruct by the end of the tape, and with Dave Mustaine they almost did.

Metal Massacre sold about 30,000 over the next few years, mainly on the strength of Metallica. James remembered a fan telling him the rhythms on "Hit the Lights" didn't sound tight, something he made sure no one could accuse him of when Metallica rerecorded it for *Metal Massacre II*. The release of "Hit the Lights" has false starts, just like the song does, a sign that even with the best song on the first-ever Metal Blade release, Metallica isn't satisfied. Some fans, such as future Celtic Frost growler Tom G. Warrior, bought the first two *Metal Massacre* records to have both versions of "Hit the Lights." There was nowhere to hear anything like it.

"While the rest of us were still finding ourselves musically and creatively, you had the sense that Metallica already knew," said Slayer's Kerry King. Slayer had heard the first two *Metal Massacre* records and were inspired to write something heavier for *Metal Massacre III*, which ended up being album opener "Aggressive Perfector," Slayer's first great song, which, in its earliest form, took its intro from and rewrote "Hit the Lights." But what really blew away Kerry was the glaring lead guitarist he saw at the Woodstock in Anaheim, shredding incredible riffs and solos without even looking at his hands.

How bad did it have to get for Metallica to kick Dave out? Metallica were a volatile band. At 2 a.m. on Monday, August 2, 1982, at the Troubadour, Metallica were cheered into their first-ever encore. Lars celebrated by playing the under-rehearsed "Helpless" instead of the planned "Blitzkrieg," showing off his drum intro, and James punched him in the gut. But Dave drunkenly wrecked the homes, hotel rooms, and friendships that Metallica counted on for places to crash on tour. He berated other bands from the audience. There are varying accounts of a fight with James over Dave's pit bulls jumping on Ron McGovney's Pontiac, but the consensus seems to be that Dave punched James in the mouth and knocked Ron to the ground. Dave was fired that day and rehired the next. "He was a very magnetic personality, very good looking, he had great hair," Lars recalled. "He had a lot of friends, of both sexes." Torben Ulrich, Lars' father who famously does not suffer fools, called Dave "always friendly, very courteous and quite articulate" in a 2006 fan interview.

But weeks after getting back into Metallica, Dave ruined Ron's bass by drunkenly pouring beer onto the pickups. Ron, whose connection to Mötley Crüe had earned Metallica an opening spot for Saxon, was already feeling used by the band for housing and transportation more than his playing. He left Metallica shortly afterward. Ron thought James would go back to his factory job and Lars would move back to Europe after Dave was fired. The other boys weren't exactly Stryper, camped out in Mark Whitaker's El Cerrito home, the "Metallica Mansion," with empty bottles and metal mags on the floor, the furniture moved out onto the lawn so it wouldn't get smashed at parties. Lars has said the three most important factors of early Metallica were music, alcohol, and girls, in that order. James and Lars shared a room with twin beds, and Dave slept on the couch. Visitors lived there for days on end, in a communal atmosphere reminiscent of Lars' boyhood home, bringing their dogs to roam free and running off when the neighbors called the cops complaining about noise or worse. James and Exodus' Paul Baloff were almost arrested for shattering streetlights with a rolling pin, but Paul's bandmate Rob McKillop took the hit so James wouldn't miss the *Kill 'Em All* tour. Metallica needed him.

And Dave needs Metallica. "I think that James and I are very much the same man. I think that we grabbed an angel, split him in half, and both of us are possessing that power," he told *Music Connection* magazine in 1983. It's a power Dave expresses in competition, envy, hatred, inspiration, and admiration, often sounding as focused on Metallica's music as his own. But every word Dave's had about Metallica may be best summed up by a quote from 2009's *Bang Your Head*. "I wanted to show [Metallica] up. As hard as I tried, though, I just couldn't do it."

Dave found enough peace to partake in the Big Four tour, joining Metallica onstage for all-star encore covers of Diamond Head's "Am I Evil?" and the Misfits' "Die, Die My Darling." More personally, he showed up to Metallica's thirtieth anniversary shows, closing the final of four nights at the Fillmore in San Francisco by playing five *Kill 'Em All* songs with his old bandmates. Dave topped a list of guests that included Jason Newsted, Lou Reed, Ozzy Osbourne, Jerry Cantrell, Bob Rock, Diamond Head, Glenn Danzig, Apocalyptica, Gary Rossington, Marianne Faithfull, and King Diamond. Kirk let Dave take the solos and they closed the four-day celebration with every living ex-Metallica member joining the band for "Seek & Destroy." Dave's chops are enhanced by sobriety, and maybe a need to compete with Kirk. Decades after he broke a string two minutes into the first song at the first Metallica gig ("Hit the Lights"), he plays with the same spontaneity and greater professionalism, as much of a Metallica obsessive as any of the fans screaming in shock at the historic moment. He hasn't cooled down entirely, still dropping the occasional barb in the press. With Megadeth still one of metal's best live bands, who'd expect him to start relaxing? But his acceptance and enjoyment of a legacy in two of metal's greatest bands seems more comfortable. "I was a violent drunk, and I was more drunk than sober," he reflected in *Louder Than Hell*. "Looking back, I would have asked me to leave, too."

For just about any other metal band, kicking out Dave Mustaine would be the most notable thing they ever did. But Metallica is not like any other metal band.

2

FIND THE HERO
OF THE DAY

Bands That Shaped Metallica

*"There's this machismo thing where guys don't want to admit
to their buddies that they don't know the song. But hopefully
they'll find out from someone what the song was and go dis-
cover the band that wrote it."*

—James Hetfield

Metallica wear their influences on their sleeves, T-shirts, jackets, in interviews, on touring lineups, on B-sides, *Garage* records, special guest appearances onstage, an official video game, and pretty much any-where people can see Metallica. Reading through interviews, Metallica's musical inspirations seem limitless, a growing list of artists that, in Metal-lica's story, shows a band that thrives on competition. Long after Metal-lica's success stopped being a surprise, Metallica shared that success with the artists that inspired them. How many people found the Misfits, Diamond Head, or Killing Joke through *The $5.98 E.P.—Garage Days Re-Revisited*? Who knew what a great song "Breadfan" by Budgie was until James Hetfield's downstrokes invigorated it? Who else could hear "Turn the Page" and think that saxophone lick would sound a lot sicker on slide guitar? If you're ever lucky enough to see Discharge, note how many fans weren't born when *Hear Nothing See Nothing Say Nothing* dropped. Guess how many of them learned "Free Speech for the Dumb" and "The More I See" from *Garage Inc.*

Anyone with a passing interest in hard rock and metal can hear how Metallica shaped the future of music. But perhaps just as remarkable is how they reshaped music's past—how, by lending their spotlight to the artists that mattered to them, Metallica effectively changed which punk and metal bands became cool, influential, important, popular, and acclaimed. The Misfits' skull logo appears on an endless amount of merchandise, inspired an intra-band lawsuit, and is more famous than anything else the Misfits have done, in no small part because Metallica wore Misfits shirts and covered their songs. Motörhead won their only Grammy thirty years into their career for a 2004 cover of Metallica's "Whiplash," a song that sounds as much like a Motörhead single as "Bomber" or "No Class." Cult bands like Diamond Head, Discharge, Sweet Savage, the Anti-Nowhere League, Holocaust, Blitzkrieg, and the Jerry Only–led Misfits all reunited after Metallica renewed interest in their songs by covering them. Reading over the songs considered for *The $5.98 E.P.—Garage Days Re-Revisited*, one wonders what kind of a career Japanese hard rockers Bow Wow or East Bay hardcore punks Fang could have had if Metallica recorded "Signal Fire" or "The Money Will Roll Right In," instead of "Last Caress" or "Crash Course in Brain Surgery."

Shortly after . . . *And Justice for All*'s release, Lars Ulrich combed through a London phone book to find artists from twenty-nine bands including Girlschool, Saxon, Vardis, Trespass, and Angel Witch to ask permission to release their music on a compilation for Caroline Records. Some of the bandmates hated each other and didn't want to cooperate, but Lars persisted and the result, 1990's two-disc *New Wave of British Heavy Metal '79 Revisited*, is one of the best encapsulations of NWOBHM, and until the internet age the easiest way to find most of these bands' music. "The English bands were more about playing what they wanted and, 'Fuck you, we don't care about our record contracts; we'll just put it out ourselves,'" Lars told *US Rocker* in 1991. "This was obviously borrowed directly from the punk thing. It was metal getting a second wind from the streets . . . here's the music, here's the attitude, and we don't give a fuck what anybody else thinks about it."

But Metallica did give a fuck when it came to showing listeners where it came from. Accepting Metallica's Rock and Roll Hall of Fame induction in 2009, James Hetfield first dedicated his award to Alice Cooper, Motörhead, Deep Purple, Thin Lizzy, Iron Maiden, Judas Priest, Rush, Ted Nugent, and Kiss, artists who inspired Metallica but hadn't been inducted yet. In the ensuing years, Rush, Cooper, Kiss, and Deep Purple have all been inducted, while Thin Lizzy, Judas Priest, Motörhead, and Iron Maiden have been nominated. While anyone can debate the prestige and credibility of the Rock and Roll Hall of Fame, Metallica clearly increased awareness of those bands. As Lemmy, never one to mince words, wrote in his terrific autobiography, *White Line Fever*, "Metallica is one of the few bands that has constantly given us credit, and I hold them in high regard for that."

THE $5.98 E.P.—GARAGE DAYS RE-REVISITED AND *GARAGE INC.*

On *The $5.98 E.P.—Garage Days Re-Revisited*, Metallica did more for underground metal than any fanzine could. Its nineties sequel expanded Metallica's range and gave a history lesson to millions of listeners. The first *Garage Inc.* disc is all covers recorded in 1998, while disc two collects Metallica's recorded covers from 1984 to 1996, a summary of how metal went from changing Metallica to being changed by Metallica. They recorded distinct but faithful tributes "Am I Evil?" and "Blitzkrieg" on the "Creeping Death" B-side, labeled "Garage Days Revisited," in 1984. But by *Garage Days Re-Revisited*, Metallica were taking liberties, changing arrangements, structure, and even progressions to make the songs theirs. It's impossible to hear Budgie's "Crash Course in Surgery" now as anything other than Metallica's hardcore version, and Diamond Head's "Helpless" gets sped up, cuts the two-minute outro, and adds a solo— with Kirk Hammett in your band, why wouldn't you? On the same record, Metallica bridged metal, post-punk, and industrial with an icy version of Killing Joke's "The Wait" (Killing Joke's Jaz Coleman: "I'll never forget their cover because I didn't know who the fuck they were").

For *Garage Inc.*, Metallica decided against covering contemporary artists. Iron Maiden was too recent, but Black Sabbath and Thin Lizzy were good, and Mercyful Fate was obscure enough to work. The only nineties song was a rendition of Nick Cave and the Bad Seeds' "Loverman," recorded at 3 a.m. with Kirk playing the song's piano part on guitar. James pushed for the song and once called it his favorite on the record ("It reminded me of the Misfits in the way it had really poppy modulations, riffs and vocal patterns but him singing about horror and ugliness"), although for all his astronomical musical talents, James cannot talk his way through a song and it's one of the record's only misfires. Better are a hard rock "Turn the Page," the rowdiest "Whiskey in a Jar" on tape, a thrash through the Misfits' "Die, Die My Darling," and an all-star "Tuesday's Gone," recorded on a San Jose radio broadcast with Skynyrd's Gary Rossington, Alice in Chains' Jerry Cantrell, Faith No More's Jim "Fatso" Martin, Corrosion of Conformity's Pepper Keenan, Primus' Les Claypool, and Blues Traveler's John Popper, having too much fun to stop as they take the song to "Free Bird" territory.

The second *Garage Inc.* disc rounds up the B-sides and one-offs, showing an encyclopedic metal knowledge—how many metalheads remember Sweet Savage, or know the difference between Blitzkrieg and Budgie? The latter's "Breadfan" turns into one of Metallica's riffiest songs in Hetfield's paws, plus a raging live staple. At Woodstock '94, Metallica opened with James yelling "Fuck you" into "Breadfan," Budgie's portrait of a scrooge and a song from which Metallica deliberately removed the hippie breakdown. They honored the performance by printing a shirt with the words "Hippie Shit: Beads & Peace" in the *Live Shit: Binge & Purge* font with the *Live Shit* "Scary Guy" image wearing a bandana, holding daisies, and, most tellingly, with dollar signs for eyes.

But it's not all antagonistic. *Garage Inc.* also collects Metallica's version of Queen's "Stone Cold Crazy," recorded with slightly altered lyrics, for Elektra's 1990 double-CD *Rubáiyát: Elektra's 40th Anniversary*, a compilation produced by Patti Smith guitarist Lenny Kaye. James would later perform the song with Queen's Brian May and Black Sabbath's Tony Iommi for the Freddie Mercury Tribute Concert in 1992. "Brian May was the harmony master," James stated in the *Garage Inc.* sleeve. "He came up with these huge parts that sounded like string sections, flamboyant orchestrations. And he was doing it all on guitar." May returned the compliment with a recorded message for Metallica's thirtieth anniversary shows. "You guys completely epitomize metal, and God bless you for it," May cheered, before thanking them for "Stone Cold Crazy" and the tribute performance. "It was quite something amazing, beyond what anyone could expect . . . by donating all your royalties [Metallica's *Live at Wembley Stadium* single, with cover art by James] to us [Freddie Mercury's AIDS fund]."

Since *Garage Inc.*, Metallica have released some stray tributes, including a raucous "The Ecstasy of Gold" for 2007's *We All Love Ennio Morricone*, and melding four Rainbow songs into "Ronnie Rising Medley," donated to the Dio Cancer Fund for 2014's *Ronnie James Dio—This Is Your Life*, ready for a *Garage IV* playlist on your preferred streaming service.

For Metallica, changing metal's past also meant changing it for themselves. Those of us who grew up with eighties and nineties rock radio can remember a time when no Metallica song earlier than "One" (and rarely even that) crossed the dial. By the 2000s, "Master of Puppets," "For Whom the Bell Tolls," and "Fade to Black" were all rock radio staples, something unthinkable in the days of airwaves being dominated by glam, grunge, or alternative. Even *Kill 'Em All* reached the *Billboard 200* in 1986, after *Master of Puppets*. Metallica's nineties success made radio a place where those songs could thrive. Maybe someday FM programmers will catch up to "Damage, Inc." or "Motorbreath."

Until then, enjoy ten of the biggest influences on Metallica's music. Or the devil he may take ya.

BLACK SABBATH

No list of any metalhead's influences can leave out Black Sabbath. If you like metal, you like something inspired by Black Sabbath, musically, visually, culturally, and otherwise. They're the only metal band whose stature can compete with Metallica's. If Metallica comes closest to being metal's Beatles, Black Sabbath (and frontman Ozzy Osbourne) are its Elvis Presley—the first megastar and biggest early influence. Ozzy, guitarist Tony Iommi ("the ultimate riff master," in James' words), bassist Geezer Butler, and drummer Bill Ward opened their first record *Black Sabbath* with their song "Black Sabbath," spawning decades of great music in seconds with a funeral toll ("Hells Bells," "For Whom the Bell Tolls," "Hallowed Be Thy Name"), a thunderstorm ("Raining Blood," "Thunderstruck," "November Rain"), and the tritone, *diabolus in musica*, the most ominous interval in all of music, quoted by the San Francisco Symphony Orchestra on Metallica's *S&M*. A young James Hetfield, raiding his stepbrother Dave's record collection, sat in the dark with his headphones and the first Sabbath record, mesmerized by the title song. "Black Sabbath was the band that just totally lit me up," he recalled years later. "I sunk right into that. I could close my eyes and be in there." It helped that James knew his friends' parents wouldn't let them own *Black Sabbath*.

Lars shared a personal Sabbath memory with *Circus* magazine in 1986, having seen the band as a twelve-year-old in Copenhagen, on the *Sabotage* tour. Being Lars, he waited with a grade school friend backstage for autographs, only to get pushed aside by older concertgoers when Ozzy and the gang walked out to their limo. "Ozzy saw us, pointed at us and said, 'Come here,'" Lars recalled. "That's the same guy we're on tour with."

Metallica would do more than tour with Ozzy and Sabbath, upping *Master of Reality* with *Master of Puppets*, covering *Sabbath Bloody Sabbath*'s "Sabbra Cadabra" (with an excerpt from "A National Acrobat" thrown in) on *Garage Inc.*, and even inducting Sabbath into the Rock and Roll Hall of Fame in 2006. James talked about finding music as a boy that expressed him better than he could express himself, stifling tears while he thanked the band that "spoke the feelings he could never put into words." Metallica capped the induction with performances of Sabbath's "Hole in the Sky" and "Iron Man," which Ozzy himself called "fucking better than great." Metallica also honored Ozzy at a 2014 MusiCares acoustic benefit, playing Ozzy's Beatles favorite "In My Life" and Ozzy's "Diary of a Madman" for the guest of honor. But like all metal bands, Sabbath's influence on Metallica was clear from the start. "Hand of Doom," a *Paranoid* deep cut touching on a prominent Metallica theme, mistreated soldiers, shows up in the lyrics to Metallica's own "Trapped Under Ice": "Hand of doom has a tight grip on me." Did it ever.

DEEP PURPLE

Not counting a few jammed out measures of "Smoke on the Water" and Kirk incorporating "Mistreated" into a solo, both on *Live Shit: Binge & Purge*, Metallica didn't officially release a Deep Purple cover until 2012, when their faithful version of the *Machine Head*–era B-side "When a Blind Man Cries" ended up on tribute record *Re-Machined: A Tribute to Deep Purple's* Machine Head, celebrating the fortieth anniversary of Purple's best-loved album. But Metallica's Deep Purple debt reaches back to February 3, 1973, when the British hard rockers came to Aarhus, Denmark, where Torben Ulrich had been competing in a tennis tournament. The players were invited to the show, and Ulrich family friend/South African tennis star Ray Moore had an extra ticket for nine-year-old Lars, who'd later declare Purple "have probably been the primary musical backbone in my body." By the eighties, Lars was sometimes introducing himself as "Ian Paice," Purple's drummer, in early Metallica interviews.

One of the first bands to perform blues-based hard rock and proto-metal, Purple are indeed a primary backbone of metal itself, breaking through with a 1968 hit cover of Joe South's "Hush." At their peak, on *Machine Head*, Deep Purple were metal pioneer contemporaries with Led Zeppelin and Black Sabbath, thanks in part to ace musicianship (particularly guitar god Ritchie Blackmore), but more so future classic rock staples such as "Highway Star," "Space Truckin'," and, of course, "Smoke on the Water," one of the simplest, most recognizable riffs in all of classic rock, as well a serious contender for most overplayed guitar store riff, ranking with "Stairway to Heaven," "Iron Man," "Smells Like Teen Spirit," and "Enter Sandman." Since *Machine Head*, Purple has endured breakups, reunions, lawsuits, lineup changes, and seeing their brand of keyboard-heavy blues metal supplanted in much of the public eye by flashier, riffier bands like AC/DC and Van Halen. But Deep Purple still plays arenas, shows up on classic rock playlists, and boasts a major imprint on countless hard rock and metal bands.

Some Purpleheads point to 1969's *Concerto for Group and Orchestra*, a live album of a Royal Albert Hall collaboration between Deep Purple and London's Royal Philharmonic Orchestra, as the spark that inspired Metallica's *S&M*. Then again, Purple reunited with the RPO for a thirtieth anniversary show in 1999, just months after Metallica joined the San Francisco Symphony in Berkeley, so maybe the students became the teacher.

DIAMOND HEAD

In the liner notes for *Behold the Beginning*, a Diamond Head anthology compiled by Lars Ulrich, Lars writes that without Diamond Head, there would be no Metallica. While these days, there'd also be no Diamond Head without Metallica—Lars convinced them to reform in 1992 and landed them the opening spot for Metallica at Milton Keynes in 1993, for 50,000 people—the UK band may have done roughly as much for Metallica as Metallica did for them. Their knockout first record, *Lightning to the Nations*, is a NWOBHM opus ranking with the best of Judas Priest and Iron Maiden, and Diamond Head might have similar success if not for label troubles, poor management, bad production, and their inability to come up with a better set of songs than *Lightning to the Nations* (though 1982's *Four Cuts* EP has "Dead Reckoning," which helped inspire "Seek & Destroy"). Instead, Diamond Head is associated with Metallica the way the Melvins are with Nirvana—a major influence and mentor who gained permanent underground cred with a boost from their much bigger protégés.

Named after a solo record by Roxy Music lead guitarist Phil Manzanera, Diamond Head formed in 1977 and earned opening spots for Iron Maiden and AC/DC on the strength of their first single, "Shoot Out the Lights" (title remind you of anyone else's first song?). Unable to find a label to release their music, Diamond Head created their own label, Happy Face Records, and printed 1,000 copies of *Lightning to the Nations*, only available at shows or through mail order in *Sounds* magazine for kids like Lars Ulrich to send away for (and in Lars' case, strike up a mail correspondence with band co-manager Linda Harris, the mother of lead singer Sean). Blending Maiden operatics with Motörhead grime, and saluting Gustav Holst with their signature, "Am I Evil?," Diamond Head created sounds heard in all subsequent thrash bands. Their riff-heavy, oddly structured songs often tackled themes of metal past, like witches burned alive or being a rock 'n' roll star who's gotta groove from night to day. *Lightning to the*

Nations hasn't outgrown its cult following, partially because it's scarce, even as an acknowledged metal classic. A 1993 Metal Blade reissue, no doubt in part due to interest in Metallica, accidentally cut the intro to "It's Electric," which subsequent reissues haven't amended. Even on streaming services, *Lightning to the Nations* is usually scattered and incomplete, making it one of those records your older sibling was right about—you needed to hear this on vinyl.

Casual metalheads associate Diamond Head with Metallica, who've covered five of *Lightning to the Nations*' seven songs onstage and recorded four of them (Metallica sensibly dropped "Sucking My Love" from their setlist by summer 1982) on their *Garage* records. At their earliest shows, Metallica didn't tell people they were covering Diamond Head until Saxon's sound guy (Paul Owen, who'd go on to join Metallica's sound crew for twenty-two years) confronted them backstage about it. Diamond Head guitarist Brian Tatler has said he never sees a write-up on Diamond Head that doesn't mention Metallica, but isn't bitter about it. "If it hadn't been for Metallica, and Lars, and the songwriter's royalties that me and [vocalist Sean Harris] get, I don't know what we would've done," Tatler told *Classic Rock* in 2016, after Metallica royalties enabled him to purchase a home. "You can't buy that sort of thing, you know?"

"They're wonderful guys," Harris added. "James frightens you a bit—I think he's meant to! But they were quite nice to us."

DISCHARGE

How many bands are singular enough to get an entire genre named after them? D-beat, the bullet-paced sound first popularized in Sweden and the UK, took its name from four Brits who pulled Motörhead's gospel a little closer to what the kids would soon be calling thrash. Headbangers can argue past any dive bar's last call over what really was the first record to blend metal and hardcore, but no discussion is complete without Discharge's 1982 debut LP, *Hear Nothing See Nothing Say Nothing* (quoted on "Dyers Eve"), twenty-seven minutes of immediately catchy slogans shouted out over speed-metal riffs. Formed in 1977, Discharge perfected their sound and solidified their lineup over several EPs (some of which, in their entirety, are shorter than most Metallica songs) before *Hear Nothing See Nothing Say Nothing* blew a proto-thrash, proto-grindcore, proto-crust punk, and proto-black metal hole in the world, leaving remnants in the music of Anthrax, Sepultura, Machine Head, Napalm Death, Arch Enemy, and Prong, among others, all of whom have covered Discharge songs. Even Beastie Boys, in their excellent *Beastie Boys Book*, reveal that their pseudo-political "Riot Fight" from their punk, pre-stardom days was inspired by Discharge. Discharge's second full-length, *Never Again* (not to be confused with their EP of the same name), compiles several of their earlier songs onto a follow-up as fierce as their debut and almost as influential, and while a failed hard rock crossover on 1986's *Grave New World* would derail Discharge and cause them to split in the same year, they have since reunited, touring and releasing music. They still sound ferocious coming from any stage or speaker, and in Discharge-inspired bands such as Carcass and Disfear. Kirk Hammett, seen wearing a Discharge shirt on the back cover of *Ride the Lightning*, cited Discharge as a punk favorite (along with Killing Joke, Minor Threat, and Black Flag) in a September 1986 *Sounds* interview, and fans who get close enough to more recent Metallica shows can count at least two Discharge patches on James' denim vest.

IRON MAIDEN

Unbeknownst to each other at the time, James Hetfield and Lars Ulrich both picked up a copy of Iron Maiden's 1980 self-titled debut without either of them having ever heard a note of the band's music. Radio wasn't touching Maiden in the eighties (and still mostly ignores them, tens of millions of records sold later), so the East London quintet made music for kids who were going to judge their records by the cover. Thus Eddie, a fantastic Derek Riggs–designed monster who graced the cover of *Iron Maiden* and nearly all of the band's records and T-shirts since, lured headbangers into taking Maiden albums home, then coming back for more songs like "Remember Tomorrow" and "Wrathchild," both of which Hetfield and

Ron McGovney covered in Leather Charm. Maiden bassist and primary songwriter Steve Harris gave his band's songs a heavy low-end that distinguished them from their NWOBHM peers, and harmonizing guitarists Dave Murray and Adrian Smith are among metal's most imitated axemen, but it wasn't until vocalist Bruce Dickinson joined for 1982's *The Number of the Beast* that Maiden jumped to the forefront of metal with classics such as "The Number of the Beast," "Run to the Hills," and "Hallowed be Thy Name," staying near the top with consistent metal hits (at least when all the crucial players are onboard) and the absolute best arena metal show in the world. As jaw-droppingly agile sixtysomethings, Iron Maiden still fill stadiums with fans who want to hear the classics faster, tighter, and louder than on record. "They, more than any other band, are responsible for opening up all the doors for heavy metal in the eighties," Lars once commented. "They've never given in, and as a result have been a big inspiration to a band like us, to stick to what we believe in and not just turn out crap to sell records or please radio stations."

Metallica have covered "Prowler" onstage, and donated a reverent "Remember Tomorrow," from Maiden's classic first record, to 2008 tribute album *Maiden Heaven*. Lars wrote in the liner notes that the song was a blueprint for Metallica classics such as "Fade to Black" and "Welcome Home (Sanitarium)." Recorded during the *Death Magnetic* sessions, one can't help but think "Remember Tomorrow" may have inspired "The Day That Never Comes" as well. But Metallica's most famous Maiden tribute comes on *Garage Days Re-Revisited*, wherein the boys thrash through a pair of Misfits covers before ending with a few off-key, comical bars of "Run to the Hills." Lars had been playing the drum intro in the studio over and over, which inspired his bandmates to jump in. "It was nothing against Maiden," James clarified in the *Garage Inc.* liner notes. "It was just a way to take the piss out of metal. And, a way to take the piss out of ourselves." Iron Maiden responded to this on the B-side to their 1992 single "Be Quick or Be Dead," with a cover of Montrose's "Space Station No. 5" in which Bruce goes into a spoken rant, "It's getting faster lads! Hurry up! Here comes Metallica in the rear-view mirror! . . . And at the finish it's prick followed by the wanker, followed by, uh, cunt with arsehole finishing a close fourth." Maiden can then be heard laughing and bantering in the studio at the song, just as Metallica did on *Garage* songs "Blitzkrieg," "Helpless," and "Crash Course in Brain Surgery."

MERCYFUL FATE

Lars Ulrich told *Headbangers Ball* in 1993 that the three bands that influenced Metallica most were Diamond Head, Motörhead, and Mercyful Fate. Formed in Copenhagen in 1981 by vocalist King Diamond and guitarist Hank Shermann, Mercyful Fate's fascination with the occult and Satanism often gets them credited as an early black metal band. But King Diamond's banshee falsetto and Shermann's sped-up prog riffs distinguished the Fate from the distorted tones and death growls that followed. "Fate would play a great riff and then never come back to it and it would piss you off," laughed James Hetfield in *Guitar World*, while acknowledging their influence in breaking verse-chorus form. "You could have a song with different parts, each of which could almost be its own song." It was Lars' relentless networking and Danish connection that first linked his band to Mercyful Fate, scoring Metallica a practice space in MF's Denmark studio while recording *Ride the Lightning*. Lars repaid the favor by inviting Mercyful Fate to open nineties Metallica shows and by playing drums on "Return of the Vampire . . . 1993," a bonus track on Mercyful Fate's reunion album *In the Shadows*. To date, it is Lars' only appearance on an album without his Metallica bandmates.

Mercyful Fate have broken up and reunited sporadically since the nineties, including a performance with Metallica at their thirtieth anniversary celebration. But their best songs are in their initial early eighties run, including one self-titled EP and two studio albums (*Melissa* and *Don't Break the Oath*) that would better soundtrack a Halloween party than a coven. Metallica melded five of those songs for *Garage Inc.* track "Mercyful Fate," taking James' words about Fate's song structures even further by drawing "Satan's Fall," "Curse of the Pharaohs," "A Corpse Without Soul," "Into the Coven," and "Evil" into one eleven-plus-minute jam, Metallica's longest studio song. Kirk might have been remembering a 1983 Mercyful Fate show in which King Diamond invited Metallica onstage. In his excitement, Kirk accidentally knocked the King offstage, and while Diamond laughed it off, Kirk's bandmates told him he was furious. Guilt-ridden Kirk didn't learn the truth until 1999.

MISFITS

In "Road Warriors," an August 1986 *Spin* profile, writer Sue Cummings remembers someone in Metallica (presumably Cliff, who carried a cassette labeled "Mezzfits" and, in Kirk's recollection, "had a way of commandeering the tape player in any vehicle") putting a Misfits tape on in the band's car. "Metallica becomes a Misfits air-guitar group in the throes of a communal epileptic seizure," writes Cummings. "They know all the words, and yell them, stomping the floor, banging the windows, jerking their heads around, asking for whiplash." In later interviews, the boys would recall listening to Ennio Morricone and having a bus sing-along to Simon and Garfunkel's "Homeward Bound," so maybe they were just playing it up for the journalist. But there's no writing Metallica history without the Misfits.

It seems almost unthinkable now, with the reunited original Misfits headlining festivals and their skull mascot (inspired by the title villain in 1946 film serial *The Crimson Ghost*) emblazoned on more T-shirts than any punk logo this side of the Ramones' presidential seal. But the Misfits were a short-lived and well-kept secret when Metallica were inflicting Cliff's mix tapes on lucky journalists and Metallica's less fortunate road crew, who were often woken up in the early morning by Misfits songs on full blast. Unable to find a label for their remarkable first album *Static Age* in 1978 (it didn't get officially released until 1996), the Misfits leaked their horror-themed, rockabilly-styled hardcore onto rare EPs like *Beware* and *3 Hits from Hell*, where young headbangers Cliff Burton and James Hetfield lapped up macabre horror-punk songs like "Last Caress." Baritone Glenn Danzig, bassist Jerry Only, guitarist Doyle Wolfgang von Frankenstein, and a revolving door of drummers based their look, lyrics, and hairstyle (the devilock, inspired by Eddie Munster) in cult horror camp—Danzig even named the band's independent record label Plan 9. Like the film and TV they devoured, the Misfits' music is often rooted in the 1950s and 1960s, owing as at least much to Elvis' rockabilly stomp and vocal stylings as the Sex Pistols' shock tactics and aggression. When recording *Garage Inc.*, Metallica considered about half a dozen Misfits songs to cover, including "Astro Zombies," "Ghoul's Night Out," and "London Dungeon" (briefly performed on the . . . *And Justice for All* box set) before settling on "Die, Die My Darling," later releasing it as a single. This decision was approved by Jerry Only, who named it his favorite of Metallica's Misfits covers and got James to sing it with him onstage in November 2000, at San Francisco's Maritime Hall.

As seen in the *Spin* anecdote, Metallica were repping the Misfits early and often. In a 1986 *MTV News* interview, James and Kirk each wore different Misfits shirts and took a moment to praise the band's horror art. But the Metallica fan most associated with the Misfits is Cliff Burton, generally credited for turning his bandmates onto them (he once named his top five bands as Misfits/Samhain, Thin Lizzy, Ozzy-era Black Sabbath, R.E.M., and Aerosmith) and the only Metallica member hardcore enough to get the Misfits skull logo tattooed, prominently, on his right arm. On Metallica's first release after Cliff's death, *The $5.98 E.P.—Garage Days Re-Revisited*, Cliff's bandmates honored their late brother by stapling "Last Caress" and "Green Hell" together into one breakneck cover. Kirk cited the Misfits' increasingly fast tempo changes on *Earth A.D.* as an inspiration on *Master of Puppets*, and named "Last Caress" as his favorite cover to play live. Black Album–era James studied Glenn Danzig's vocals while teaching himself to sing. Nirvana, whose frontman put Metallica's "Last Caress/Green Hell" on his famed "Montage of Heck" mix tape, once saluted Metallica on MTV, in their caustic fashion, for repping the Misfits (Krist Novoselic: "James Hetfield gave the legions of rockers the okay to like punk rock!"). Metallica and Misfits have since collaborated in the studio and onstage, with James singing uncredited backup on "Twist of Cain" and "Possession" on Danzig's self-titled 1988 debut and inviting Danzig to support Metallica's 1994 Shit Hits the Sheds tour. More recently, Danzig performed a few songs with Metallica at their thirtieth anniversary shows in 2011, including all the Misfits covers Metallica have released.

MOTÖRHEAD

They never had a platinum record in the United States, spent less than two years on a major label, and didn't reach the *Billboard* Top 40 until 2013. But all thrash metal without Motörhead is, simply put, unfathomable. Former Hawkwind bassist and Jimi Hendrix/Pink Floyd roadie Ian "Lemmy"

Kilmister, the most badass man ever to pick up an instrument, led his band of road dogs through numerous lineup and label shifts, before pairing with guitarist Phil Campbell and drummer Mikkey Dee, the only constant being Lemmy making everything in his way sound like Motörhead. Since 1975, Motörhead's speed metal has been melting faces with its punk flair and warrior attitude. They toured and put out records almost every year until Lemmy's death in 2015, always sounding the same and always kicking ass. Any metalhead worth his or her horns has that moment of getting a first Motörhead record, coupled with the thrill of finding out all their other records sound just like it.

Metallica have been outspoken Motörhead fans for as long as they've been giving interviews. According to *So What!*, their favorites were *Overkill* (Lars), *Ace of Spades* (Kirk), and *Another Perfect Day* (James)—James picking the only Motörhead record to feature Thin Lizzy guitarist Brian "Robbo" Robertson. "Lemmy in particular was an icon, sort of a godfather for people who love heavy metal," James has said. "He was the captain of the ship. . . . There's certainly no Metallica without a Motörhead." Lars, who can be seen passing out drunk in the liner notes for Motörhead's *Orgasmatron*, has stated that Metallica music was a combining of heads—Motörhead and Diamond Head. Metallica have used their success to give back to Motörhead, inviting Lemmy to perform onstage with them in several times, singing his praises in the outstanding 2010 documentary *Lemmy*, and even giving the master an appearance as himself in *'Tallica Parking Lot*, a silly animated short co-created by Robert Trujillo and co-starring Bootsy Collins, Mike Judge, Trey Parker, Matt Stone, Brendan Small, and Metallica. But perhaps Metallica's best tribute to Lemmy came December 14, 1995, at Whisky a Go Go in West Hollywood, where Motörhead was playing Lemmy's fiftieth birthday celebration. Motörhead's opening band, billed as the Lemmys, showed up in Lemmy regalia, long black wigs, aviator shades, and all-black attire, setting up their equipment in front of the stunned crowd. They raged through "Overkill," "Damage Case," "Stone Dead Forever," "Too Late Too Late," and "The Chase Is Better Than the Catch" before bringing Lemmy himself out to perform "(We Are) The Road Crew," with a visibly thrilled Jason Newsted sharing lead vocals in his Lemmy costume (studio versions of the first four songs appeared on a limited edition "Hero of the Day" single, titled "Motörheadache"). "That was the biggest compliment anybody has ever paid me," Lemmy recalled. "But they got their tattoos on the wrong arm, every one of them."

RAMONES

How distinctive are the Ramones, one of the most imitated acts in American music history? Punk rock, even at its best, exists in part as a failed imitation of the Ramones—anyone can play three-chord songs with simple lyrics, but nobody can play them like the Ramones. Check out Metallica's awful Ramones covers on various editions of the "St. Anger" single, and hear how even a great band like Metallica can't capture the mania Joey, Johnny, Dee Dee, and Tommy Ramone delivered on their first three records. Metallica covered six songs from those records—"Now I Wanna Sniff Some Glue," "53rd & 3rd," "Today Your Love, Tomorrow the World," "Commando," "Cretin Hop," and "We're a Happy Family"—for *We're a Happy Family: A Tribute to Ramones*, a 2003 tribute record compiled by Rob Zombie and including liner notes from Stephen King. Only the garage ruckus of "Commando" channels the Ramones' energy, giving listeners the pleasure of hearing Metallica rhyme "Don't talk to commies" with "Eat kosher salamis" while Lars, Bob Rock, James, and Kirk take turns on vocals. In a *Some Kind of Monster* outtake, the boys are surprised to hear the tribute organizers prefer "53rd & 3rd" to the band's pick, "Commando," shortly before getting the news Dee Dee Ramone has died of an overdose. "Drugs suck," mopes James. "53rd & 3rd," Metallica's stilted version of a Dee Dee original, makes the record. In the liner notes to their "St. Anger" singles, Metallica call the songs "Garbage Days Revisited" and get self-aware about their covers' quality ("Sometimes pride goes out the window for the sake of contractual . . . well, you get the picture!"). They could have taken a lesson from Dee Dee himself, who proved even legends can screw up great songs when he dumped a terrible version of "Jump in the Fire" on messy 2001 record *A Punk Tribute to Metallica*.

Metallica honored the Ramones more effectively from the stage, playing a surprise 2002 club show (their first in two years, with Bob Rock on bass) in San Francisco, billed as "Spun," opening with four of their Ramones covers. Metallica also booked the Ramones to play Lollapalooza's main stage with them in 1996, ensuring thousands of people would see them perform each day and causing Johnny Ramone to complain to Kirk that he'd be retired and playing golf in LA if his band hadn't been invited to tour. But it was the least Metallica could do for longtime fan Joey Ramone, who as early as 1988 was spreading the Metallica gospel in interviews. "I think they're great," Ramone told Terry Gross on NPR. "I like their attitude."

THIN LIZZY

Thin Lizzy's influence on Metallica is most audible in the mid-1990s, when Metallica adapted more of the Dublin band's hard rock tendencies and even took Thin Lizzy's arrangement of "Whiskey in the Jar" back to the charts. But Lizzy had been showing up in Metallica's music for years—the lyric "Honesty is my only excuse" in "Damage, Inc." (also a popular Metallica T-shirt slogan) was taken from Thin Lizzy's "Honesty is No Excuse." Kirk Hammett workshopped his "Enter Sandman" solo with Thin Lizzy guitarist "Robbo" Robertson in mind, and revealed his "Master of Puppets" solo opened with a variation on a lick from Robertson's replacement, Gary Moore. Cliff Burton would tell friends the guitar harmonies he wrote for "Orion" were learned from Thin Lizzy's melodies. "[Cliff] planted a harmony seed in me that I've never forgotten," James told *Newsweek* in 2017. "He was a big, big Thin Lizzy fan. . . . he brought in a little more musicality."

That musicality was learned in part from a multicultural rock quartet immortalized by hits like "Jailbreak" and "The Boys Are Back in Town," and bolstered by a tremendous back catalogue that blended hard rock, heartland rock, folk, psychedelic, and metal. Bassist/songwriter Phil Lynott grew up worshipping Jimi Hendrix and Bob Dylan, and took his band, originally a power trio, to the charts with a 1972 arrangement of the traditional Irish folk song "Whiskey in the Jar." Lynott was reluctant to release "Whiskey" over one of his band's originals, but spent the next decade shooting out enough great records to rewrite pub jukebox playlists for eternity. Lizzy are at their most metal in deep cuts—"Emerald" is pulverizing enough for Mastodon to cover it for their first record—though hard rock standards such as "Waiting for an Alibi," "The Rocker," and "Cowboy Song" helped earn Lynott a Dublin statue erected in 2005. Lynott died in 1986, and sadly didn't live to see the statue, but he did briefly meet a starstruck budding American guitarist, who would recall the episode years later in his band's fanzine. "The only sounds I could produce were caveman grunts," James Hetfield lamented.

3

PURSUIT OF TRUTH, NO MATTER WHERE IT LIES

James Hetfield

"I get to put my loves, fears, hates, question marks into this music, and it definitely helps me."

—James Hetfield

It's 2004, and James Hetfield is on Country Music Television. Maybe he's trying to improve on Metallica's 1996 country rock aberration "Mama Said," which he performs off-broadcast with country veteran Jessi Colter. Maybe he's remembering his inebriated appearance in the dreadful unauthorized fan movie *Metallimania*, where he tells a fan he sees himself playing country music in ten years (this is the metal equivalent of Bob Dylan telling reporters he'd sell out for "ladies' garments," forty years before he appeared in a Victoria's Secret ad). More likely he's on CMT to pay tribute to the man called Hoss, a favorite of James' father, Virgil. James and Waylon were acquainted years earlier, when Hetfield interviewed Hoss for a college radio station, trading autographs for James' father and Waylon's son. Waylon also appeared on select dates of Metallica's Lollapalooza tour, apparently at James' suggestion.

Hetfield takes the stage. How is this metalhead going to honor Waylon Jennings? "I've Always Been Crazy"? "Only Daddy That'll Walk the Line"? "Theme from *The Dukes of Hazzard*"?

James sings, "Don't You Think This Outlaw Bit's Done Got Out of Hand."

That's right. James Hetfield, in the inaugural *CMT Outlaws* performance, sharing a bill with Tanya Tucker and Shooter Jennings, struts out with a song about how he's not the tough guy people think he is. Over twenty years after announcing himself to the world on *Kill 'Em All*, James still brings a sense of reality, demystifying any bullshit in his presence, even his own. It's the most James Hetfield thing he could do.

On top of that, James totally owns "Outlaw Bit." He turns the song into a raging country-metal stomp. He adds his signatures "Ye-ah!," "Ooh!," and even his evil laugh (there's a studio version, on the 2003 Waylon tribute record *I've Always Been Crazy*, with James playing all the instruments, but the song is best experienced live, bulling into the cheers of a captive audience). The crowd screams back in terror and joy, and James plays right off them. And in case you didn't think he was having fun, he closes with a few measures of the *Dukes of Hazzard* theme.

Maybe if you're a big enough James Hetfield fan, you won't be surprised by "Don't You Think This Outlaw Bit's Done Got Out of Hand." James contains multitudes. At most Metallica shows you're likely to see him play the characters in "One," "Master of Puppets," and "Nothing Else Matters" just a few songs apart, among numerous other voices. In James' first solo *Rolling Stone* cover story ("The Leader of the Real Free World"), David Fricke introduces him as a loner who spends hours talking to his fans, and a mix of political and philosophical ideas. Kirk Hammett's first impression of James was wondering how this "shy, mellow guy" became a "screaming banshee" onstage. In Metallica James embodies a combination of machismo and vulnerability, living out his struggles in song. James' favorite film, the one with a score that's been opening Metallica shows since 1983, revolves around three distinct characters that James has said he sees himself and the world through. In a 2008 Fricke interview, James and Robert take their families to the Hermitage Museum in St. Petersburg to see Rembrandt's *The Return of the Prodigal Son*. James tells his daughter it's his favorite painting. He first saw it in a rehab workshop, refreshing him on the Luke parable his Christian Science upbringing drummed into him. When the workshop called on James to say which figure he saw himself in—the father, the prodigal son, or the jealous brother—he picked all three. The father and repenting son are two of James' most public personas, to the point where forgiveness themed one of his biggest songs, the only Metallica song he had to exorcise by turning it into a trilogy. But the jealous son? To James, that was his relationship with one Lars Ulrich.

James is a master of voices, shifting narrators in songs like "Creeping Death," "Master of Puppets," "Disposable Heroes," and "Enter Sandman," and sometimes shifting species, in the curious case of "Of Wolf and Man" (he later voiced a lycanthrope musician named Wolfgang on children's TV show *Skylanders Academy*). "For Whom the Bell Tolls" switches from third to second person, the attacks getting closer with the narrator. In *Some Kind of Monster*, Bob Rock sums up one recording session by noting that James went into another voice. James eyes Bob. "Which one of me are you talking to?" He smiles, but he's not kidding. I was me, but now he's gone.

YE-AH!

If James can be summed up in a word, it's "Ye-ah!" The hyphen and exclamation point are all a part of it. Amanda Petrusich described it in a *New Yorker* profile, "he sings as if he's gritting his teeth, and finishes each line with a curled snarl, the Satanic version of Valley Girl up-speak." It's a word and phrasing associated with James almost as much as "Enter Sandman," enough to inspire parodies as varied as "Every James Hetfield 'Ye-ah!'" audio clips or April Fools' news stories about James joining the Yeah Yeah Yeahs. Anyone with a metal record in their collection or at least a passing familiarity with modern rock radio has their own James Hetfield "Ye-ah!" impression. Like Elvis' "Uh-uh," the more exaggerated a James impression is the more it sounds like him. An artist like Rob Zombie can build an enduring, influential metal career based on the James "Ye-ah!" According to studies, James has said "Ye-ah!" more than 200 times on record, depending on how many extra "e-ahs" you count. When something in *Cunning Stunts* makes him laugh mysteriously in, of all songs,

"Nothing Else Matters," James recovers with a quick "Ye-ah!" Even with the San Francisco Symphony on *S&M*, James can't resist James-ing— "San Francisco Symphony man, let's hear it baby, ye-ah! Maestro Michael Kamen at the helm, ye-ah!"

But no one really sounds like him, which is part of why he's James. His quirks and enunciations make him an atypical singer, as do his melodic lines—imagine the verses to "For Whom the Bell Tolls" without vocal patterns. He's not possessed with noticeable rock god features, like Robert Plant's voice or David Lee Roth's looks. Having one of the most imitated and identifiable metal voices doesn't make James seem like much more than a guy who writes great songs. There are no messianic poses, no world-saving or intellectual pretenses, no makeup or costume changes (or even costumes, for that matter). No act about how what torments him is deeper than what torments you. Just a staggering blend of energy and intensity, from that rare performer who can pull an arena to its feet while telling them to die by his hand.

"THERE WAS NO OTHER OPTION"

James was born in Downey, California, to Cynthia and Virgil Hetfield. His mother was an opera singer and painter, and his father was a truck driver who also taught Sunday school, which James remembered as "part of my regimen." Virgil married Cynthia when she already had two teenage boys from a previous marriage, one of whom Virgil eventually threw out of the house. The Hetfields didn't have many house guests, something James didn't think much about until encountering the hippie-like social community in Torben Ulrich's home. Virgil loved the wilderness and hunting, making his own bullets and rubber-band guns for his son Jamie. Every summer they'd live on a boat for two weeks and dine off the fish they caught in Lake Powell. Virgil had grown up fatherless on a Nebraska farm with his aunts, his traveling musician father Virgil Sr. splitting before his son was born.

"When he talked to me, it would be in scripture," James recalled. Virgil would get teary-eyed reading the Bible while James watched. "I felt like an outcast from the beginning," James remembered. "It was hard to explain to my parents that I didn't understand this, because they were so immersed in it. . . . I felt very alienated from school, from my family, and spent the rest of my life looking for family."

Like his father, Jamie Hetfield loved the outdoors, in particular biking, skateboarding, hiking, and smoking. He crushed out on Tatum O'Neal in *The Bad News Bears* and dreamed of growing up to be Fred Biletnikoff of the Oakland Raiders. He played football for the Downey Vikings as a high school freshman and wanted to again as a sophomore, until his coach told him he needed a haircut to qualify. Eddie Van Halen and Michael Schenker didn't have short hair, so James left Coach Cummings and football behind. James wouldn't graduate, but he'd return in 2011 as an honorary inductee to the Downey High School Hall of Fame.

James' Christian Scientist parents raised him without doctors or dentists, instead taking their family to a practitioner who'd find scripture to help with health problems. They gave James a waiver to get him out of PE and other health classes, telling James to put his faith in a god he felt unsure of. His first medicine was an aspirin from his half-brother when James was in late high school. James remembered church years later. "We had these little testimonials, and there was a girl that had her arm broken. She stood up and said, 'I broke my arm but now, look, it's all better.' But it was just, like, mangled. Now that I think about it, it was pretty disturbing."

"I was pretty much afraid of everything," he'd say in 2014. "Afraid of the world, afraid of speaking, you know, a really, really shy kid. Music was a way to speak, simple as that. Music was the voice I didn't have. . . . There was no other option."

Cynthia signed nine-year-old James up for classical piano lessons, but James preferred teaching himself drums on his older brother David's kit. Growing up a frustrated drummer later helped him bond with a frustrated frontman, who mouthed along with James' words from behind the kit and sometimes switched instruments (Lars on vocals, James on drums, Kirk on bass, Jason on guitar) for "Am I Evil?" Playing both piano and drums helped James develop complex rhythm and timing skills, acing the ability to do different things with his left and right hands while singing.

Kirk would later say James was the rare guitarist he'd never heard say he couldn't play and sing something at the same time. "I wanted to play drums on guitar," James has said. "I wanted a really percussive sound, one that really reacts quickly and is punchy, but also if you hang on a chord it's going to fill the room."

He bought sheet music for his lessons at K Music, a mom-and-pop store in Downey, but more importantly found his first record there, Lynyrd Skynyrd's "Sweet Home Alabama" 7-inch. On *Kill 'Em All*, James would slide a "Sweet Home Alabama"–like progression in "The Four Horseman," helping liberate the song from the version Metallica's departed guitarist had originally written.

James' first rock show—humorously enough for people who know their Metallica history—was his stepbrother taking him to see Jethro Tull with Uriah Heep. Already expressing interests beyond hard rock, sixteen-year-old James got his mom to drive him to see Blondie at the Greek Theatre as well. But at the California World Music Festival on Sunday, April 8, 1979, James watched Aerosmith bring their hardest game, still formidable enough to follow Van Halen and UFO. "There was something magical about seeing them as actual live people, not just pictures on an album," James recalled years later. He was wowed by Joe Perry's coolness, and shocked to hear Steven Tyler call the crowd "motherfuckers."

James' favorite Aerosmith record was obviously the loudest one, *Rocks*, and his favorite song was "Nobody's Fault," the heaviest thing Aerosmith ever recorded. He loved that Aerosmith kept the sound of a door opening in the studio in the final take, giving "Nobody's Fault" a DIY atmosphere James could relate to. James adorned his bedroom wall with a poster of Steven Tyler and Joe Perry singing into the same microphone, though he couldn't decide whether he'd rather be the frontman or guitarist. Maybe he'd have to be both. Cynthia painted a silhouette of her son posing like his heroes in his room. James inherited and developed her visual skills, designing T-shirts, logos (he drew the iconic Metallica logo on a napkin in their Norwalk, California, rehearsal room), and his own drawings, which veer toward Kustom Kulture (think Pushead taking an Ed "Big Daddy" Roth class).

James wrote letters to Aerosmith asking for a lyrics sheet, addressing each individual member in hopes of a response. Someone at the Aero Force responded with an order form for a *Draw the Line* T-shirt. James wasn't thrilled, but all was forgiven by 1993, when Metallica friend and Aerosmith fanatic Rich Burch (the guy credited with the quote "Bang the head that doesn't bang" on the *Kill 'Em All* sleeve, as well as the friend who gave Metallica the mix tape with Killing Joke's "The Wait") was dying of AIDS. Lars and James, visiting Rich in the hospital, got Steven Tyler on the phone with him shortly before he died.

Like many adolescents, James loved Van Halen's debut ("It oozes of youth and rebellion"), and he'd slow the turntable down on UFO records to copy Michael Schenker's solos by ear. He discovered the Ramones and AC/DC around the same time, but unlike his peers he didn't pit punk and metal against each other. "'Well, fuck you man, I like 'em both.' That's the feeling behind the early Metallica songs," James states in *American Hard-core*. He found the ultimate with Motörhead.

James started teaching himself guitar on a five-dollar instrument he picked up at a garage sale, before Cynthia helped him buy an old SG Gibson from a classmate. James dreamed of running around onstage, which he couldn't do with drums or a piano. As an adult, James would say he wished he could play lead guitar like Kirk Hammett. But unable to compete with Kirk, he joined him as the best rhythm player metal had seen.

SURVIVAL TECHNIQUES

"I'd say that in every child's life there is some form of abuse, there's some form of traumatic experience that happens and scars and helps form your survival techniques later on," James has said.

At thirteen, Cynthia Hetfield told her kids their father was on a long business trip. Over the next few months, James noticed more and more of his dad's possessions were gone, taken while the kids were away. He never learned what went down between his parents, or how their marriage got so bad that they would divorce against their religious beliefs. Virgil's note to the family didn't address James, who would later acknowledge his own "big character defect," suspecting people of hiding things from him after Cynthia covered up Virgil's abandonment. Cynthia told thirteen-year-old James to cut his hair so he could get a job to help support the family, and James told Cynthia he wouldn't go back to Sunday school.

Three years later, Cynthia fell ill with cancer and refused medical help. James' stepbrothers insisted on helping her, but it was too late, and Cynthia died when James was sixteen. James remembered it as the angriest he'd ever been. "As soon as you acknowledge the pain you are giving in to the negative aspect of the error, or the evil or whatever. So she's withering away in front of us and we can't say anything." Christian Science didn't allow a funeral or grieving, leaving James to spend hours at his mother's mausoleum ("Why didn't you let us help you?," he'd remember asking) and interpret death on his own, in his writing. He didn't want to touch the inheritance his mom left to be divided among James and his older siblings. ("It was like that was still Mom. I didn't want to mess with that.") James left school for ten days and moved in with his half-brother in La Brea to finish high school. He didn't fit in at school, where being long-haired and introverted meant forfeiting your social life, or at home, where his siblings were too old to be the brothers he craved but not old enough to be paternal. "I hid as much as possible in my music," James remembered.

Music for James included playing Black Sabbath covers in bands named after UFO records (Obsession) and Rush songs (Syrinx). His short-lived band Phantom Lord, whose name he'd later raid for a song title, became Leather Charm. James wrote original songs with names like "Hades Ladies," "Handsome Ransom," and "Let's Go Rock 'n' Roll," all reportedly as bad as their titles, though the latter two were reworked into "No Remorse." James knew his songs weren't great ("I couldn't write a lyric to save my life"), but when his bandmates preferred to keep playing covers, James decided he needed new bandmates. On his high school yearbook page, James wrote "Play music," "Get rich," and "Long Live Rock."

"I wanted it to be freedom from school, from work, from the typical music that we were hearing," James told NPR. "It was a way to get away from my screwed-up family."

"I DON'T BELONG"

"I'm always feeling like I don't belong, no matter where I am. So I'm just searching for a family nonstop," James told *Time Out* in 2012.

James has used the term "father figure" in interviews to describe Ray Burton, Bob Rock, and Phil Towle. It's not a view his bandmates share— Kirk has said Bob was more like a fifth member or big brother. But James roves and wanders for that connection, telling *So What!* he wished he'd known his parents and family history better, or commenting "Our parents are proud" about *S&M* when both of his were dead. Asked by *Heavy Metal Mania* in April 1986 whether Metallica's parents like their music, James responded that Cliff's, Kirk's, and Lars' parents do. "My dad, you know, whatever," he laughs.

He came closer to finding home with his bandmates, rooming with Ron McGovney at Ron's parents' place and helping Lars pack newspapers for his *Los Angeles Times* delivery job. James worked as a high school janitor and made pharmaceutical stickers in a Santa Fe Springs factory, carrying around a small recorder to sing riff ideas into. At lunch James would write songs. He was unnerved when an older coworker promised him if he kept working, someday he could be the foreman of the factory. But James would keep trying to get closer to his lost family, adapting many of his father's frontiersman habits ("Proving manhood to myself. A lot of the things I felt my dad didn't teach me.") over the years while developing new ones. James currently lives on a ranch where he harvests his own meat and vegetables, and is more recently an expert-level beekeeper. Though he got closer to Virgil near the end of his life, James couldn't bring himself to tell his father how much he appeared in James' songs. "Until you both die, it's gonna go on," James told Marc Maron in 2017, twenty years after Virgil's death. "I still battle with him, voices appear in my head."

Interviewed by preteen journalist Elliott Fullam for Little Punk People in 2017, James takes a moment to think about what his chosen superpower would be. He settles on "to heal people . . . Not just outside, but inside, too." When the kid asks him a fart question, James indulges him— he's a pro, and good with kids—but also shows the boy how to make a realistic sound by flicking his fingers on the leather seat. "My dad taught me," James says.

"FORGIVE YOURSELF"

In a 2009 interview, comedian Jim Breuer asked each bandmate to name the most sensitive member of Metallica. Rob, James, and Lars all pick Kirk. But Kirk knows best, and picks James. "His heart can probably wrap around this building."

James has changed much in Metallica. But in the public eye, fans watch James seem to outgrow or move on from things that come back to him—spirituality, drinking, rage, insecurity, mental health issues. Since starting therapy, he has often talked about a need for validation, trying to rock audiences into liking him. On the Worldwired tour, he usually ends "The Unforgiven" with a wave of his hand and states, "Forgive yourself." It's hard to think of another metal god who would say such a strange and important thing to a stadium crowd. But it's also part of why Metallica connects.

James once recognized his calling as "identifying with people's broken-ness and singing about it and bringing it into a stadium and on record," notably citing the venue size his band is most likely to play but also the one that makes people feel least alone. By articulating that perceived broken-ness, James shows an empathy and awareness that reaches millions. "If I could exorcise all those demons I would have, but it's just something you embrace," James said in 2017. "It's a part of me, and I get to celebrate it in my music. I get to communicate it, I get to use it as a therapy to help my own insanity, and other people do, too."

The demons don't go away. But neither does Metallica. "There's always gonna be stuff that bothers us," James said in 1993. "And we'll write about it."

4

FULL SPEED OR NOTHING

Kill 'Em All

"We learned pretty early on that there was no party for us, so we made our own."

—James Hetfield

The drummer played too fast. James tells it like a scene from *That Thing You Do!*—"Lars was always nervous onstage, so he'd just play faster and faster. Nobody wanted to wimp out and tell him. We figured, 'Hell, we'll just play faster too.' And that's what we did on the record as well."

One of the great pleasures of being a metalhead is playing *Kill 'Em All* for your punk friends, who have no idea how much they're about to love this band. Slap a different band name on *Kill 'Em All*'s cover, and you've got an opener for Bad Brains at the 9:30 Club or Black Flag at the Ritz. You can hear mathcore from before Kurt Ballou or Ben Weinman had ever plugged in a guitar. It's a fully realized Melvins record three years before their debut EP, and a Motörhead best-of with all new songs. It's the record Justin Broadrick and Nicholas Bullen bonded over before Napalm Death recorded *Scum*. It sounds like it was recorded in Cerberus' doghouse. World, meet Metallica.

Serious metalheads and punks didn't know what to do with them. An early *Kerrang!* review guessed that a standout in Metallica's set was titled "She Can Destroy," unable to believe this band was rising above metal sex clichés. Popular fan-made bootlegs such as the *No Remorse* vinyl and the

Power Metal demo (featuring the *Metal Massacre II* version of "Hit the Lights," and a possible basis for Pantera's transitional 1988 record *Power Metal*) had covers with mythical beasts and naked women that resembled scenes from *Heavy Metal* comics instead of Metallica lyrics. Kirk went from being taunted for his long hair at a CBGB Agnostic Front show to being celebrated there a year later. *Kill 'Em All* had united hardcore and metal kids.

"All we had was music, you know? And then when we got into the music, all we had were each other," Kirk says in *Murder in the Front Row*. "I think that the anger of being in a place that just didn't have enough to offer—you know, the frustration of being bored—I think a lot of that got channeled into our instruments."

"The rock clubs wouldn't book us because they thought we were punk," James told *Guitar Player*. "And the hardcore clubs would say 'They're metal, they have long hair, get 'em out of here!'" But any club, bar, high school, or roller rink Metallica could play was good enough. On September 18, 1982, they played their first San Francisco show, a last-minute substitute gig for "Metal Massacre Night" at the Keystone. For a sense of how much Metallica stood out, they played between bands called Hans Naughty and Bitch, an S&M themed band. But Metallica were still part of the scene they were about to demolish and revolutionize. Two hundred or so fans went nuts, many of them joining Metallica onstage and leaving after their set. When Metallica brags about their fans on *Kill 'Em All*, the word isn't "cool" or "smart" or "tough." It's "insane."

Metallica introduced themselves by turning off the lights. The show's about to begin. The dream is about to start. It's a theme they'll revisit on a much bigger album that starts with a song about turning off the lights. But Metallica was already hell-bent for metal, reinventing themselves and their songs on *Kill 'Em All*. The final "Hit the Lights" starts with a fade-in, almost unheard of in metal, light years away from the version James and Lars recorded for Brian Slagel in October 1981.

Amazingly, the songs on *Kill 'Em All* average over five minutes—ten songs in 51:20. In Metallica's hands they race by like the horsemen drawing nearer. The songs break from their original guitarist and *No Life 'Til Leather* versions, fleshing out "Phantom Lord" and giving "The Four Horsemen" a new middle eight. Beginner drummers teach themselves double bass with "The Four Horsemen," Lars having set his kit like Motörhead's Philthy Animal Taylor. Three thousand miles away, in Springfield, Virginia, young Dave Grohl pored over *Kill 'Em All*'s booklet and felt his life changing by the decibel. Twenty-five years later, he'd introduce Metallica as "My favorite band in the world" at *Death Magnetic*'s radio premiere. "Just by looking at you we thought, 'Oh my god, we could be in a band too!'" Metallica were the first of countless kids to learn the ropes with *Kill 'Em All*, playing with a DIY energy that couldn't be taught or harnessed. Kirk's solos bend out of pitch, but they still make "The Four Horsemen" his own and inspire guitarists to spend hours trying to replicate "Seek & Destroy." The latter song, written by James in his truck outside his workplace, is one of Metallica's most-played songs but never rehearsed, only played live, getting a different swing every time. Sometimes there's a false ending or extension, and sometimes James jumps into the pit to get hugged and let kids sing the rejoinder into his mic. Playing it different at every show is the closest it gets to the spontaneity of *Kill 'Em All*.

Metallica is a four horsemen army on *Kill 'Em All*, writing mission statements in ways they never have since. It's hard to listen without getting swept up in Metallica's "we," the plural pronoun showing up more times on this record than all the rest of Metallica's records combined, in five of its ten songs. "*Kill 'Em All*'s lyrics created as much excitement as the band's music," wrote sociologist Deena Weinstein. "It is a call to arms to a new generation of metalheads, many of whom were already armed and ready." There's a "Metal Militia" by the time the record closes, Lars' multitracked footsteps on the studio's wood floor creating an army march that doubles as the sound of your speakers blowing out. "No Remorse," which predates the Motörhead compilation people assume it's named after and is brutal enough for a Cannibal Corpse cover in 2002, took lyrical inspiration from an ad for Time Life's *World War II* book series and musical life from Kirk's solo, which jumps in before the first verse. The punk onslaught of "Whiplash" and James' pre-Metallica "Motorbreath" inspired everyone from Morbid Angel to a Seattle *Ride the Lightning* fan who'd befriend Kirk after his band's debut *Bleach* had been released by Sub Pop. Kirk later saw Kurt waving his arms in the snake pit of Metallica's 1992 Seattle show. "I went over there to see what he had to say," Kirk told *NME*. "His one question to me was 'Are you guys gonna play "Whiplash" tonight?'" They closed their first set with it.

"*Kill 'Em All* was the first really consistent thrash album where every song was just a razor blade," Pantera's Dimebag Darrell recalled. "James' fuckin' rhythm playing is unbelievable, especially for his first record. They wrote fantabulous songs and it made me motivated."

Kill 'Em All showcases the bassist, bounding over the *No Life 'Til Leather* low end. Cliff unpredictably ascends the bassline in "Jump in the Fire," before blowing everyone away on "(Anesthesia)—Pulling Teeth." He is one of the only rock bassists to get a solo track, and one of even fewer to deserve one. At Metallica shows through the mid-eighties, James introduces "our freak space cadet bass player." "How about a fuckin' bass solo?" James asks. The crowd always roars, ravenous for more Cliff. How many bass solos get that?

"Cliff had all kinds of shit that he wanted to record on his bass, and the producers would say, 'Well, it doesn't sound right,'" James stated in *Metallica Unbound*. "Of course it didn't sound right! It wasn't fuckin' normal. But it's how we wanted to sound."

Metallica sounds unbreakable. It's their least anguished record—no "Fade to Black" or "Welcome Home (Sanitarium)" yet. But in a Spotify documentary, James described *Kill 'Em All* as "a lot of anger, a lot of questioning things. What the hell am I doing? What do I do? Do I matter? A lot just wanting to go crazy." Off record, Metallica were still finding their identity, occasionally auditioning third guitarists, and actively seeking a new singer, particularly Armored Saint bellower John Bush. But Armored Saint was thriving, and Bush didn't want to leave LA. At Metallica's thirtieth anniversary show, James introduced Bush as "The person we always had in mind to be singing for Metallica. . . . This is a big dream for us. I hope this means as much to him as it does to us." Bush, who found his voice as Anthrax's best frontman, doesn't regret it. ("I remember saying, 'You guys don't need anybody. James is awesome!'")

Metallica weren't above self-mythologizing, writing about how crazy their fans were before they even had fans. Cliff's "Anesthesia" was not the first take, and the "take one" intro was scripted for the engineer (for a more manic intro, check out young James introducing Cliff's "Anesthesia" solo at Hollywood Palladium: "The fucking freak himself will pull your fucking teeth right out of your face!"). Early "live" B-sides were alternate takes of "Phantom Lord" and "Seek & Destroy" with crowd noises dubbed in. Stories about Music America, the Rochester basement studio where Metallica recorded, being haunted may or may not have been true, but sounded great in interviews (they also flexed their horror fixation on the "Jump in the Fire" single, with artwork taken from Les Edwards' cover for British horror novelist Graham Masterton's 1978 book *The Devils of D-Day*). In truth, Metallica slept in U-Haul packing blankets at the Music Building in Jamaica, Queens, a former furniture warehouse next to a railroad track where trains passed by every twenty minutes. They begged Music America for a repair budget for the equipment. On tour they slept four to a room, sharing towels and beds (in Kirk's recollection, Lars took all the blankets and Cliff had pointy elbows). They learned which fast food places let four guys eat off the same $2.99 all-you-can-eat plate and borrowed a toaster and refrigerator from Queens residents Anthrax.

"METAL UP YOUR ASS"

Megaforce's executives, financing the record and Metallica's upcoming tour (mom-and-pop founders Jon "Jonny Z" and Marsha Zazula mortgaged their home), saw distributors balking at the album's proposed title, *Metal Up Your Ass*. Metallica were not happy about this. "We should just kill 'em all," suggested Cliff, in response to the label's concerns. His idea was never carried out, but it did serve Metallica with a new album title. The bloody hammer on the cover was Cliff's idea, too. Nobody can tell if the hand is letting go of or picking up the hammer on the album cover, or whose bloodshed it caused. On tour, Cliff carried a hammer in his luggage, in case he needed to destroy something. Going through customs from the UK to France, airport security took the band's porn but let Cliff keep his hammer, presumably to avoid any situation that might involve wrestling a violent tool from Cliff Burton's hands.

"Metal Up Your Ass," later a popular Metallica shirt and the name of a death metal fest in Fort Worth, is a good argument against Metallica's autonomy. It's a funny name, and the Metallica T-shirt image of a dagger rising from a toilet bowl is pretty cool. But as loud as the music on *Kill 'Em All* speaks, it would be harder to take seriously under the name *Metal Up*

Your Ass, a title more in line with the metal bands that Metallica were dis-tinguishing themselves from. Officially releasing *Metal Up Your Ass* would not have kept Metallica from being one of American music's greatest claims. But they might not have changed rock music as effectively.

Four decades have done nothing to lessen the ferocity of *Kill 'Em All*. If anything, it sounds heavier now, knowing how many thrash and metalc-ore bands couldn't emulate it without sounding watered down. The per-fectly raw production hits the sound that black metal bands aim for. Were *Kill 'Em All* released today, its authors could hop on a tour with anyone from At the Gates to Nile to Pig Destroyer to Sleep. *Kill 'Em All* is peak metal madness, a lesson in motorbreath for people who tell you not to take chances. When alt-country star Jenny Lewis finally finds a partner who's as much trouble as she is in "The New You," she shows it by revealing they listen to *Kill 'Em All* together.

Megaforce pressed 15,000 copies, and *Aardschok* magazine gave *Kill 'Em All* a 99/100 review, holding out on a perfect score only because the critic thought the new Steeler record (with the first major appearance of masturbatory guitar hotshot Yngwie Malmsteen) would be heavier. "Metallica are a lot from LA but fortunately nobody has told them that!" *Metal Mania* raved. Other listeners were less generous. "The whole thing was kind of innocent," James recalled. "I remember hearing the album and going, 'Oh my God, that sucks!'"

"I remember getting the test pressing and listening to it and thinking, 'Oh my god, no one can hear this! This is not good enough!'" Kirk ago-nized, wishing he could play like Jimmy Page on Zeppelin's debut. "After I listened to it for about two or three weeks, I thought, 'This is me' . . . I just have to be myself and let people hear me."

Not many people heard just yet. A scheduled spring 1984 tour with Exciter and the Rods was canceled when they sold only fifteen tickets for the 3,400 capacity Hammersmith in London. Worse, before a January 1984 show in Boston, Metallica's U-Haul went missing. The truck had been hotwired and stolen. It was found a month later, missing the gear Metallica recorded *Kill 'Em All* with, including the Marshall amp James' mother had bought him shortly before her death. (A box of Metallica shirts that was in the truck, of no value to the thieves or anyone outside Metallica's small circles in 1984, would go for at least four figures today.)

Metallica rescheduled the Boston show and borrowed gear from Anthrax, but the dream of playing where their NWOBHM heroes had in Europe crashed. The pain stayed with Metallica even years after they could afford to replace all their equipment many times over. In 2017, when Spokane-based Metallica tribute act Blistered Earth had their gear stolen after a Portland show, word got out to four Bay Area thrash legends who quietly replaced Blistered Earth's gear, free of charge.

At least one person was still thinking ahead, and Metallica started recording again in February 1984. "You have all your life to write your first album," said a young Lars on *The Metal on Metal Show*. "But you only have, you know, eight months to do the second album."

5

POUNDING OUT
AGGRESSION

Lars Ulrich

"The reason most people get off on what we do is that they know it's totally real. Whether they like it or not is a different thing, but they can never take that 'real' thing away from it. I think as an artist that's the best you can do."

—Lars Ulrich

Metallica's 1996 Fan Can, the first in a sporadically released collection of fan club boxes, comes with a "Making of *Load*" video. The best segment is a short called "Lars' (Reckless) Driving Skills." "I've been flipped off more than, like, anybody," Lars says, between swerves. "But it gets me from Point A to Point B quicker than most other people."

Lars doesn't care about being the bad guy. In metal, that's supposed to be a good thing. But Lars cares even less than metal gods are supposed to care, who might at least think twice before suing their fans. Much of Metallica's inner circle wanted Lars' art auction scene removed from *Some Kind of Monster*. Lars insisted it stay in, showing the viewers who he really was. His logic was that the art preview showed the focus was on more than money, and watching Lars discuss Dubuffet, Basquiat, or Jorn one sees an appreciation for the paintings as art and not a status symbol (Lars drinks himself numb watching the paintings go). But there's no getting past watching a leading voice in angry, alienated music pulling over $13 million off his wall.

In another scene, Lars and Kirk watch their departed bassist Jason Newsted's new band Echobrain play a club show. It's hard to imagine anyone, much less someone with Lars Ulrich's music sensibilities, seriously thinking that Echobrain, whose music is about as good as their name, were replacing Metallica in any way. But there's Lars in *Some Kind of Monster*, watching Echobrain and openly distraught that more than twenty people showed up to see Jason's new band. "I feel like such a loser," he moans, putting his head in his hands. "I can't hold my band together. I start records I don't finish . . . Jason's the future, Metallica's the past."

This didn't turn out to be true. But this is part of what makes him Lars. In Lars' Metallica there's always more to do. Being in the world's biggest metal band is never enough. It might be part of why he relates to James, who admitted, post-therapy, that he feared Jason would enjoy being in another band more than Metallica. For as long as Metallica has been together, Lars has been by far its most outspoken member. When Metallica finish their duties with the press and start to go their separate ways, Lars sticks around. He's the only member of Metallica who gives interviews on his day off. "Sometimes I wish I could shut Metallica off, like James and Jason can," Lars has said, "but I can't." There's only one Metallica fan in the world who would question the commitment of James Hetfield, the songwriting heart and soul of the band, and Jason Newsted, the superfan who threw his life into doing everything he could to play with his heroes and put up with their worst tendencies for fourteen years. But that one fan is on the kit behind Metallica every night.

More than James or Kirk, Lars openly enjoys being famous. "Certain people like to play up for the camera more than others," James says in *A Year and a Half in the Life of Metallica*, while air drumming. People who want to be rock stars don't like what they see of themselves in Lars. Metallica has an impressive record of charity work, but only Lars does it on *Who Wants to Be a Millionaire*. He's the only member of Metallica known to have dated a famous actress (*Gladiator*'s Connie Nielsen), or married a fashion model (Jessica Miller). He's also the only member of Metallica that people hate. People will never forgive him for suing Napster. It's still the first thing many fans associate him with. Any Lars Ulrich news story or photo that gets posted on the internet is likely to get flooded with ridicule or hate comments, more than twenty years after the debacle. VH1.com once published a list titled "10 Times Everybody on Earth Got Pissed Off at Lars Ulrich." When drone metal hipsters Sunn O))) covered "For Whom the Bell Tolls" in 2002, they subtitled it "(I Dream of Lars Ulrich Being Thrown Through the Bus Window Instead of My Mystikal Master Kliff Burton)." Several unauthorized online merchandisers sell Cliff Burton T-shirts and stickers with "It Should Have Been Lars" printed on the front, a decision that's perhaps more inconsiderate to Cliff Burton's family than it is to Lars.

To hear some fans tell it, Lars is Metallica's Mike Love, the ruthless, megalomaniacal businessman who exploits his position in one of America's greatest bands by taking advantage of the tormented genius who writes the songs. At best, some fans see him as almost Metallica's Mick Jagger, the rock star poseur businessman who shares creative duties with a cooler partner. (Like Jagger, Lars has been knighted in his home country, accepting the title from Denmark's Crown Prince in 2017.) But the way Lars manages business and his creative duties is not quite as awful or as admirable as people want it to be. People love to play what ifs with Lars, imagining what the band would be like if they fired Lars in 1986, as they were rumored to be considering. Fans joke about Metallica sounding their best at their 2004 Download festival shows where Slayer's Dave Lombardo and Slipknot's Joey Jordison replaced him. (Lars, who was hospitalized following a panic attack, couldn't bring himself to look at pictures or press of the show, while being game enough to emit, "If seeing Dave Lombardo and Joey Jordison playing with Metallica isn't a great show, then I don't know what is.") But as much as some fans wish it, there is no Metallica without Lars Ulrich, the guy who called James Hetfield back and promised "Hit the Lights" to Metal Blade.

"I would say that Lars is a manager who also likes to play drums," James has said. "He will think of ways that people don't play drums and try to do it. . . . It's really mathy for him. He will figure it out, but once he's figured it out, it's unbelievable. He can pretty much play anything if he just puts his mind to it."

It's hard to see success ever satiating Lars. "You think one day some fucker's gonna tell you, 'You have a number one record in America,' and the whole world will ejaculate," Lars stated after the release of the Black Album. "I stood there in my hotel room, and there was this fax that said,

'You're number one.' And it was, like, 'Well, okay.' It was just another fucking fax from the office."

TORBEN AND LONE'S BOY

Lars was born December 26, 1963, in Denmark to Lone and Torben Ulrich. Torben was a second-generation tennis star described by *Sports Illustrated* as the circuit's "most fascinating, most captivating figure. Win or lose, he provokes reaction and constant comment." An artistic, iconoclastic hippy, Torben stood out among the Wimbeldon crowd, in which he competed for over twenty years. Torben wrote about jazz for Copenhagen papers, playing Miles Davis and Ornette Coleman in the house, and befriending artists like Sonny Rollins, Don Cherry, Ben Webster, and Lars' godfather, Dexter Gordon (Lars found a childhood friend in Cherry's stepdaughter Neneh). Torben later become a metal celebrity in his own right, sometimes called "Metal Gandalf" by fans, even by Lars himself, for his pensive, wizardly demeanor. He's stayed involved in Metallica's business, writing for *So What!* and giving harsh input on his son's music. In *Some Kind of Monster*, Lars plays an ambient new Metallica song for Torben, inspired by seeing Sigur Rós at the Fillmore. Lars thinks it might open the new record, but Torben strokes his beard and states, "Delete that." Lars protests, but Torben is firm. "For me it doesn't cut it." Lars, already pained by James leaving for rehab the day before, says there's nothing personally worse for him than Torben knowing his music sucks, though Lars would later tell interviewers he couldn't remember what song his dad didn't like (this episode inspired an Iron Reagan song called "Delete That").

But the Ulrichs gave Lars a flexible upbringing. He grew up quick with no siblings, spending much of his time with his father's artistic and literary friends. In California, Lars would be surprised his young metal peers considered parents the enemy. Torben was a drinking buddy who took his son to shows, including the Rolling Stones' free Hyde Park show in 1969, when Lars was five. "Americans would call it 'spoiled,'" Lars admitted. "But I was very independent. . . . As far as my parents were concerned, I could go see Black Sabbath twelve times a day. But I had to find my own means, carrying the paper or whatever, to get the money to buy the tickets." He also had to find his way there and back, sometimes falling asleep on the ride back and getting woken up by the conductor.

Lars dreamed of playing tennis like his father. But after a Deep Purple show at Vejlby-Risskov Hallen, Lars' tennis racket became an air guitar. Young Lars made his own drum kit out of cardboard boxes and paint stirrers, pretending to be Ian Paice. Lars didn't know the guitarist's name, but was impressed that he rubbed his instrument on his ass. Purple inspired him to pick up *Fireball*, and later to buy platform boots like Ritchie Blackmore's to wear to school, which got him teased by classmates who called him "Smoking Joe." But Lars, a self-described "Type A personality," was unfazed. "It just never dawned upon me that I would not be able to be myself," he's stated. "That never registered."

But as a teen Lars was still figuring that person out. He was wowed by a family visit to New York ("Everything in America was just bigger and cooler and faster"), later telling a Guitar Center interviewer that he was drawn to America's goal-oriented culture. Upon finishing school in Denmark at sixteen, Lars flew to Florida to attend a tennis academy before settling in LA. Lars was humbled on the West Coast, going from being a top youth tennis competitor in Denmark to not even making local teams. But his travel experience gave a confidence that later helped him manage three unruly guys who hadn't been far outside Southern California. He also stayed on top of metal by subscribing to Bullet Mail Order, becoming such a dedicated customer that the company started shipping and billing him for all their new releases. Lars brought friends over and schooled them in the ways of NWOBHM.

One student of Lars' unofficial music students was a shy boy from Downey, who stayed overnight, poring over demonic-looking records and making mix tapes. He'd remember finding himself through the music, taping over his old AOR cassettes, being amazed by all the different-sounding metal bands that came from the UK—in LA, most of them sounded the same to him. "You were pretty much able to hand the tape around, it'd be like tenth generation copy but you would still hear the magic in whatever was happening there and think 'Wow, I've discovered yet another piece of my puzzle,'" James recalled.

BEAT THE DRUM SLOWLY

Lars would tell people he got his first drum kit from his grandmother. To this day, Lars is mocked for not having the technical skill of some of metal's most accomplished timekeepers. He's made some atrocious production decisions, but much of the hate comes from people not liking him personally. "He plays exactly enough to make the riff kick ass and stay heavy," Exhumed's Matt Harvey wrote of Lars for Invisible Oranges. "No matter how fast a riff or song is, it always retains power. He never forces his drumming on the listener like so many modern players who use drum fills excessively."

People who complain about Lars' drumming might also tell you Kurt Cobain is a bad guitarist, or that David Lee Roth is not a good singer. Lars is often sloppy, and simplified his kit down to a six-piece after the Black Album, but Lars has a distinguished feel and endurance that Metallica's classic records are unimaginable without. He's a better writer than he gets credit for, coming up with motifs and arrangements as well as helping Kirk pick solos. He famously asked Kirk to repeat the riff that would become "Enter Sandman" three times and put a tail on it. Those song-driven instincts are clear in his drumming, and Metallica's technical accessibility is a major part of their ability to connect. By making the right choices with a few fills, Lars has inspired countless hopefuls to sit behind the kit.

"He's really song-oriented, in the way he does everything," says *Hardwired . . . to Self-Destruct* producer Greg Fidelman. "In the way he plays his drums, he's playing the song, not playing the drums."

Lars seems aware of his reputation, telling drummer jokes ("Q. What has three legs and a cunt on top of it? A. A drum stool!") and talking up guys like Dave Lombardo or the Mars Volta's Jon Theodore. "I'm not a particularly accomplished drummer but I am very, very, very good at understanding the role of the drums next to James Hetfield's rhythm guitar," he told *Rhythm*. "I guarantee you I'm the best guy in the world for that, and that's enough for me."

James might agree, answering a question in 2009 about Lars being a subpar drummer. "He will admit that," James reflected. "And I'm not a very good singer. But something happens when we play together."

ENGLAND'S DREAMING

Like James Joyce leaving Dublin to write *Ulysses*, Lars had to get away from Europe to appreciate it more, to write, play, and arrange with an outsider's view of European bands. He read *Sounds* and *NME* and looked for ways to connect with bands. (Lars: "I think Danes, by nature, are inquisitive and curious," adding his best advice: "Ask questions.") He followed Motörhead around California, finding their hotel room and introducing himself as the head of America's Motörhead Fan Club. It was an unofficial club with only one member, but Lemmy remembered him. "He wanted to have a drink with me, and clearly wasn't used to drinking my measures, so he threw up," recalled Lemmy. "It wasn't that bad, and I didn't make him clean up or anything, but I did insist that he wear a bib for the rest of his time with me in the room. Oddly, he threw up the next time we met as well." Finding Lemmy more approachable than the golden gods of Led Zeppelin or the superhumans in Kiss, Lars booked a trip to England.

"I'd sit there and learn from the Motörheads and Diamond Heads and Iron Maidens, because I was so far up their asses all the time," Lars remembered. He introduced himself to Diamond Head backstage at London's Woolwich Odeon and talked himself into getting invited to crash on Brian Tatler's floor in a sleeping bag. Lars ended up staying with Sean Harris for a month, squeezing in the back of Harris' compact car and watching the band write songs. Lars called his friends back home to tell them he'd been throwing up from drinking too much with Diamond Head, occasionally putting Harris on the line. Tatler would remember Lars being the most driven person he'd met.

SHOW BUSINESS

Few bands have someone other than the frontman as their unofficial spokesman, and even fewer have the drummer. If history is written by the people who give interviews, Lars wants to make history, hunting out platforms the way James and Kirk search for riffs. In his earliest interviews, Lars already has a staggering sense of the music business, singles, radio, and more. He's shrewd enough to recognize Metallica's "weakest market" in Europe

(England, really?) at an age when most bands can barely manage drink tickets. He kept a journal, starting with Metallica's first-ever show (March 14, 1982, at Radio City), in which he would mark who played well, who needed to improve, pay, crowd size, and whether he got to meet the head-liners. At twenty he sent Q Prime management a five-point letter about why the packaging for *Ride the Lightning*'s US release was unacceptable, from misspelling Kirk Hammett's name to listing the wrong song titles, barely giving himself a moment to bask in the fact that he'd just cowritten and gotten an advance copy of fucking *Ride the Lightning*. Lars is so ingrained in Metallica's business that it can seem recreational for him. (Lars: "I'm not particularly driven. . . . For people that really work, saying that Metallica is a job—that's kind of insulting.") In *A Year and a Half in the Life of Metallica*, when Lars learns the Grateful Dead have their own MGM luxury plane, he's not just impressed. He knows it's the same plane Guns N' Roses has.

Lars cares. He's the most image-conscious member of the band. In *Some Kind of Monster*, his hair changes with nearly every other scene. He complains when his bandmates smile too much, from Kirk in *S&M* to Bob Rock in *Some Kind of Monster* to Jason in photoshoots (Lars: "Every time he poses he looks like someone from Anthrax!"). It's not like anyone thinks Metallica is less badass if someone smiles. Maybe Lars has calmed down since the 2000s, with Robert all smiles onstage. But that's the kind of thing Lars worries about.

"Apart from the guy in Nirvana, who'll lie to you and say, 'Uh, we don't want anyone to buy our records,' 99.9 percent of people in bands would like people to hear their music and get into their band," Lars said in the early nineties. "That is a fucking fact." Lars was right about the Nirvana frontman, who publicly complained about MTV overplaying his videos while privately telling his managers they weren't getting played enough. But Cobain knew his fans wanted to see him differently from his managers, and Lars is a similarly savvy rock star, playing up his band's outsider cool-ness while striving for the biggest successes. He made sure to point out "One" was successful without radio or MTV in his Grammy acceptance speech, but he still showed up to accept the award. In a press release for "One," Lars emphasizes that MTV's decision makers are troubled by their dark new video. "We want them to play the long version because we think it explains the story line a lot better than the short version. But we need you to call in and request it to make it #1 so they'll play it in super duty rotation (that means a lot)."

"The way we're gonna be big, hopefully, in four or five years, is gonna be quite a different way than any other band has done it, except maybe Iron Maiden," Lars told *Kick Ass* magazine in July 1985. "It's gonna be a sort of thing where you don't have to follow any trends or get airplay, you don't need to make videos, you just sort of do it through a really good street buzz. Keep a down-to-earth thing going with kids, doing what you wanna do. . . . The public will change for us in a few years, instead of us changing for them."

Metallica is the first band Lars joined, at seventeen, and the only band he's ever been in. He struggles to live outside of it. When James, in a scene filmed for *Some Kind of Monster*, says that in rehab and therapy he had to learn he was more important than Metallica, Lars is incredulous. "Why does it have to be either/or?" To Lars, anything less than 100 percent is phoning it in. Being restless and unsatisfied doesn't make Lars an easy bandmate. But it does make Metallica. Jason Newsted, who knows a thing about Metallica obsessions, marveled in a 1994 *Brave Words & Bloody Knuckles*, "He eats, sleeps and breathes Metallica! I don't think he enjoys his time away from the band."

Whether or not he enjoys it, he applies the same curiosity and dog-gedness he brings to Metallica, through indulgences in film ("definitely my favorite escape"), art galleries ("my place of sanctuary"), and music, hosting groundbreaking artists on Sirius XM show *It's Electric!* since 2017. Watching Lars interview members of the White Stripes, the Dillinger Escape Plan, and LCD Soundsystem, as well as peers from Alice in Chains, Tool, or his own band, one sees the tireless fandom that his friends compared to music school all those years ago in LA. "I don't consider myself any less turned on by the things that turn me on than I did 10, 20, 30, or 40 years ago," he told *Kerrang!* in 2018. "I absolutely still have this crazy thing about music and art in general." One senses that decades from now he still will, even in the unpredictable life of Lars Ulrich.

6

TAKE A LOOK TO THE SKY

Ride the Lightning

"If you came here to see spandex, and fuckin' eye makeup, and all that shit, and the words 'rock 'n' roll, baby' in every fuckin' song, this ain't the fuckin' band."

—James Hetfield

Seventy thousand people saw Metallica at Donington on August 17, 1985, when James made this proclamation. It was at Monsters of Rock, more than ten times the size of Metallica's previous biggest crowd, with Metallica hilariously stuck between Ratt and Bon Jovi. Jack Black recalled this story in 2014 at the Concert for Valor, in Washington, DC, promising a band even better than Tenacious D. "With the fire and force of a thousand suns they changed the landscape of rock 'n' roll forever," he intoned.

The story of Metallica at Donington has been told in various forms. The Hetfield quote has been cleaned up, rewritten, and appears in nearly every Metallica book. But few of these histories quote the next line. Taking in the cheers from a crowd that's still catching their breath from "Ride the Lightning," James yells, "We came here to bash some fuckin' heads for 50 minutes!"

Not "We came here to rock," or "We came here to kick ass." What Metallica does to the fans is more immediate than what they do for themselves. They felt more like fans that day, trying to catch glimpses of ZZ Top backstage and being escorted out by security. Metallica only connects the bashing and the heads, and both will be exalted. Metallica also kept their word about lyrics. On Metallica's *$5.98 E.P.—Garage Days Re-Revisited* version of Budgie's "Crash Course in Brain Surgery" two years later, they ripped out the original's "Ooh baby, I can rock and roll / Ooh baby, get out of my soul" couplet and replaced it with Metallica's own rowdy banter.

"There's nothing cooler, no better moment, than you getting 20,000 to 40,000 people singing along," James told *The Village Voice*. "You feel a part of something, you feel like you're doing the right thing."

Metallica epitomized thrash on *Kill 'Em All*, but on *Ride the Lightning* they stopped depending on it. For *Kill 'Em All*, they might have written "Speeding Death" or "Galloping Death." On *Ride the Lighting*, they set the pace at "Creeping." The first song on *Ride the Lightning* is already heavier and lighter than anything on *Kill 'Em All*, moving outward and tackling bigger themes. *Ride the Lightning* is not as consistently heavy, but it's darker and more varied. Moderately paced metal stomps like Pantera's "Walk" and Gojira's "Vacuity" are rooted in "For Whom the Bell Tolls." It's also the first Metallica record that isn't about how much Metallica kicks ass, though that's abundant in the music.

Even before Metallica had a reputation for metamorphizing, it makes sense that they'd change on their second record—they were almost a different band. *Kill 'Em All* was primarily written by James, Lars, and Dave; *Ride the Lightning* was mainly James, Kirk, Cliff, and Lars, with two Dave cowrites ("Ride the Lightning" and "The Call of Ktulu") left. Getting Kirk and Cliff on record means making the most of them. Today the classic lineup seems entrenched, but as late as 1984 James and Lars were still talking about getting a singer. On *Ride the Lightning*, we're hearing James growing into his frontman role and realizing it. Cliff pulled the band to a more harmonic and melodic side, expanding on the classical influence started on "(Anesthesia)—Pulling Teeth." He'd sometimes play or sing the third part of a two-part harmony along with their music, in Kirk's memory, "a living, breathing harmonizer." Cliff gets six of eight cowrites on *Ride the Lightning*, marking himself on the record's best known songs, everything except "Trapped Under Ice" and "Escape." Kirk was leaving his mark on a band that still had Dave Mustaine's fingerprints on its songwriting. The harmonies and solos put to rest any wonder whether Dave or Kirk

would be Metallica's best lead guitarist, or which band, Exodus or Metallica, could do best with the Phrygian segment and "Die by my hand" chant
that Kirk wrote when he was all of sixteen years old.

Ride the Lightning has dynamics, fast and loud movements near slow
and quiet ones, the speed and sound mixing slow and loud parts too. "Even
in the same songs, we're trying two or three different things. . . . We're not
satisfied to just do one thing well," Lars told *Hit Parader* in 1986. "We're
always looking for new ways of playing heavy metal." *Kill 'Em All*'s rules
are out the window. Metallica imagined thrash as something huge, with
unlimited potential. *Ride the Lightning* pioneered thrash ballads, complex
metal instrumentals, and getting fans mad at Metallica, already unafraid to
piss off the metal kids as much as they offended any parent, preacher, or
politician. Life's for my own to live my own way. *Ride the Lightning* also
marked the beginning of metal bands evaluating themselves by Metallica's
standards. "People said, 'They wrote a ballad, they sold out, it's over for
them, I'm going to Slayer.'" James told *The Washington Post*. "There were
metal bands out there saying 'Thirteen new songs and no ballads!'"

It's a record of death, by nuclear warfare, capital punishment, armed
conflict, suicide, suffocation, biblical plagues, and Cthulhu. It's also a
record of alienation, made by four outsiders, at least three of whom were
getting homesick recording in Denmark, reflected in the solitude of "Fade
to Black," "Trapped Under Ice," "Ride the Lightning," and "Escape."
"Everything I write about has something to do with me," James said of
Ride the Lightning, describing the lyrics as more punk-inspired and opinionated. "I write about a lot of fears and things that bother me." Not that
James had been given the chair, but he'd tell David Fricke that putting
himself in other people's situations helped get his own feelings out. Being
James, he didn't tell listeners what the "Ride the Lightning" narrator's
offense was, or even if he'd committed it, or whether being freed from a
frightening dream meant dying or waking up. James condemns the situation but doesn't clarify whether he's damning the conviction or the sentence, although in a 2012 *The Village Voice* interview he joked that the guy
getting the chair had stolen music online.

"Since fucking Black Sabbath, there's nothing like that, with that level
of attitude and intelligence in lyrics," Sepultura's Max Cavalera said in
2005. "James Hetfield wrote the most amazing lyrics in metal, ever."

Cliff's Bach-inspired acoustic intro to "Fight Fire with Fire," coaxing listeners in before the attack, is also a first. At the Keystone on the *Kill 'Em All* box set, Metallica labors over the intro and stumbles into a song they've barely developed the chorus to. But they have to let it out. The arms race–themed song shoots down eye-for-an-eye politics over a rapid off-tempo rhythm, falling bombs marked by descending harmonics. The title track shoots out a melodic minor intro before crushing it with cranked up distortion, James yelling out cries for help in a death sentence narrative that ranks with Johnny Cash's crime fiction and Devin Townsend's extremity (Heavy Devy once named it his favorite Metallica song, citing Lars' double kick to toms salvo at the end of the solo).

Lars strikes an anvil bringing out "For Whom the Bell Tolls," echoing the start of *Back in Black* years before Metallica followed it with their own all-black album. "For Whom the Bell Tolls" sounded nothing like a smash, at least until Metallica's later successes helped make it one (it scores the excellent intro to 2009 film *Zombieland*), but the series of riffs that build with Cliff's chromatic, propulsive bass intro are undeniable, as are James' most commanding vocals and strongest lyrics to date.

"Fade to Black" is the first single. It's at least as strong a shock to fans of *Kill 'Em All* as "Enter Sandman" will be to . . . *And Justice for All* fans. James wrote the suicide tale at a friend's house in New Jersey, teaching himself to mute acoustic guitar squeaks while he composed. The recorded version uses a confessional steel string acoustic, and Metallica showed they could be as emotionally violent and heavy as they were musically. The cinema-themed title is one of Metallica's first uses of film influence, and it's a harbinger for songs like "Welcome Home (Sanitarium)" and "One," though unlike those two, "Fade to Black" has no vocal chorus hook, as lost as the narrator. Some *Kill 'Em All* fans were disgusted. Black Sabbath, Judas Priest, and Iron Maiden had all used acoustic guitars, but Metallica were supposedly above that. But fans like journalist Donna Gaines heard something else, described in her book *Teenage Wasteland: Suburbia's Dead End Kids* as, "The hour-of-darkness lamentations of a dying human soul. Alone, defeated, depleted, hopeless and stranded but for one last exit. . . . This song goes to the bottom but *comes back up*. It gives you the will to power, to triumph, it's cathartic, it's killer."

The panicked "Trapped Under Ice" starts side two at Metallica's fastest, a horror story about being trapped and silenced, four years before "One." *Whiplash* founder Brian Lew remembers Lars being inspired by *Never Cry Wolf*, although Lars tried to sell his band's intellect by telling interviewers "Trapped Under Ice" was about cryogenics. "The main theme of teenagers is that they are not being heard, and by making music so loud, someone has to hear it," James said in *A Year and a Half in the Life of Metallica.* "Escape" is famous for two things, (a) being a deep cut on a perfect metal record, and (b) Metallica hating it. Fans have theorized that James dislikes it for its simplicity, catchiness, last-minute inclusion, pushing James' voice by being written in the key of A, and its lyrics (whose "so-called standards" is James talking about?). Metallica acknowledge this, lovingly teasing art rock guitar hero St. Vincent about "Escape" when she professed her *Ride the Lightning* love on social media (for a good time, check out her subsequent interview with Kirk Hammett). But everyone's Metallica is different, yours and mine, ours and theirs. "Escape," James' most-hated classic-era song, called "the one Metallica song I really hate" by none other than Cliff Burton, played a total of once live (2012 at Orion Fest, the only time they played *Ride the Lightning* in its entirety), is a great song, boasting some of Lars' best accents and inspiring bands such as Gojira, who covered "Escape" for the *From Mars to Sirius* import.

James unleashes an alarming main riff, and Cliff drives his Rickenbacker into the war zone for a detailed, descriptive version of the Plagues of Egypt that thrashes hard enough for Gwar's Oderus Urungus to cover a Bible story song in 2010 (Oderus: "Metallica is one of the greatest bands ever, and because of everything they've done, because they wrote 'Creeping Death,' I will never diss them." Not quite, but who checks Gwar for integrity?). Whoever sets up Lars' crash cymbal every night must pray that Metallica doesn't play this song, but the star is Kirk, whose crowd-inciting bridge helped make "Creeping Death" Metallica's second most performed song, behind only "Master of Puppets." Cliff harmonizes the third chorus and often sang it himself live, as did Cliff's biggest fan, Jason Newsted. These days it's sung by Metallica's biggest fans, the audience. The evocative instrumental "The Call of Ktulu" closes, a transformative piece for Metallica and metal in general, marking Dave's last songwriting contribution while flexing Cliff's classical chops and Lovecraftian instincts, purposely misspelling the beast's name rather than bring it closer by writing it down. On *Ride the Lightning*, Metallica sound like they can summon the cosmic.

FLEMMING RASMUSSEN

Lars called engineer Flemming Rasmussen, intrigued by his work with Rainbow and the prospect of a trip back to Denmark. Unable to afford a hotel, Metallica lived in Rasmussen's studio free of charge while Flemming's wife, Pernille, complained about the boys in Danish, to Lars' discomfort. For about a month and a half, the boys worked from 7 p.m. until about 4 or 5 a.m., going out for beer and poker afterward. Vocals were double-tracked, strengthening the metal militia, and Rasmussen remembers a minimum of six guitar tracks on all songs, the kind of stunt you pull when you're recording a guy who can make multiple tracks sound like one guitar as convincingly as James Hetfield. Rasmussen would join Metallica for two more records, and other bands have flocked to him for that white whale, holy grail sound, but Rasmussen stays firm. "To get that sound, you had to have been that band at that moment, because they were inventing it all on the spot."

A MIDSUMMER'S NIGHT'S SCREAM

Michael Alago, a twenty-four-year old A&R rep for Elektra, thought Metallica were "the most charismatic band that I had ever seen." He had seen Metallica at Brooklyn's L'Amour in 1983 and was blown away by *Kill 'Em All*. "It wasn't just loud and aggressive, it had elements of British heavy metal, punk rock, and classic rock, but more than anything it had speed," he wrote in *I Am Michael Alago: Breathing Music. Signing Metallica. Beating Death*. He gave Lars a business card and was still in touch by the time Metallica announced an August 3, 1984, show with Raven and Anthrax at Manhattan's Roseland Ballroom, billed as "A Midsummer's [*sic*] Night's Scream." Metallica rode to New York drinking themselves to sleep on a foul-smelling bus whose AC broke down in Texas, but arrived in time for a sold-out crowd of 3,500, including Alago, Elektra CEO Bob Krasnow, and Pere Ubu manager Cliff Burnstein, who had founded Q Prime with Peter Mensch in April 1982 (Def Leppard was their first client). James celebrated his twenty-first birthday that night by climbing up on the monitors above a raging sea of headbangers. They all absorbed the live debut of a strange new song that dealt four increasingly heavy progressions, each riff cycle accentuating the previous one, before presenting a reinterpretation of an Ernest Hemingway story. Burnstein stuck to the walls, shielding himself from multiple erupting mosh pits, some in the crowd wearing homemade Metallica shirts. "I felt old for the first time," Burnstein recalled. "There was a whole new breed of fans." Supposedly headliners Raven played afterwards.

In Alago's memory, he ran backstage to Metallica's dressing room, hugged and kissed each member, and insisted they meet him at his office the next day. Over beer and Chinese food, the group listened to *Ride the Lightning* and watched Alago bait them to Elektra with stories about the Stooges, MC5, and Queen (Cliff was curious about the more obscure stuff from Elektra's subsidiary Nonesuch). Elektra's lack of metal bands was seen as a way for Metallica to stand out, as well as get more attention and support, and they were promised artistic control. "They were so focused it was kind of easy on my end," Alago recalled. Metallica joined Q Prime and signed an eight-album deal on the condition that the first 75,000 *Ride the Lightning* copies would be on Megaforce. This worked fine for the Zazulas—Elektra's boost helped double *Kill 'Em All* sales by November, rescuing a label that earlier in 1984 hadn't been able to fund *Ride the Lightning* without help from its British partner label, Music for Nations.

Elektra A&R man Brain Koppelman, known for promoting Tracy Chapman, described *Ride the Lightning* as "a perfect album." Years later he wrote a *Ride the Lightning* discussion into his TV show *Billions*, making antihero Bobby Axelrod (Damian Lewis) a fan and giving Metallica an appearance in the episode "Short Squeeze." "It takes guts to make change. It's also called progress," a musician tells Axelrod, having clearly learned from her favorite band. *Ride the Lightning* stays an exemplary firebrand, showing up in everything from a joke in *Silver Linings Playbook* to M.I.A.'s T-shirt in the "Paper Planes" video. But in the months after the record's release, Metallica already sounded ready to move on.

"I think the day that you're totally happy with what you've done is the time to sort of rethink what's going on," Lars told *Metal Forces* in November 1984. After writing and recording forty-seven perfect minutes of metal history, Metallica was still trying to get better.

"I'M PICKING OUT A THERMOS FOR YOU"

By *Ride the Lightning*, Metallica was big enough to spur interest in Spastik Children, a punk collective that included James on drums with Cliff, and sometimes Kirk or later Jason, playing venues like the Stone or Ruthie's Inn (described by James as Metallica's *Cheers*), on weeknights. While metal usually does comedy better than any other rock genre—look at Gwar, Stormtroopers of Death, Dethklok, Spïñal Tap, Tenacious D, *Ziltoid the Omniscient*, Wayne and Garth, Bill and Ted, Beavis and Butt-Head, and Cheech and Chong's "Earache My Eye" (an early bass influence for Rob), for starters—Spastik Children is almost unlistenable. Band protocol included never rehearsing and performing drunk, to the dismay of fans who showed up to see James and Cliff. Worse, they'd sometimes intro a *Kill 'Em All* song before segueing into some original SC garbage or a reworking of the Steve Martin song from *The Jerk* about buying a thermos. Shoddy footage is available online, but you'll be sorry.

Metallica's comedy project didn't last. But even if Metallica had broken up and pursued new paths in 1984, no amount of Spastik Children reunions would dilute the impact of *Ride the Lightning*, a record that upended the entire history of metal, Metallica's part included. James (in 2017), Lars (1990), and Jason (2002) have all named it as their favorite Metallica record, as have countless fans taken in by the magic of a record that can sell six million copies and still feel like it was written exclusively for each listener. "We knew it would freak people out," James said later, considering "Fade to Black." "But we also got hundreds of letters from kids telling us how they related to the song and that it made them feel better."

7

HIT THE LIGHTS

Metallica at the Movies

"There's a train of thought that . . . the public needs to be beat over the head with your mission, your intention behind the movie. I don't follow that all the time. I think people, when they're in their right space, and the right time, art speaks to them."

—James Hetfield

Metallica's greatest cinematic exploits are, of course, in their music. Movies have inspired some of their best songs (see chapter 17), and Metallica has been creating movies for our ears for as long as they've been releasing music, with theatrical flair and dramatic delivery. Yet for a band of their stature, Metallica has taken precious few trips to the silver screen. Other than a few talking head appearances in music documentaries (most often Lars), brief cameos in films such as *Get Him to the Greek* and *Hemingway & Gellhorn* (almost always Lars), and even the occasional voiceover work (yes, that's James telling Kenny he's going to Hell in *South Park: Bigger, Longer & Uncut*), the band is not well known for their screen presence. Someone must have blackmailed them into appearing in the 2006 straight-to-DVD flop *The Darwin Awards*, in which the boys reenact a concert urban legend and get to share an IMDb credit with Winona Ryder and Lawrence Ferlinghetti. Bless the person who sat through the movie just to upload Metallica's screen time to YouTube—they play parts of "No Leaf Clover" and "Sad but True." For a band sometimes thought of as the metal Beatles, it's hard to imagine Metallica making *A Hardwired Day's Night* or *The Thing That Should Not Let It Be.*

Metallica's passion for film reaches their live performances, music videos, and outside pursuits, from the show-opening blast of Ennio Morricone's "The Ecstasy of Gold" from *The Good, the Bad and the Ugly* to the use of *Johnny Got His Gun* in the "One" video to Kirk Hammett's horror collection. Lars is enough of a film buff to get an in-depth conversation with the *New York Times* film critic A. O. Scott, inspired in part by Lars' music critic father. That said, Metallica have contributed and inspired a few gems in the rockumentary and music film canon. Most of the films described here are aimed at Metallica's base, with only a few likely to appeal to anyone who couldn't tell "The Unforgiven" from "The Unforgiven II." In short, most of these Metallica films are for fans only—but who could hear Metallica and not be a fan? Here are sixteen movies and videos to include in your Metallica film fest.

CLIFF 'EM ALL (1987, DIR. JEAN PELLERIN AND DOUG FREEL)

For a Metallica fan raised in the smartphone era, it might be hard to see why *Cliff 'Em All* was one of the most popular and important metal films of the 1980s. Search "Metallica live" on YouTube and you'll find any number of shaky-cam clips from Metallica shows, as well as many more high-definition and pro-shot clips than the ones in *Cliff 'Em All*. But for those of us who spent most of our lives with no way of immediately accessing Metallica footage, *Cliff 'Em All* was a marvel. Metallica made *Cliff 'Em All* one of the only concert films to look more like something a fan would give their friends than something a band could give their fans.

Released in 1987, a little over a year after Cliff Burton's fatal bus accident, *Cliff 'Em All* packed an hour and a half of video footage from Metallica's first few tours in a bootleg-style release that reflected Metallica's DIY ethos at the time, somewhat like a video companion to *The $5.98 E.P.—Garage Days Re-Revisited* (it's even subtitled *$19.98 Home Vid* on the cover). Most of the video is fan-shot, and Lars called fans personally to request footage and to assure them that Metallica wasn't trying to prosecute bootleggers or exploit Cliff's name. Segments get their own band-created, unprofessional-sounding names (see the "Still drunk on Ozzy tour" performance of "Master of Puppets," or the "Four Horseman" performance billed as "Headlining with Venom, Nazareth, beer"). Short, drunken interludes from Hetfield, Hammett, and Ulrich create a demystifying atmosphere that helped distinguish Metallica from their more produced and self-important peers. Where else can you get a free roach-smoking lesson from Kirk Hammett, or watch James explain the "*Metal Up Your Ass/Kill 'Em All*" story to a crowd that was hearing it for the first time before getting caught up in a chant (James: "Say 'Me-tal-up-your-ass!'")? Aesthetically and historically, *Cliff 'Em All* is a relic from a time long gone.

Yet even when overshadowed by the internet (but not the 1999 DVD reissue, which thankfully can't clear up the mix), *Cliff 'Em All* is a valuable document. There is no better video tribute to Cliff Burton's incredible talents as a bassist. With respect to Metallica's spectacular box set releases, this is the best video collection of the band's rise to fame. Whether blowing away headliners Raven just weeks after *Kill 'Em All*'s release with "No Remorse" and "Metal Militia," or stunning Roskilde Festival attendees hearing "Welcome Home (Sanitarium)" and "(Anesthesia)—Pulling Teeth" while waiting for Phil Collins, Metallica had a lot worth capturing. Watch the camera trying to find the most exciting thing onstage to focus on—no easy task when you're shooting James, Lars, Cliff, and Kirk playing songs from three perfect records. By the time the film closes, with a photo tribute to Cliff set to "Orion" (the last acknowledgment in the "Hey man, think of a name for the thank list" end credits—"And of course—Jan and Ray Burton!!"), Metallica have shown themselves capable of both power and poignancy.

The back of the *Cliff 'Em All* cassette case reads in part, "Well we finally went and did what we always talked about not doing, releasing a vid!! Before you throw up in disgust let us (except K__) tell you the idea behind this . . . it's really a look back at the 3 1/2 years that Cliff was with us and includes his best bass solos and the home footage & pix, that we feel capture his unique personality and style. The quality in some places ain't that happening but the feeling is there and thats what matters!!" "K" is assumed to be Kirk, but the band has never commented on why he didn't want to talk about *Cliff 'Em All*.

2 OF ONE (1989, DIR. STEVEN GOLDMAN)

Metallica stayed away from music videos for years. Lars even told an interviewer in 1988, "There's no thoughts about it. Having one is pretty useless anyway. *Headbangers Ball* is a fucking joke." But as we all know, Metallica started making videos shortly thereafter, starting with one of the most affecting clips ever to grace a video channel. If only a handful of music videos deserve their own video album, "One" is among them.

 2 of One might be best remembered for Pushead's iconic cover art, a skull tangled in a mummy-like papoose, which has since appeared on several Metallica T-shirts and posters (including the one on the gang's wall in *Point Break*). The film itself runs less than twenty minutes, starting with a black-and-white Lars interview (he talks us through writing the song, acquiring the rights to *Johnny Got His Gun*, filming the video, and gets interrupted by a phone call) before playing two versions of the "One" video, one full-length and one with just the band performance, cut down two minutes for hesitant programmers and to give Metallica a sense of whether the video worked better with or without film dialogue. "Neither me nor the band think much of it," says Ulrich of the latter edit, inexplicably called the "Jammin' Version," and chances are you'll agree with him. Who wants to see a condensed version of an epic like "One," much less a video that removes the *Johnny Got His Gun* scenes?

 In 2006, *2 of One* was supplanted by Metallica's video collection *The Videos 1989–2004*, which included *2 of One* in its entirety on the DVD (somewhat like how Metallica supplanted *The $5.98 E.P.—Garage Days Re-Revisited* with *Garage Inc.*). But for the Metallica collector, *2 of One* is a must, mainly for the Pushead cover.

A YEAR AND A HALF IN THE LIFE OF METALLICA (1992, DIR. ADAM DUBIN)

One of the busiest times in Metallica's history is captured in this two-part, four-hour documentary. *A Year and a Half in the Life of Metallica* depicts the world's best metal band becoming the world's biggest metal band, following Metallica in the studio, on the road, and in their down time, whether watching President George H. W. Bush announcing the invasion of Iraq or welcoming a visit from a Make-A-Wish Foundation teen, who is flabbergasted that he gets to spend a few hours in the studio and play "The Four Horsemen" with his heroes. The band even meets heroes of their own, including Tony Iommi, Brian May, and best of all Spinal Tap, who are not impressed that another band has released an album with an all-black cover. "Where did that idea come from?" asks an indignant David St. Hubbins.

A Year and a Half catches Metallica in thoughtful adolescence, over-coming their reservations about working with Mötley Crüe and Bon Jovi's producer, or filming music videos. The songs are so entrenched in the rock and metal canon that it can be a revelation to see them in their compos-ing, recording, and mixing stages, not to mention in their onstage debuts. Almost as good as the live footage is seeing fans hearing and reacting to the songs for the first time, including the band's record-breaking listening party at Madison Square Garden. None of the gushing fans in line for the Black Album seem to agree on what "The Unforgiven" is about, and some of them sound like they're still trying to figure it out in their heads while explaining it ("Finally, someone in metal is saying something right!"), but it's fun to watch them try.

There are uncomfortable moments, like some tasteless jokes about the Who's Cincinnati concert disaster and a sound crew roadie's groupie sto-ries. The band gets cranky with Bob Rock's studio carping. The now-infamous scene where James mocks Axl Rose's tour rider makes Hetfield look more like a rock star struggling with his own notions of fame and success than the rebellious everyman he was probably imagining himself. But nobody comes to Metallica for a sanitized version of the truth, and *A Year and a Half in the Life of Metallica* provides a comprehensive look at the band, down to the color of Kirk's briefs (red).

Bonus: *A Year and a Half in the Life of Metallica* includes all of Metal-lica's Black Album music videos, artfully planted throughout the film as interludes. Future *Black Panther*, *Creed*, and Childish Gambino com-poser Ludwig Göransson purchased and studied *A Year and a Half in the Life of Metallica* after seeing the "Enter Sandman" video as a boy. "It felt to me like an *X-Files* episode," he stated on *Bullseye with Jesse Thorn*. "I'd never heard anything that sounded dangerous and scary before. . . .

Unfortunately, I didn't become the lead guitar player of Metallica, but it was the lead way into my musical career."

PARADISE LOST: THE CHILD MURDERS AT ROBIN HOOD HILLS (1996, DIR. JOE BERLINGER AND BRUCE SINOFSKY)

Paradise Lost is an almost unbearably sad look at the trial of Damien Echols, Jessie Misskelley Jr., and Jason Baldwin, three teenagers known to much of America as the West Memphis Three. But before that, they were metal-loving kids accused of the grisly murder of three eight-year-old boys. A plea bargain will free them after eighteen years in prison (documented in the equally potent sequels *Paradise Lost 2: Revelations* and *Paradise Lost 3: Purgatory*), but knowing that doesn't make *Paradise Lost* easier to watch.

Charged with murdering the boys in a Satanic ritual, the West Memphis Three were tried for their clothes, music preferences, and faith (Echols dabbles in Wicca) more than anything incriminating. Prosecutors bring in Metallica lyrics as evidence, and the designated WM3 spokesman Echols speaks of loving their music, especially "Welcome Home (Sanitarium)." The kids can't defend themselves well, and the 72-IQ Misskelley is pressured into confessing and implicating his companions after twelve mostly unrecorded hours of interrogation without legal representation or family. DNA evidence from the crime scene gets destroyed, and the boys are dealt death row and life sentences.

Metallica had never licensed their music to a film before, but brought national attention to the West Memphis Three's case by donating three songs—"Sanitarium," "Orion," and "The Call of Ktulu" to *Paradise Lost*'s soundtrack, years before the release of punk and alternative star-studded benefit albums such as *Free the West Memphis 3* and *Rise Above: 24 Black Flag Songs to Benefit the West Memphis Three*. *Paradise Lost* also served as Metallica's introduction to Berlinger and Sinofsky, before giving ten songs to 2000's *Revelations* (the film's entire soundtrack) and three to 2011's *Purgatory* (including "The Day That Never Comes" over the end credits), as well as approximately 1,600 hours of footage filmed over nearly two years for a groundbreaking band documentary.

SOUTH PARK: BIGGER, LONGER & UNCUT (1999, DIR. TREY PARKER)

Metallica's frontman has an uncredited cameo in the *South Park* movie, singing "Hell Isn't Good" to the recently departed Kenny. One of the film's only musical numbers that doesn't appear on the soundtrack, "Hell Isn't Good" gives James a chance to tell this sinful boy he's going to Hell, where he's apparently getting better music than the angels. Metallica's relationship with *South Park*'s Trey Parker and Matt Stone dates back to performing at Parker and Stone's *Orgazmo* premiere party in 1998, but that didn't stop *South Park* from mocking Metallica for suing Napster in their "Christian Hard Rock" episode in 2003. No one in Metallica lent their own voice that time, though Trey Parker appreciated them enough to add a "Ye-ah!" to the end of James' sentences.

CLASSIC ALBUMS: METALLICA—METALLICA (2001, DIR. MATTHEW LONGFELLOW)

It makes sense that Eagle Rock's stellar *Classic Albums* series, which has produced documentaries on classic rock albums including the Beach Boys' *Pet Sounds*, Fleetwood Mac's *Rumours*, the Jimi Hendrix Experience's *Electric Ladyland*, and more, would choose the self-titled Black Album for its Metallica entry over the more critically acclaimed *Master of Puppets*. Not only is the Black Album way more popular, selling over twenty-one million copies worldwide to *Master of Puppets*' six million, but its controversial status in Metallica's discography leaves more room for discussion than the irrefutable *Master*. Thus, Metallica's entry in the *Classic Albums* series is the Black Album.

Metallica die-hards will be familiar with much of the footage, some of which is culled from *A Year and a Half in the Life of Metallica* and various VH1 tapes, including Metallica's *Behind the Music* feature. But distilled to their Black Album insights for *Classic Albums*, the documentary offers a concise look at the album's creation and the band's creative process, emphasizing, in Lars' words, "We didn't go to the mainstream. The mainstream came to us."

David Fricke provides many of the film's best scenes, articulating how revolutionary the Black Album's singles were when they stormed the airwaves, and Bob Rock explains how a Bon Jovi producer got talked into working with Metallica. Metallica themselves offer insights into their songwriting and creative process, but equally enlightening are the moments at the mixing board. The isolated tracks of songs like "Nothing Else Matters," "Holier Than Thou," and "Wherever I May Roam," graced with band commentary, show the extraordinary amount of thought and theory went into every song. Say what you will about the Black Album's success, it wasn't through lack of effort.

ST. ANGER *REHEARSALS* (2003, DIR. WAYNE ISHAM)

How much do you love Metallica? Enough to sit through eighty minutes of rehearsals for their most derided album? If you've sat through and enjoyed all of St. Anger *Rehearsals*, you will probably enjoy every second of music Metallica has recorded.

Inspired by the packaging of Tom Petty and the Heartbreakers' *The Last DJ*, Metallica released a DVD with copies of *St. Anger*. The *Rehearsals* video is a studio performance of the album front to back, helmed by frequent Metallica video director Wayne Isham. S*t. Anger* may be a mess, but it's a fascinating one, and so is watching the band run through the songs on video. Contrasted with the multimillionaire settings of *Some Kind of Monster*, *Rehearsals* shows Metallica working through takes and banter like your average garage band. Kirk has revealed that they created *St. Anger*'s songs by jamming and using ProTools, and in St. Anger *Rehearsals* they're more or less learning all the songs on camera. Bob Rock's suggestion that the record should sound like a band getting in the garage for the first time, even if that band is Metallica, gets taken to heart.

The music gets a better mix on the DVD than on the record, a small reward for those of us who worked hard to find something to like about the *St. Anger* songs. Four of them ("Invisible Kid," "My World," "Shoot Me Again," and "Purify") enjoy the novelty of never having been played on tour, and possibly never again after this rehearsal video. James at one point mumbles, "I just want to get the fuck out of here"—can you relate? Trujillo's chemistry with the band seems to develop as the film progresses (he's the only one who looks like he's performing for a crowd), and, freed from the album's tinny production, many of *St. Anger*'s best riffs hint at the kind of comeback album it could have been, had the band not been trying, in one of the title track's lyrics, to just "flush it out."

SOME KIND OF MONSTER (2004, DIR. JOE BERLINGER AND BRUCE SINOFSKY)

The first of Metallica's two theatrically released films, *Some Kind of Monster* is unquestionably the most famous Metallica movie, and one of the best rockumentaries ever made. *Some Kind of Monster* captures Metallica in crisis, reeling from infighting, fallout from the Napster scandal, Newsted's departure, and Hetfield's rehab, and that's just the first half hour. Hiring the self-described "performance coach" Phil Towle, Metallica goes through on-camera group therapy as the bandmates try to pick themselves up and get back on track.

The premise sounds preposterous for a bunch of famously gruff guys like Metallica. Critics struggled to find real-life precedents, and many compared it to the classic hard rock mockumentary *This Is Spinal Tap*. Scenes from *Some Kind of Monster* have been subjected to analysis and debate among metalheads for years after the film's release, including a tearful reunion between Lars and Dave Mustaine, cringeworthy fights between James and Lars, and a lavish Christie's Auction in which Lars sells some of the world's most valuable paintings. The gritty kids scowling at you from the *Kill 'Em All* sleeve are barely visible in *Some Kind of Monster*. Yet few documentaries depict human vulnerabilities as clearly as *Some Kind of Monster*, through therapy and even the band's personal home videos (Hetfield picking his daughters up at ballet class is a highlight).

It's an intimate, sometimes voyeuristic, often humanizing look at Metallica, but the painful moments are offset by the band's integrity. Metallica were both praised and mocked for *Some Kind of Monster*, in particular for enlisting a controlling therapist, going for each other's throats on camera, and exposing their insecurities for a mass audience. But for many viewers, Metallica's willingness to confront and publicize their darkest moments reminded us of why they earned millions of fans to begin with. Being richer than God, creatively dry, and constantly at odds with one another, Metallica couldn't be blamed for hanging it up in the early aughts, but *Some Kind of Monster* gives insight into the drive that's kept Metallica alive and thriving for forty years. It's almost inspiring enough to make you want to put on *St. Anger*.

THE VIDEOS 1989-2004 (2006, DIR. VARIOUS)

Of the twenty-one videos collected in *The Videos 1989-2004*, at most "One," "Enter Sandman," and "The Unforgiven" could be called classic, while the rest range from "good" to "adequate" to "misguided" (see chapter 29). On top of that, other than the Black Album's hits, little of *The Videos 1989-2004* chronicles Metallica's best music. Anthologizing Metallica's music videos means getting only one song from the four thrash masterpieces but four from *St. Anger*. Unlike most artists' music video collections, *The Videos 1989-2004* doesn't play like an anthology of the best, or even their best-known songs—how many people remember "The Unnamed Feeling"? And yet *The Videos 1989-2004* presents a fascinating trace of Metallica in an underloved era—you're not going to get another Metallica movie that employs "My Friend of Misery," "Bleeding Me," "The Outlaw Torn," "Carpe Diem Baby," and "Prince Charming" on the DVD menu. Many of their videos are better than you remember, like "The Memory Remains" getting an appropriately artsy rendering with Marianne Faithfull, or the classic action movie homages in "I Disappear" (Metallica may not have written a summer movie banger on par with Guns N' Roses' "You Could Be Mine," but unlike GNR they obtained the rights to secure their song for their music video collection). Even the classics might look different to you—did anyone even notice there were *Playboy* centerfolds in the background of "Nothing

Else Matters" until *The Videos 1989–2004* blurred them out? *The Videos 1989–2004* may not show much of Metallica's best, but it's a thorough portrait of their MTV years.

GET HIM TO THE GREEK (2010, DIR. NICHOLAS STOLLER)

Get Him to the Greek is a raunchy comedy that adds up to everything one could expect from a Judd Apatow–produced Jonah Hill movie about the music industry. Some of the jokes have aged poorly, and in hindsight the film lays out the music biz abuse and corruption the Me Too movement would highlight years later, but for the most part it provides the mindless laughs and entertainment the trailer promises. *Get Him to the Greek*'s best real-life artist performance comes from Sean Combs as a deranged record exec, but the film earns a place in this book for a couple of scenes with Lars Ulrich playing himself, showing his sense of humor about his rock star lifestyle and Napster. Perhaps he took solace in the knowledge that he never wrote anything as bad as "African Child."

ABSENT (2010, DIR. JUSTIN HUNT)

Absent is mixed bag, a poorly edited film that sometimes carries the weight of its subject matter well. There are a few compelling interviews, including late Arizona boxer Johnny Tapia, but the best parts would be better served in a half-hour TV special than a full-length movie. Again, metalheads can find all the Metallica scenes online.

That said, *Absent* has some of the most candid James interviews on tape. He doesn't come out unscathed from the director's choices. James gives spoken-word readings of "Dyers Eve," "The God That Failed," "All Within My Hands," "The Unforgiven," and "Where the Wild Things Are" his best shot, but only proves his acting chops are in singing and not talking. But James' interviews about his father are among his most gut-wrenching and personal to date, revealing a tension he brushed over in nineties interviews after the two reconnected. He recalls his father not saying goodbye to his children in the note he left ("I fuckin' hated him for that"), and admits, despite bonding with his father as an adult, that they were never close, wondering aloud whether he bought his father a house because he really wanted to or because he felt obligated to. In a devastating segment, James recounts confronting Virgil about Cynthia's death ("She died because you left. She didn't know what to do.") and taking time to learn to love his family. James signs off on an uplifting note, finding closure with his mother at her mausoleum and setting goals for his own family. ("I wanna make it to grandpa. . . . No matter how silly the question is I'll take time to answer them.") Even the most cynical Metallica fan can be moved by how much he's overcome and how healthy he sounds in *Absent*. James' experience was rewarding enough that he decided to work with director Justin Hunt once more, narrating his 2017 documentary *Addicted to Porn: Chasing the Cardboard Butterfly*.

HEMINGWAY & GELLHORN (2012, DIR. PHILIP KAUFMAN)

Hemingway & Gellhorn's notable story, directing, sets, acting, and costumes are ultimately failed by the script, which doesn't approach the writing standards of Ernest Hemingway or Martha Gellhorn (much less John Dos Passos, depicted by an underused David Straithairn). The title characters are portrayed by Clive Owen and Nicole Kidman, and while the film portrays the married writers' behavior rather than style, it should be commended for making Gellhorn a star in the story and not the footnote she's often relegated to in Hemingway depictions. The weak spot in the cast is Lars Ulrich, who puts on a terrible Dutch accent as documentarian Joris Ivens, but Lars has said that he preferred his *Hemingway & Gellhorn* role to his cameo as himself in *Get Him to the Greek*, noting that he missed out on Halloween as a boy in Denmark and enjoys art that lets him be somebody else. Keep an eye out for Metallica associate Steven Wiig as the Finnish World War II sniper Simo Häyhä. Wiig also appears in *Some Kind of Monster*, played drums with Jason Newsted's side band Papa Wheelie, and worked as Lars Ulrich's personal assistant from 2001 to 2009 before suing Lars for unpaid overtime. The matter was settled out of court.

MISSION TO LARS (2012, DIR. JAMES MOORE AND WILLIAM SPICER)

"Tom's never asked for much," says journalist Kate Spicer, introducing her brother near the start of English independent film *Mission to Lars*. But there's one thing, Tom, a Metallica fanatic who suffers from Fragile X, a genetic disorder that commonly causes autism, longs to meet Lars Ulrich. If you've seen more than one road trip movie, you can probably tell where *Mission to Lars* is heading. But the film lifts itself above the average triumph of the human spirit story with its heartfelt, evenhanded look at the characters, plus the all-consuming fandom that drives a guy like Tom to plaster his room with Metallica memorabilia. Kate, Tom, and their brother, William, trek from Great Britain to the United States, pulling strings and looking for openings to meet Lars while Metallica rolls through the World Magnetic tour. The siblings rely on tips from their parents and the occasional expert to help them through the trip, and present an entertaining look at fan culture. (Kate recapping Metallica's stage pyro: "It was very safe, but it was really clever!") But the film's highlight, in as spoiler-free terms as possible, is the eventual meeting with Mr. Ulrich, one of the most touching moments in any music documentary filmed. Lemmy Kilmister, always metal's wisest sage, said it best in the film's press release: "I cried."

METALLICA THROUGH THE NEVER (2013, DIR. NIMRÓD ANTAL)

Metallica's second theatrically released film is their best concert movie. Sure, *Live Shit: Binge & Purge* catches them closer to their career prime, and *S&M* shows a more novel experience, but *Metallica Through the Never* is their best concert *movie*, made for a big screen and a large crowd. It's an engaging, perplexing, and most of all hard-rocking narrative concert film in the vein of Prince's *Sign O' the Times* or Tom Waits' *Big Time*. Described by Robert Trujillo as *Mad Max* meets *The Twilight Zone*, *Through the Never* keeps the viewer on edge with strange interludes between footage of one of America's musical treasures in their element—onstage.

Don't think too hard about the "plot," a surreal, almost dialogue-free story about a roadie named Trip (a glowering Dane DeHaan) who tries to get a mysterious package to the band. Director Nimród Antal provides some arresting scenes, with nods to the band's music (there's a horseman drawing nearer, and the stage disaster is right out of *Cunning Stunts*) and history (Trip suffers both a skateboard wipeout and a self-immolation—remind you of one undaunted metal frontman?). But Antal knows the real plot is Metallica unleashing a ferocious, career-spanning show on thousands of fans. The film's staging would distract from a lesser performance but enhances Metallica's, from a literally electrifying "Ride the Lightning" with Tesla coils to a gigantic, marble Lady Justice that comes crashing down during ". . . And Justice for All." Not that anything in *Metallica Through the Never* is superfluous—the action creates the atmosphere of a Metallica show by conjuring something more than the music itself, a thrilling, larger-than-life exploration of humanity, set to the sound of what Antal described as "'fuck you' music." "Growing up in a broken home, and certainly not having an ideal childhood, it was my soundtrack. I think for a lot of kids they represented that," Antal elaborated. "I was blessed to have the gift to work with the greatest band in the world."

As with every Metallica show, the audience takes a lead role, emphasizing Metallica's lyrical prowess as much as any of Antal's stage props. (RogerEbert.com's Sheila O'Malley noted, "Some of the best moments in the film involve footage of the concert audience . . . arms were in the air, eyes closed, lost to everything else but that immediate moment.") Antal appreciates Metallica enough to be able to convey their live unpredictability, the distinct personas of each performer, and a setlist that includes deep cuts and "Fuel." James, Kirk, Lars, and Robert are in top form, blasting through their set like a bunch of SoCal dads who turn into heavy metal superheroes when they pick up their instruments. Only a band as talented as Metallica could stick a ballad in between "Battery" and "Enter Sandman" without it getting decimated. If you were to show Metallica's greatness on film, *Metallica Through the Never* is about the best you can do.

Finally, how about those end credits? Yes, that's Metallica, over a quarter of a century removed from *Cliff 'Em All*, once more ending their film with a moving performance of "Orion."

RADIO DREAMS (2016, DIR. BABAK JALALI)

What made Lars Ulrich appear in *Radio Dreams*, a little-seen Iranian-American film about a radio station manager organizing a jam session between real-life Afghan rock band Kabul Dreams and Metallica? Lars hasn't commented on it much, and mostly spoke to Danish press, but maybe he's being uncharacteristically taciturn to help preserve the sanctity of this mysterious movie. The plot centers around the station manager, Hamid, a wild-haired, sometimes temperamental idealist who often communicates through storytelling, including tales about a strange encounter with a penguin and a suicide attempt on the Golden Gate Bridge. Hamid (played by the Iranian songwriter-musician Moshen Namjoo, currently in exile in America for using Quran verses in his music) believes the Kabul Dreams and Metallica collaboration stands for more than a meeting of musicians and cultures, and gets anxious about his vision for this team-up slipping away, but holds onto his faith through something that's been helping countless musicians and writers since the eighties. "Metallica is my voice," he narrates. "They screamed whatever they didn't let me scream. It's the voice of my generation." Several critics have compared *Radio Dreams* to Beckett's *Waiting for Godot*, who described his work as a way of finding "a form that accommodates the mess." Kind of like Metallica's music.

EXTREMELY WICKED, SHOCKINGLY EVIL AND VILE (2019, DIR. JOE BERLINGER)

Joe Berlinger released two Ted Bundy films in 2019, the documentary series *Conversations with a Killer: The Ted Bundy Tapes* and the crime drama *Extremely Wicked, Shockingly Evil and Vile*. While the former builds on Berlinger's crime doc stature, the latter works as a vehicle for its star/producer, Zac Efron, who gives an award-worthy performance that dismantles his teen idol reputation. Based on Bundy's ex-partner Liz Kendall's memoir, *The Phantom Prince: My Life with Ted Bundy*, the film trades murders and theories for home life and courtrooms, as Efron chillingly shows how a man who has been accused of multiple murders, sexual abuse, pedophilia, cannibalism, and necrophilia could win the hearts of dozens of admirers and be described as "the kind of guy you want your sister to marry." James Hetfield shows up in a small part as Officer Bob Hayward, the man who arrested Bundy, giving a license-and-registration speech like the one James was on the receiving end of in *Some Kind of Monster*. While James doesn't seem destined for bigger acting roles, he convincingly disappears into a humble state trooper with the blue-collar sensibilities he brings to Metallica. "James Hetfield, to his credit, he came in and absolutely nailed the part," Efron remembered. "When I got pulled over by James Hetfield, it was kinda like a dream come true. . . . 'No friggin' way. You?'"

8

BASS SOLO, TAKE ONE

Cliff Burton

"The difference between the rest of the metal field and Metal-lica is the difference between punching your fist in the air rather than at a specific target."

—Cliff Burton

Somewhere in 1983 there's a struggling, adolescent band, playing music with almost no commercial potential. They can barely keep a lineup together and have no record deal in sight. The alpha males in the group can't stop fighting and are getting more violent. The fiery lead guitarist, a crucial songwriter and stage presence, is tearing the band apart with his alcoholism. Their bassist has infuriated the drummer by printing business cards that call the group "power metal." They can't find a manager. And now, these guys are moving their band approximately four hundred miles north, taking an eight-hour drive from Los Angeles to El Cerrito, for the sake of a new bassist.

"Now that I think of it, it was real wild that we did that," James said in 1985. "All of a sudden just move up to San Francisco, no place to stay or nothing." But Cliff Burton is a bassist you drive four hundred miles for. If Cliff is joining your band, you need to get wilder. Even if that band is Metallica.

"He oozed this confidence, this 'I don't give a fuck'-ness that I felt but didn't know how to do," James elaborated years later. "There was this punk rock celebration, but there was a sophistication in his playing, harmonies, theory, melody . . . Cliff was able to take all that schooling and bring it into our world."

Punk rock sophistication doesn't go anywhere near capturing the bundle of eccentricities piled up in one Cliff Burton. He wore bell-bottoms and a jean jacket throughout high school, even on hot summer days, not giving a shit that his friends and eventually his bandmates in Trauma (who wore stage costumes) and Metallica (who did not) made fun of him. He drove a car with a taped-up steering wheel and occasionally donned a moldy cowboy hat his sometime bandmate Jim Martin called "the hat that lives." He had an abnormally long middle finger that shoves itself into photos, like a punk metal hippie Johnny Cash at San Quentin. Lars spent months badgering Cliff to join Metallica, and once onboard Cliff stayed a loner among loners. He never lived in the Metallica Mansion, moving straight from his parents' house to the road, and played the cool stoner in a band that was more into drinking. Sometimes while his bandmates partied Cliff could be found in the house's lower level, reading fairytales to the Zazulas' young daughter. "Cliff would use the word 'I' a lot more," says Lars. "We would use 'we.'"

"FLOPPY-FINGER TECHNIQUE"

The youngest of schoolteacher Jan and engineer Ray Burton's three kids was born February 10, 1962. He didn't walk until he was about twenty-two months old, which worried his parents until they figured out he was tricking them into carrying him around. Cliff was a good student and an introvert, preferring to curl up with a book or a record than play with other kids. Outside of school, he liked hunting and fishing with a homemade spear. Once Cliff severed a tendon trying to cut a carp on Clear Lake, damaging his right pinky. As a result, he hammered bass strings with his fingers in the style of his hero Geezer Butler, which Cliff called "floppy-finger technique." More specifically, being unable to bend his pinky gave Cliff intrinsic metal horns on his right hand, flashing metal in any room blessed by his presence.

Cliff was thirteen when his sixteen-year-old brother, Scott, died of a cerebral aneurysm. The Burtons' youngest son would only live eleven more years, but did so with a sense of duende. Cliff started taking music lessons shortly after Scott died, practicing for about six hours a day. He quickly outgrew his teachers and headbanged feverishly while he practiced. His liberal parents supported him and enthusiastically attended his shows, something they'd do through his time in Metallica. Cliff picked up a Rickenbacker like Lemmy and an Alembic like Stanley Clarke.

He formed his first band, EZ Street, in high school with future Faith No More musicians Jim Martin and Mike Bordin. Cliff and Jim continued studying music at Chabot College in Hayward, where they renamed their band Agents of Misfortune and developed more of a space rock sound, watchable in a Hayward Battle of the Bands video online. But it was in the San Francisco metal band Trauma that Cliff caught a fledgling LA band's attention.

"A BIG PSYCHO"

Aiming for success, Metallica wanted a bassist who'd write more than Ron McGovney. Ron had been skipping band practice to spend time with his girlfriend. More outrageously, he'd been going to Mötley Crüe shows. He'd sell most of his gear after leaving Metallica and not play much music again, though he's been cool about answering Metallica questions ever since. He's thanked, along with Dave Mustaine, Exodus, and Trauma, in the *Kill 'Em All* liner notes, and was flown out to the Rock and Roll Hall of Fame, along with ex-guitarist Lloyd Grant, for Metallica's induction. In 2010, Ron noted that his family still gets invited to Metallica shows. "James went out of his way to make my kids' first concert experience one that they will never, ever forget."

Trauma had some minor successes, opening for Saxon at the Keystone and contributing a pretty bad sub-Maiden song, "Such a Shame" to *Metal Massacre II*. At a gig at LA's Whisky a Go Go in the fall of 1982, James and Lars watched Cliff in Trauma, playing bass with a wah-wah pedal. "They had a certain look," James recalled. "And he was just . . . Cliff." James was impressed that Cliff didn't care about the crowd—he was looking down at his bass, not the audience. "You couldn't fuck around with him. I wanted to get that respect that he had." After the show, Cliff's bandmates wondered why he talked for so long with two metalheads who approached him.

"We're in this band, and we're looking for a bass player, and we think you'd fit in," James recalled telling Cliff. "Because you're a big psycho."

Cliff played his first Metallica show on March 5, 1983, at the Stone. He left his job at a Castro Valley rental yard and made a pact with his parents that if Metallica hadn't made it after five years, they could stop supporting him and he would quit to be a studio musician (he'd later take them out for sushi with his first big Metallica check). Enlisting Cliff changed Metallica more than it changed Cliff. In early interviews, Dave Mustaine calls him "the new Steve Harris of metal"—indicating, holy shit, that Steve Harris wasn't metal enough for Metallica. "We'd discovered Kate Bush around that time," said Cliff's roommate Kirk. "We listened to the Police all the time, because Cliff was a big fan of Stewart Copeland's drumming." Reading Cliff interviews, one sees a love for Creedence Clearwater Revival, the Velvet Underground, Roxy Music, Blue Öyster Cult, the Dictators, Anthrax, Thin Lizzy, the Sex Pistols, Yes, and Peter Gabriel, not to mention driving Kirk crazy with the Eagles. Cliff gushes about U2 and R.E.M. so much ("Have you heard of them?") that it's easy to forget he died in 1986, before *The Joshua Tree* and *Document*.

"We learned stuff from Cliff pretty much right away," says James in *Back to the Front*. "We learned moral integrity and how to stand up for ourselves."

As the oldest member of Metallica, Cliff often seems like the cool older brother teaching music theory to the kids. A classical music enthusiast ("Bach is God"), Cliff was the only member who could learn a time signature by ear, then transcribe it for his bandmates. He wrote many of his melodies on a detuned classical guitar. Employing arpeggios, tapping, triads, and downpicking, Cliff stood on the shoulders of Geezer Butler, Lemmy, and Steve Harris to make bass a lead instrument in Metallica.

"A lot of times the rest of us would defer to him in times of insecurities," Kirk remembered. "He just seemed so much wiser and much more responsible than the rest of us." Being mature didn't mean being soft—longtime Metallica photographer Ross Halfin says Cliff was the biggest pain in the ass to photograph, because anything remotely staged was poseur bullshit. Cliff couldn't be confined by poses, rock star trappings, tastes, fashion, or even his own music. Sometimes live he'd let out an audible roar while playing. By the time they'd get back to their hotels wasted at 3 a.m., Cliff still wanted to play, talking an exhausted Kirk into figuring out Skynyrd or Thin Lizzy songs. Amid all the noise, he still had more to release.

"I felt such an immense sense of pride about Cliff being on our team," James said in 2016. "It was like, 'Look at that unique human being out there, flying the flag for us. I'm so glad he's in our corner.'"

"There's many factors involved here, but that would be the main one," Cliff explained in an interview. "To absolutely devote yourself to that, to virtually marry yourself to that—what you're going to do—and not get side-tracked by all the other bullshit that life has to offer."

Cliff's most famous fan, Jason Newsted, has called him "the Jimi Hendrix of bass." On *Live Shit: Binge & Purge*, Jason honors Cliff the way Cliff sometimes honored Hendrix, with a few measures of "The Star-Spangled Banner" in his bass solo. Cliff played the solo on his last-ever gig, September 26, 1986, in Stockholm, heard on the *Master of Puppets* box set. The show ends with "Fight Fire with Fire," eliciting the loudest screams of the night.

LJUNGBY

Leaving Stockholm, the band drew cards to see who would get the best bunk. Kirk shuffled the deck and Cliff cut it. In Kirk's memory, Cliff drew the ace of spades. Kirk drew the two of hearts, went to his new bunk, and fell asleep with the book he'd been reading, Stephen King's *It*, published less than two weeks earlier.

Earlier that day Cliff had called Corinne, his girlfriend, whom he'd met at an Iron Maiden show in 1984. She was going to see R.E.M. at the Greek Theatre in Berkeley and promised to call when she got home to tell him know how the show was. A thunderstorm canceled the show, so she went home and called the hotel Metallica were scheduled to stop at in Copenhagen. The bus hadn't arrived yet.

Cliff was thrown through the glass window closest to his bunk and was crushed when the bus fell on him. Bloodied and bruised, and covered in coffee from the spilled dispenser, James kicked out the emergency exit.

After three years of hard-living, all-nighters, stage diving, and getting famous, Metallica was dealt a heavy sense of mortality.

Cliff was taken to a Ljungby hospital where the official cause of death was chest compression with lung damage. Shocked and stranded in the freezing cold, James started screaming and crying. That night he smashed up his hotel room and had to be taken out into the street (manager Peter Mensch told the hotel manager he'd pay the bill if nobody called the police). The bus driver was questioned but never charged, and his name has not been released to the public. The crash is sometimes thought to have been caused by ice, although the police reportedly described it as "exactly like the pattern of asleep-at-the-wheel accidents." Across the Atlantic, twenty-three-year-old Jason read the news. "I remember my tears hitting the newspaper."

Cliff's passport was mailed back to his parents, and the rest of Metallica's tour was canceled. James, Kirk, and Lars sat in Cliff's bedroom crying and drinking on the eve of his funeral, October 7, 1986, in Castro Valley. James wore a cast, Lars was on crutches, and Kirk's faced was visibly bruised. They passed around Cliff's ashes and scattered them in Maxwell Ranch. James, Lars, and Kirk dealt with losing Cliff by holding their first bassist auditions the day after his funeral. "The last thing Cliff would've wanted us to do was quit," James told MTV. "He'd be the first one to kick us in the ass and make us wake up."

"My relationship with death is different," James reflected in 2006. "I grew up with Christian Science where you don't believe in funerals. In a way it's very unhealthy not to get closure, time to mourn. But the idea behind it is to let the person live on within you." He'd later tell *Rolling Stone* the death-inspired lyrics on *Ride the Lightning* and *Master of Puppets* meant more to him after Cliff died. Cliff lives with James, who's been known to reach out to younger artists facing trauma and loss, such as calling Baroness' John Baizley in the hospital after his band's bus accident in 2012. James also approached Slipknot's Corey Taylor and Jim Root on a festival bill in Greece twenty-odd years after Cliff's death, asking them about their recently deceased bassist Paul Gray. "He said, 'If you need an ear, if you need somebody to talk to, you know where I am,'" Root stated. "He said in some ways they really didn't deal with it [losing Cliff]. He wanted to make sure we didn't make some of the same mistakes they made throughout their grieving process."

CLIFF 'EM ALL

The shaken metal community paid its respects. Metal Church and Anthrax both dedicated their next albums, *The Dark* and *Among the Living*, respectively, to Cliff. Dave Mustaine wrote the music to "In My Darkest Hour" after finding out Cliff had died. Jim Martin wore a shirt reading "A Tribute to Cliff Burton" in Faith No More's "Epic" video. And Cliff stayed a part of Metallica's future. James named Metallica's music festival after Cliff's "Orion," the song played at his funeral (Cliff might've loved knowing his song named a festival that hosted a dazzling range of music). It's hard to see Metallica trying the *S&M* shows without Cliff's influence, or to listen without wondering what they would have sounded like with Cliff's classical instincts. Watching Kirk and Jason talk up their Bach, Handel, Scarlatti, Mozart, and Paganini influences for *S&M*, one hears Cliff. "We never would have written guitar harmonies or instrumentals or songs with very intricate melodies and orchestrations without Cliff," states James.

Kirk cries remembering Cliff in a *Back to the Front* video. "I respect everything he stood up for, and it's what I try to stand up for."

It's easy to romanticize Cliff, and the early band with him. He represents the purest era of Metallica, the ageless icon of a band that aged so publicly, and often unflatteringly. People take what they like from his life and interpret it how they want, honoring him with memorials and an official "Cliff Burton Day" (February 10) in Alameda County. Everyone makes their own Cliff, projecting their own view of him and pointing to anything to support their idea of where Cliff would be. In the eerie, low-budget 2018 documentary *The Salvation Kingdom*, Cliff's born-again sister, Connie, and her devout friends project their faith onto her brother, certain that Cliff got the title "To Live Is to Die" from Billy Graham. Some fans insist that Metallica would've made more records like *Master of Puppets*, and that Cliff would never have let his bros stoop to something like a radio hit or a music video, although Cliff himself hinted that the band would get more melodic and maybe even film a video in the future. Cliff was unpredictable, and so was Metallica's future with or without him. "We do what we wanna do, you know," he says in *Cliff 'Em All*. "If they consider that selling out, whatever." The rough, fan-compiled video was a better tribute to Cliff than any written or taped statement from the band could have been, although those came later.

But no one serves Cliff's legacy better than Ray and Jan Burton. (James: "When I grow up, I wanna be Ray Burton.") The couple stayed in touch with Metallica (as did Connie, who credits Lars with helping her through addiction), befriending the new bassist, Jason, and corresponding with fans. The Burtons privately donated Cliff's posthumous royalty payments to a scholarship fund for Castro Valley music students. Jan passed away in 1993, and Ray still made sure to talk to fans, sign autographs, take pictures, answer questions, and respond to letters until his death in 2020. He knew Cliff would have done that, too.

9

MORE IS ALL
YOU NEED

Master of Puppets

*"I think you could safely say we've matured musically, if not
any other way, a bit over the past three years."*

—Cliff Burton

The best evil laugh in music history comes near the end of "Master of
Puppets." The song drifts into a melodic, dreamlike interlude, only
to distort under Hetfield and Hammett's assault, like the mood swings of a
trip. At about 8:15 the guitar cuts out and there's an otherworldly laugh, a
dark "Muah-ha-ha-ha." Almost as suddenly, it's crushed by the final smattering of chords, ringing out like a punch to the head.

And then, the members of Metallica laugh.

They break into a cackle that sounds like gas-huffing hyenas. But more
important, they sound like Metallica. It vanquishes the Disney-villain aesthetic of the previous laugh within seconds. Metallica make human laughs
sound scarier than a processed one, just as they presented a reality that
was scarier than any of the demonic imagery previous metal bands had
written about. No band has articulated it better than Metallica on *Master
of Puppets*.

Master of Puppets is the greatest metal album of all time. It's not everyone's favorite, and it's not even everyone's favorite Metallica record. But
it's the greatest of all time, the way *Citizen Kane* is the greatest film of
all time. Okay, maybe Black Sabbath's *Paranoid* is *Citizen Kane*, but

in that case *Master of Puppets* is definitely *The Godfather*. Yes, people hold up *Back in Black* or *Led Zeppelin IV* or *Appetite for Destruction*, all classics and even the greatest in some areas. But *Master of Puppets* is a greater metal record than any of them. Nobody argues that it's actually hard rock.

Like the very best artists, Metallica proved that you don't succeed by outplaying your peers. Not that Metallica are slouches, but even in the showiest moments on *Master of Puppets*, each of them can drop out or slow down to complement the song. Lesser bands prefer to spend the entire song showing how great they are with their instruments, but Metallica gets to the top by knowing how to make choices in their compositions. Listening to Dream Theater play *Master of Puppets* in its entirety in 2002, one hears a band that can play circles around Metallica but doesn't personify those songs. James, Kirk, Cliff, and Lars step back into simpler grooves, giving each instrument and the lyrics full effect, blowing away the best shredders in the world.

James' original cover concept was Howdy Doody sprawled out in a gutter with track marks up and down his arms, proving someone can write staggeringly advanced music and be twenty-two at the same time. His sketch for the final cover was given to artist Don Brautigam, who created the graveyard of white crosses and master hands that decorated T-shirts and spawned tributes all over the world. The cover's hands were originally feminine, but were purposely degendered by Metallica for the sake of universality in the final art, reflecting the record's manipulation themes, from the title track through "Welcome Home (Sanitarium)," "Disposable Heroes," and "Leper Messiah." Metallica were also thinking of Iron Maiden's ability to make album covers that came alive in a stage set, and were maybe getting big enough to have real crosses extend from their *Master of Puppets* backdrop. How the fuck would Howdy Doody be put into the stage show?

Metallica also liked Iron Maiden's concept of ambitious record covers with silly in-jokes and quips in the liner notes, giving "extra fucken yahooz" to *The Young Ones* and *Teenage Mutant Ninja Turtles* (still only a comic book series in 1986) while nicknaming their roadies "Sclarbmeister," "Gimme Four," "Don Vito," "Gussetus Maximus," "Lick my Syphilletic [*sic*] Piles," and "You're on glue, Mon." More famous names pop up, including Rush's Geddy Lee, Alex Lifeson, and Neil Peart (plans to get Lee to produce *Master of Puppets* never materialized, though Rush is honored with a "Tom Sawyer"–esque progression in "Sanitarium"). Thanked last, "and most of all," is Edna, the nickname for one of Kirk's guitars but also Metallica slang for a woman eager to spend time with the boys on the road. Metallica were political activists in their music and party animals in their record sleeves.

Metallica had been sparse with sound effects like the explosion in "Fight Fire with Fire," but on *Master of Puppets* they'd gotten rid of them. All sounds were made by the four men who wrote the record. They'd considered battle sounds for "Disposable Heroes," and Lars had to be talked out of ending the record with a Sam Kinison quote. Metallica, instead, honored George Carlin on a sticker gracing early editions of *Master of Puppets*: "The only track you probably won't want to play is 'Damage, Inc.,' due to multiple uses of the infamous 'F' word. Otherwise, there aren't any 'shits,' 'fucks,' 'pisses,' 'cunts,' motherfuckers' or 'cocksuckers' anywhere on this record." Somehow, this didn't stop the PMRC from including Metallica on their 1986 blacklist.

But *Master of Puppets* shows a band transcending good and evil, confronting mental health issues, mass incarceration, addiction, institutional religion, the military industrial complex, and government chickenhawks. When you hear the cliché about Metallica being "the thinking person's metal band" (forget that—isn't metal the thinking person's music?), you can thank *Master of Puppets* for spearheading it. Metallica also distinguished themselves from more popular bands by not falling into chauvinism, at least in their music, instead creating a sound and image that was masculine without being macho. "There were no T&A videos, no lecherous leering, and certainly no pop pandering," wrote Hannah Levin in *Kerrang!* "When I listened to 'Disposable Heroes' or 'Leper Messiah' I felt emboldened to take on things I found frightening and comforted that there were others who preferred their metal rendered in its most pure and powerful form."

It's the first record Metallica wrote for a major label, without the financial restrictions of a deadline, although writing was completed in approximately eight weeks. (James: "I think *Master of Puppets* was all we ever thought about.") It's also their first record without any Dave Mustaine cowrites, and the first and only Metallica record written exclusively by James, Lars, Kirk, and Cliff. "We didn't just want to be better than every other band," James remembered in *Back to the Front*. "We wanted to be better than each other."

Playing along with Gabriel Fauré's "Pavane," the sign-off music for San Francisco's channel four station, James came up with the intro to "Battery," a minor flamenco that promises brutality even before the electrics kick in. The lyrics are forceful but ambiguous. Is "Battery" an assault? An artillery? Battery St., where Metallica played at the Old Waldorf in San Francisco? Is the circle of destruction a circle pit? Metallica's lyrics ensure multiple listens almost as much as the pummeling music does.

James started seeing friends shoot speed and heroin as his band found greater success, inspiring the lyrics of his *Master*-piece. The slower movement was written before *Kill 'Em All*, but Metallica saved it for the right song. James thought the "Master of Puppets" main riff, written in his living room, was "too obvious," once again showing a band that never does anything the easy way. But Lars heard its catchiness, and Kirk dropped it from D to E for heaviness, unleashing Metallica's most beloved classic from their thrash years. Over 1,600 performances later, it's Metallica's most performed song, yet no one gets sick of it. When Metallica let fans pick the setlist on their 2014 Metallica by Request tour, "Master of Puppets" was the most requested song at all twenty-six shows. And like "Battery," the song leaves fans with more questions than answers—is the "Fix me" lyric about getting a fix or being fixed? What's the high note in the solo after the mellow part, which Kirk himself says he's never been able to re-create? Chekhov might say that Metallica doesn't have to solve problems, they only have to formulate them correctly.

"The Thing That Should Not Be," once named by James as his favorite Metallica song, is tuned so low that Jason remembers the bass strings shaking on the neck when he learned it. The creature in "The Thing That Should Not Be" is scarier, and more Lovecraftian, than other songs describing famous monsters. Metallica prefer to keep the beast vague, nameless and lurking beneath the sea, watching. The lyrics get deep into the Cthulu mythos, nodding to Nyarlathotep, *The Shadow over Innsmouth*, *The Necronomicon*, the fallen city R'lyeh, and the sailors drained of sanity, all the more strange when one realizes Metallica's resident Lovecraft fan

Cliff Burton doesn't have a writing credit on "The Thing That Should Not Be." Stranger eons . . .

"Welcome Home (Sanitarium)" showed Metallica reinventing the metal ballad with degrees of heaviness, melodic enough to be considered for a video although the idea was quickly scrapped. (Lars: "We don't need one as bad as a lot of other bands.") James, still finding and inventing his voice, had trouble singing it as high as he wanted, so instead he put a high harmony on it, one of Metallica's best. James was a master of destigmatizing alienation, making "Sanitarium" an unofficial anthem for fans like Damien Echols, the distinct, quickly changing movements conveying the inner turmoil of its narrator. "We realized from working with a lot of different moods and dynamics that there are other ways of being heavy," Lars stated years later.

The incendiary "Disposable Heroes" was inspired by the British TV documentary series *The World at War*, adding the military to the number of controlling forces addressed on *Master of Puppets* (see the Army hat and dog tag among the album cover's graves). Kirk has said he wanted the guitars to sound like something military bagpipers would play, striking with speed-picking wizardry to turn into Metallica at their most unrelentingly heavy, heard in the crossover thrash of bands like Power Trip and inspiring Angela Gossow to write "Despicable Heroes" for Arch Enemy's *Anthems of Rebellion*.

Starting and ending with DIY-style banter that was more prevalent on punk records than metal, "Leper Messiah" builds off a Lars-written motif to attack evangelical corruption, with a "Spreading his disease" lyric possibly referencing the record Anthrax released the previous year. The title is from David Bowie's "Ziggy Stardust," something Kirk would apologize for while fanboying in front of the amused Thin White Duke years later. Kirk found David Bowie through "Fame" as a boy and loved being confused by *The Man Who Fell to Earth*, writing about the ways it explored xenophobia, acclimation, climate change, and "the inability to cope" after Bowie's death in 2016. "I wonder if Bowie was always there in a creative sense himself," Kirk wrote on his Fear FestEvil website. "Perhaps that's why he was always seen to be moving, always changing, and my thought is that maybe those were questions that lingered in his mind as well. . . . Let's just say that his range of empathy was greater than the average human being." Kirk would know.

Opening with a heavily distorted organ played through a rotary speaker, "Orion" was built around Cliff's middle section waltz, originally part of "Sanitarium" until Metallica could write a song that lived up to Cliff's classical instincts. Cliff wrote all the two- and three-part harmonies in his haunting bassline, fully arranging the song and playing two of its four solos. It might be the strongest case for Cliff's brilliance on record, enough for James to tattoo the middle bassline on his arm years later. Sadly, Cliff never got to play "Orion" live, and Metallica themselves didn't play it in its entirety until the *Master of Puppets* twentieth anniversary shows in 2006. "That was the highlight of the set for me," James told Swedish newspaper *Dagens Nyheter*. "I cried every time I played it, but it was good tears. I was overwhelmed with gratitude for the fact that I had the opportunity to play in the same band as Cliff and learn things from him."

Master of Puppets closes with two Cliff cowrites, hightailing out on the recalcitrant "Damage, Inc.," heavy enough to be Kerry King's favorite Metallica song. The reversed intro is an unsolvable Cliff puzzle, riffing on the Bach chorale "Come, Sweet Death," which Cliff surely appreciated having the same title as a Misfits lyric. Once more, Metallica keep the lyrics cryptic (is it referencing the National Crime Syndicate's Murder, Inc.? What's the razorback we're not supposed to fuck with?), but there's no denying some of Lars' best variations, up to twelve tracks of bass, Kirk's full metal solo, and James seizing immortality by making the case that his right hand should be enshrined in a museum, near Axl's larynx and Ozzy's liver. *Master of Puppets* slams out on a song composed by all four members, and Metallica have made one of the only scarily great metal records.

THE OZZMAN TOURETH

"Trying to act cool but knowing that there's this god in front of you, of sorts, who has changed your life, and has put you on that stage," James told the BBC. "It was really hard to not just follow him around and ask him every Black Sabbath question under the sun."

Metallica were invited to open for Ozzy Osbourne, a greater honor than any single or video release would have been. The Godfather of Metal proved a fatherly figure, giving career advice one moment and hurling a bottle across the room minutes later. The gawky boys hung onto his every word, and were shocked to learn he liked "Sanitarium." Metallica tried impressing the Godfather by soundchecking Black Sabbath songs, hoping he'd join them, but Ozzy thought they were making fun of him, until his assistant pointed out they thought he was a god. "It was genuinely one of the first times that I realized people actually liked Black Sabbath," Ozzy recalled. Metallica only got seven songs in their main set, but when they'd leave the crowd would chant for them to return. (UK fans, perhaps showing appreciation for Metallica's punk sensibilities, gobbed on them.)

Ozzy's handlers warned Metallica that the boss was supposed to stay sober on tour, though one Metallicat whose name rhymes with "Riff Rurton" smoked a joint with Ozzy and hid the boss under the hotel bed when management tried to find him. Not that Metallica were always the instigators—another time, drunk Ozzy approached Kirk and Lars' table and asked them to jam. Ozzy's handler frantically shook his head "no," but of course Metallica couldn't resist. In the elevator to his room, Ozzy took his penis out and started peeing while everyone else tried to avoid the spreading puddle. The boys ran out the door with Ozzy coming after them, urine dripping onto the floor.

The tour expanded Metallica's audience and soon more thrash bands were supporting legendary acts (Slayer opening for Judas Priest, Anthrax for Kiss, and Megadeth for Alice Cooper among them). But Metallica helped Ozzy nearly as much as he helped them, giving him cred from newer hard rock bands who'd been watering down the sounds Ozzy pioneered on *Blizzard of Ozz* and *Diary of a Madman*. "I didn't help them on their way, they helped them on their way," Ozzy said in 2017. "They fucking went for it and they're still better than any of these fuckers out there now."

Touring and word of mouth helped make *Master of Puppets* the first gold thrash record, bringing metal to the mainstream while staying musically underground, with thrash compositions and hardcore-inspired lyrics. It barely registered on radio or MTV, but Metallica were improving on their own terms, calling their own shots, forming, destroying, and reinventing their own identities. "I thought it might be a little too crazy for most people," Cliff said in a 1986 *Hit Parader*. "I'm glad I was wrong."

Upon learning he'd earned enough in Metallica to put down payments on a house, Cliff was reportedly pumped to finally have a place where he could shoot his knife-launcher.

As Metallica got bigger, so did the consequences of their actions. Promotor Bill Graham chewed out James for wrecking his dressing room, which James would recall as the first paternal talk he'd had since his father left (he also took uncomfortably long to realize Graham wasn't kidding). Later, at a New Year's show, James threw his mic stand into the crowd during "Seek & Destroy" and clocked a kid in the head. Metallica tried appeasing him with merch and alcohol, but he sued them anyway. Most famously, a skateboard accident (the "break" in the action hinted at in the *$5.98 E.P.—Garage Days Re-Revisited* booklet) made Metallica miss a potential *SNL* appearance. James had played in bandages before, cutting his hand on broken glass during the Venom tour, but this time Q Prime made James sign a form that he wouldn't skateboard anymore. (Lars: "If he is, he's doing it far away from any of us.") It did give James the distinction of confounding metal's greatest wildman (Ozzy: "He must've broken it about four times!"), who gave Metallica a longer soundcheck so Metal Church's John Marshall could practice and fill in while James ran around onstage. Years later, James' exploits would be honored by making him and Robert playable characters in *Tony Hawk's Pro Skater HD*.

As late as 1986, James was laughing in interviews about not being identified backstage. But Metallica's entourages and fan groups were growing. Metallica started checking into hotels under pseudonyms—James was "Jimmy Vodz," Lars was "Richie Rippensmoke," Cliff was "Samuel Burns," and *Mad* magazine fan Kirk was "Melvin Potrzebie." Diverting from Ozzy in May to play with Armored Saint, Metallica were now headlining theaters instead of clubs, with their crowd expanding past metal circles (Johnny Cash brought his son to a theater show). Having sold James and Lars' San Francisco home to live on the road, Metallica kept a rule about not shitting on the bus—go in a towel and dump it outside. Now when Cliff dumped in a towel, fans wanted to keep it. Some of Metallica's old acquaintances had trouble understanding the new rules. "There's not enough room for everyone we've ever spoken to," Kirk stated. "They go for the predictable response of, 'Wow, he's a rock star, he doesn't have the time of day. He's too big for his friends, he doesn't know who his friends are.'" Tour manager Bobby Schneider (the drum tech on David Bowie's Serious Moonlight tour) was designated to keep people off the bus while Metallica struggled to sleep, leaving the TV on to fight the ringing in their ears.

"You just find out who your friends are after a while," James remembered. "All of these people tell us, 'Wow, we don't like you anymore because you're not an underground band' . . . Which is bullshit, because we'd be doing the same shit if we were still hanging out with Megaforce." Metallica also started taking pains to protect their image, fighting with a Houston promotor over whether they'd get limo'd to the venue (Lars compromised that Metallica could use a limo as long as their fans didn't see it).

Mainstream critics didn't know what to do with them. A mixed review from *Spin* derided Metallica's "intellectual" pursuits and slammed their "corporate-deathburger-influenced 'creative direction.'" Self-proclaimed "Dean of American Rock Critics" Robert Christgau gave *Master of Puppets* a B–, praising their energy and politics while scoffing, "But the revolutionary heroes I envisage aren't male chauvinists too inexperienced to know better; they don't have hair like Samson and pecs like Arnold Schwarzenegger. That's the image Metallica calls up, and I'm no more likely to invoke their strength of my own free will than I am *The 1812 Overture*'s." Like most people, Metallica critics tend to assume the music they detest is enjoyed by their enemies from high school.

But to paraphrase Howlin' Wolf, the little girls understood. The 1986 *Spin* Metallica profile found two girls fighting over a poster. ("Before you met me, you didn't even *know* Metallica. Look at Kirk. He's in love with me, and he just doesn't know it yet.") Middle schooler Brent Hinds borrowed a cassette from a friend and took it to the basement so his parents wouldn't know he was listening. His future bandmate Bill Kelliher spent hours playing along with *Ride the Lightning* and *Master of Puppets* after school. Thirteen-year-old beginner guitarist Mark Morton found the best music he'd ever heard and clasped his headphones to his ears. Over in Norway, Vegard Sverre Tveitan labored to learn James' down-picking from a taped cassette of *Master of Puppets*, years before he'd go by Ihsahn in black metal innovators Emperor. Young Corey Taylor waited for the last verse "Damage, Inc." to jump up and scream along with the lyric he'd pull for Slipknot's "Surfacing" years later. Scott Ian compared hearing

Master of Puppets in 1986 to $E = mc^2$, creating something entirely new that formulated the world it was in ("Seriously, did they find a bottle of Beethoven pills?"). In France, Joe Duplantier ran home from school to watch *Cliff 'Em All* and listen to *Master of Puppets*, years before his band Gojira would medley ". . . And Justice for All," "Fight Fire with Fire," "Enter Sandman," "Master of Puppets," and "Sad but True" in encores. "Metallica was my life!" he recalled in 2013.

"Everybody knew they were the big dog on the block, and they never had to watch out for anybody," said Pantera's Vinnie Paul, citing *Master of Puppets* as his favorite record. "They were a band to measure your accomplishments by."

"The tonalities they chose, intentional or otherwise, were of such a foreign and antagonistic quality that it stood alone in a sea of fantasy inspired and image-centric heavy metal," Strapping Young Lad's Devin Townsend stated in 2017.

Metallica changed more than the metal landscape. *Master of Puppets* mixer Michael Wagener engineered Janet Jackson's R&B metal hit "Black Cat" for *Rhythm Nation 1814*. "Orion" gets sampled on DJ Shadow's groundbreaking *Endtroducing . . .* in "Number Song." Hum the main progression of "Welcome Home (Sanitarium)" to yourself. How does Weezer's "Undone—The Sweater Song" go? (Rivers Cuomo acknowledged this in 2009.)

"I don't think, in this band, we can ever be fully, artistically satisfied," says Kirk in a 1986 *Sounds* interview. His music proves this, although twenty years later he was content enough with *Master of Puppets* to name it as his favorite Metallica record. "If you released this today, it would be right up there with all the newest releases in terms of sound, quality, production, concept . . . Even the things James was writing about back then are still relevant. And you get the feeling it will all still be relevant tomorrow."

10

A FREIGHT TRAIN COMING YOUR WAY

Metallica Live

*"When a fan walks out of a Metallica concert, I want them
to feel content pain. I want them to feel completely drained
of physical energy, mental energy, their throat is to the point
where they can't talk anymore. I want them to feel what we
feel every night, where we've given it our all and more. When
someone leaves, I want them to say 'You know what, that was
the best concert I've ever seen. Good luck topping that one.'"*

—James Hetfield

Stories of young Metallica blowing away their headliners are numerous,
a beloved part of Metallica lore. Venom's PA and pyrotechnics were
strong enough to send plaster coming down from the ceiling in Metallica's Zurich dressing room, but not enough for them to get so severely
upstaged by their openers that fans walked out. W.A.S.P. didn't fare any
better, drinking fake blood from plastic skulls and insisting they close
every show of their 1985 North America tour, only to watch Metallica
fans either leave (including young Jason Newsted in Phoenix, walking out
with a $14 Metallica shirt he'd eventually wear out) or stick around to spit
on W.A.S.P. frontman Blackie Lawless. By the time Metallica got to Holland with Twisted Sister, Dee Snider knew well enough to insist Metallica
closed. Twisted Sister were coming off *Stay Hungry*, and had a bigger hit
than *Kill 'Em All*, but there was no way to out-thrash Metallica.

"Going on after Metallica was definitely humbling," Dokken's George Lynch stated in *Bang Your Head*. "We were pretty much demoralized." Metallica held fourth billing on the 1988 Monsters of Rock tour, headlined by Van Hagar with support from the Scorpions, Dokken, Metallica, and Kingdom Come. Fifteen thousand fans stampeded the LA Coliseum floor when Metallica started midafternoon, welcomed back to the town where they'd been scorned in clubs for thrashing too hard a few years earlier. A young Tom Morello, years away from Rage Against the Machine, was in the crowd. "I thought it was music for crazy people," he recalled in 2011. "I guess that turned out to be right. . . . I've never seen one band kick every band's ass as bad as Metallica did on that day. They came out and absolutely destroyed the place, caused a huge riot where tens of thousands of fans poured from the stands of the stadium down onto the field, tore up the fences, tore up all the chairs, and then poor Dokken had to come on."

Even the Godfather of Metal was caught off guard when Metallica supported Ozzy's *The Ultimate Sin* tour in 1986. "Every night the crowd was going nuts for them, stealing the show most nights," Ozzy recalled on a *Behind the Music* episode. "They're really hard to follow."

Metallica doesn't need tourmates to fill a stadium anymore. But they support newer bands and older influences by bringing them on the road. Many of Metallica's more recent openers—Lamb of God, Mastodon, High on Fire, Gojira, Kvelertak, Down, Baroness, and Local H (picked through a 2017 fan contest) among them, as well as global stars like Korn, Slipknot, Linkin Park, and Ghost—are better than the bands that headlined over Metallica in their club days and prime songwriting years. Some of those supporting acts were pushing better records than Metallica's recent albums when they opened. But none of them can trounce Metallica onstage. In their decades as headliners, you never hear about Metallica's openers blowing away the kings.

In Metallica's hands, a stadium needs the intimacy of a club and aging is a reason to play tighter, not slower. Getting exponentially bigger is no reason to stop experimenting. Moving into arenas, Metallica used their enormity to reinvent and break the confines of rock stages, from the Damaged Justice tour's Lady Justice statue to the Wherever We May

Roam tour's snake pit to Poor Touring Me's collapsing stage to World Magnetic's lighting rig coffins. Free to take their time and speak their mind anywhere, Metallica break geographic and political boundaries, taking thrash metal across the Iron Curtain in 1987 and bringing arena metal to China in 2013 (they were barred from playing "One," "Master of Puppets" or "Battery," though somehow "Blackened" and "Seek & Destroy" were okay). Lars logs and creates every setlist, making sure Metallica never plays the same show twice. "I'm more interested, personally, in how you present guys playing music to an audience and fuck with that," says Lars in *Cunning Stunts*. "The sort of trappings that come with what you supposedly can do and what you can't do and breaking those barriers."

This includes where they play (Antarctica in 2013, making them the first artists to perform on seven continents), how they play (hosting the two-day Orion Music + More festival with bands, a film festival, car show, horror museum, guitars exhibit, standup, and more), what they play (2014's By Request tour let fans vote the setlist over the internet), who they play with (Lady Gaga at the 2017 Grammys? Babymetal on the Worldwired tour?), and what they do when an international emergency puts the world on lockdown (2020's "Pandemica" drive-in show). "We don't know what the hell we're doing," James said, before shaking up the concert movie format with *Metallica Through the Never*. "But we know we want to try."

"We were always a live band, always. Since day one, that's how we got our fanbase," James has told VH1. By not releasing a music video or a live album for years, Metallica ensured fans could only get a sense of live Metallica by showing up. It's the best way to hear them, more than any record or film. No matter what release they're touring on, no matter what size the venue, the trove of available live Metallica music shows they're nearly always a powerhouse onstage. Recent performances uploaded by the band are often as riveting as anything you can find from their early years. On the *Kill 'Em All* and *Ride the Lightning* box sets, young James gets winded, sometimes sounding like a lion cub learning to roar, sometimes missing most of a verse in the fervor (his rhythm playing, sans solos and vocals on the demos, is something else). The wallop of *Ride the Lightning* songs months away from release overpowers how off-key, under-rehearsed, or poorly mixed they sound. But Metallica's early sloppiness is no match for their modern tightness, a controlled chaos like one of Lars' beloved Pollock paintings (Lars once picked Pollock's Number 32, 1950 as the painting that best embodied Metallica). Watch how assured James Hetfield has grown on the microphone, developing and changing his persona over the years, building an intensity and connection, expressing himself musically in ways he never does offstage.

"Nobody else commands the same kind of respect and attention without it being self-seeking or egocentric," James' longtime friend and collaborator Jerry Cantrell has noted. "He's been at the top of his game for so long and he continues to search for a deeper meaning. . . . He's the godfather, man."

It doesn't hurt that these days Metallica has more contagious crowd energy, an electricity that jolts the stadium into a chant over the "Breadfan" riff, before whipping them off course with the time change. Sometimes they'll draw out the progression before the last "The Four Horseman" verse, charged by the bounding arena when Lars' drums kick back in. Early tapes often show dumbstruck fans wondering what just annihilated their senses. This ain't the NWOBHM. "It wasn't really until James started getting some European shows under his belt in the spring of 1984, where he started being able to command the big, European crowds," Lars notes in *Murder in the Front Row*. "That's when he became James Hetfield, the frontman."

"You don't stay relevant in metal for 36 years without learning how to make every seat count," Craig Jenkins reviewed the Worldwired tour in *Vulture*. "Whenever you get it into your head that Metallica has shown you everything it's capable of, it reaches out with just a little more."

Maybe one night it'll be "Disposable Heroes," or "Trapped Under Ice," or maybe even "Dyers Eve." Maybe they'll play the audience participation classic "The Memory Remains"—what other band is cool enough to let their fans be Marianne Faithfull on any given night? Maybe they'll play a new song, before the studio version is out. Maybe it'll be Rob and Kirk covering a song by a surprise local artist, as they've been doing on the Worldwired tour. Maybe it'll be something they've never tried before, as

Metallica is prone to do. But if it's Metallica, the best bet is that you're in for something phenomenal.

ADRENALINE STARTS TO FLOW

Metallica has one of the most sprawling official live discographies of any metal band. Other than the *Some Kind of Monster* EP, which features James' worst-ever singing and peaks with him forgetting the words to "Ride the Lightning," Metallica's live records are usually great—how could they not be? But even their best live records can only conjure the chaos of their shows, never quite capturing the exhilaration of seeing Metallica in the flesh. Maybe there's a definitive Metallica live record hiding in Lars' vault, but until then, here's some of the best documented proof of Metallica's prowess.

LIVE SHIT: BINGE & PURGE (1993)

Dropped on the heels of the Nowhere Else to Roam tour, Metallica's first live record gave something back to the fans who craved exclusivity. You can own the Black Album without being much of a metalhead— no chance of that if you bought *Live Shit: Binge & Purge*. Inspired by Queensrÿche CD/video package *Operation: Livecrime*, Lars saw live albums becoming obsolete and fans paying more attention to video, thus he packaged two full video shows (1989 Seattle and 1992 San Diego), one full audio show (1993 Mexico), and a photo book into a set channeling Metallica's massiveness. Metallica are on top of the world, five for five in classic albums (if you haven't come around to the Black Album, stick to the Seattle show) on *Live Shit*, tearing through anthem after anthem over three-hour shows where you wouldn't take a second for a bathroom break, even during the solos (you're going to miss Kirk's "Little Wing"?). *Live Shit* testifies that success and the Black Album didn't soften Metallica—their songs are louder and faster than on record, and filthier (James changes a "Whiplash" lyric to "dick rash"). You won't get everything you love about Metallica on *Live Shit*, but you won't miss anything while it's playing.

CUNNING STUNTS (1998)

Supporting *Load* and *Reload* on the Poor Touring Me tour is no one's idea of the best Metallica era. But *Cunning Stunts*, filmed over two 1997 Fort Worth nights, shows another side of Metallica that still pulls off a great show. From the start Metallica distances themselves from their past, not taking the stage to "The Ecstasy of Gold" but rather jamming out on "Bad Seed" before breaking into an apt "So What." The Anti-Nowhere League cover and spoonerism title may look like Metallica clinging to their faded youth, but the centered stage on the Convention Center floor demolishes the fan and band barrier, helping give the arena the intimacy of their early shows. Even when they fill two arena nights, Metallica find ways to turn the floor into a stage, bringing fans close enough for security to have to tackle a stage crasher during "For Whom the Bell Tolls" and for Kirk to dodge a thrown drink during "So What." The "Enter Sandman" stage collapse loses some of its fun on video, although in person it was realistic enough for fans and journalists to believe the EMTs and burning roadie were real. But the most explosive thing on *Cunning Stunts* is a unique, frenetic Metallica show, including some of James' best singing, additional blast beats from Lars, and perhaps best of all a gorgeous short Jason solo that interpolates "My Friend of Misery" and "Welcome Home (Sanitarium)," one of his most affecting recorded moments. Check out the DVD for interviews, a documentary, and a photo gallery.

S&M (1999)

Metal had been symphonic before Metallica recruited the San Francisco Symphony Orchestra for *S&M*, but never quite the way Metallica did it. Metallica's horror symphony is more Elfman than Emperor, influencing score composers like Ramin Djawadi (*Iron Man, Game of Thrones*).

S&M is mostly a hit-filled affair, but the songs were picked with conductor Michael Kamen (famous for his film scores, including *Brazil*, *Lethal Weapon*, and *Die Hard*) based on what sounded best with a symphony. Metallica wanted to leave out "Enter Sandman," but were impressed enough with Kamen's arrangement to keep it, whereas "The Unforgiven" didn't work as well as hoped, and was eventually canned. Likewise, there's no attempt to symphonize anything from *Kill 'Em All*.

The orchestra (the "S," a mirrored treble clef joining the Metallica logo's "M" on the cover, is for "Symphony") complements Metallica beautifully, performing the "Ecstasy of Gold" intro and even matching the gunfire in "One." The artists shine most on more constructed works like "The Call of Ktulu," "The Thing That Should Not Be," and "Bleeding Me." The terra incognita includes two new songs—the excellent "No Leaf Clover," which sounds written for the orchestra, and the stoner rock-inspired "-Human," which hasn't been performed since the *S&M* shows, selected in Lars' words, to give the performers music that was "not just foreign to them, but foreign to us." Most of all, the show was foreign to the seated attendees, inspiring season ticketholder Francis Ford Coppola to walk out early but inspiring younger fans like eleven-year-old Sonny John Moore, who allegedly can be seen attending the show, ten years away from his debut EP *My Name Is Skrillex*. Orchestra musicians regretted not bringing a change of clothes for the intermission, working as hard as the thrash kings, the sweat pouring out like the music they play. On record, baroque fan Kirk might be the MVP, pulling out an electric sitar for "Wherever I May Roam" and fusing Chopin's Piano Sonata 2 (Funeral March) with Montrose's "Bad Motor Scooter" (yes, the song Mötley Crüe nicked for the "Kickstart My Heart" intro) between Metallica originals. But the film shows James in command, lurking in the orchestra pit for "Hero of the Day" and laughing for unknown reasons on "The Thing That Should Not Be." In madness he dwells, so much that none of his dad jokes ("Of Wolfgang and Man," really?) can take away from the magnitude of *S&M*.

Watch the DVD extras for an *Animal House* homage starring Jason and wisdom from the show's lighting designer, only known as J.B.: "Like Wordsworth said, poetry is a motion recollected in tranquility. You have to go and take the song and go sit in a closet and listen to it, and then you hear how to light it."

THE BIG FOUR: LIVE FROM SOFIA, BULGARIA (2010)

Maybe the craziest decision Metallica ever made in a career full of crazy decisions was to not only book an entire fourteen-date tour going onstage after Slayer, but film it for all to see. Metallica released four excellent concert films for the World Magnetic tour (*Français Pour une Nuit, Orgullo, Pasión, y Gloria: Tres Noches en la Ciudad de México, The Big Four*, and *Quebec Magnetic*), while outdoing every band at the Big Four shows, themselves included. *The Big Four* edges the other films for lineup, historical significance, and Metallica's setlist. Each band brings their A-game, including Megadeth playing through rain and one of Jeff Hanneman's last Slayer shows, but Metallica claims their headliner status from the first notes of "Creeping Death." Some of the biggest cheers come for "Fade to Black," a reminder that Metallica didn't have to be the loudest Big Four band to be the heaviest. But just as remarkable is seeing by far the most popular metal band on Earth match their more niche peers' aggression on "Blackened," "Hit the Lights," and "Sad but True," which James dedicates to his Big Four tourmates (who enjoyed a boost—the Big Four tour earned some of their biggest audiences to date, and *Live from Sofia* gave both Slayer and Anthrax their first platinum-certified full-length). The all-star jam on "Am I Evil?" is the tour's most viral moment, but just wait for the cheers when James, hunched on his knees at the ripping crescendo of "Nothing Else Matters," holds up his pick for the stadium's LED screen to show the logos of all four of the night's bands. He flips it over—"THE BIG 4."

The extras include a woman who asks James to sign a homemade *Death Magnetic* pillow so he can be in her dreams, plus a cordial, semi-awkward conversation between Lars and Dave Mustaine. But Dave Ellefson remembers a friendly atmosphere in his autobiography, *My Life with Deth*. "James was standing outside the dressing rooms, cheering on everybody and shouting, 'Have a great show!' A band that big doesn't have to do that . . . But that wasn't Metallica's style."

METALLICA THROUGH THE NEVER (2013)

Promoting Metallica's best concert film, movie director Nimród Antal noted, "This is a Metallica film, first and foremost. The last thing I wanted to do was step on some awesome songs with dialogue." The songs-only official soundtrack doesn't have the film's IMAX 3D thrills, but it does have a top-level, impeccably mixed Metallica performance you can play in your car. It even one-ups the film by adding Kirk's gorgeous "Nothing Else Matters" intro solo, one of the loveliest moments of any Metallica show yet never released in a studio version and absent from the movie. Just one more *Through the Never* enigma.

BOX SETS, *KILL 'EM ALL, RIDE THE LIGHTNING* (2016), *MASTER OF PUPPETS* (2017), . . . *AND JUSTICE FOR ALL* (2018)

Metallica has long been the world's biggest metal band, but their box set series makes the case they're also the world's biggest metal fans. Metallica put the kind of obsessive care and detail into their first four album box sets that they'd want for *Paranoid* or *Lightning to the Nations*. Like *Cliff 'Em All*, the box sets are in part scraped together by fans, who sent in recordings, photos, and stories. Each set contains a classy book of intricate collages and oral histories from pals ranging from El Cerrito party guests to Ozzy Osbourne, plus records and DVDs of live music and interviews showing a portrait of the artists as a young band. It's fun to hear young Metallica doing radio IDs for underground metal stations, decades before they could afford to mock the radio promo opportunities in *Some Kind of Monster*. The boys try to make the call letters sound extra tough by adding grunts and "Ye-ahs!" "I'm talking to Mike Griff from fuckin' loud Cleveland," asserts Cliff Burton. "*The Headbang Metal Show*, WCSB 89.3 on your FM . . . knob."

In an April 1986 WYSP Philadelphia *Metal Shop* interview, James and Lars celebrate releasing the most groundbreaking metal music to date by singing "Bath-o-ry" and "Bath-a-room" to the tune of "Battery" before James settles on "Country Bear Jamboree." "That's what it's about, man," James vows. "Those bears get way out of control." Unlike some metal artists, Metallica don't use overdubs on their master tapes, show-ing works in progress like "Orion" with a synth intro, "Welcome Home (Sanitarium)" when it was called "Orion, the Hunter of the Sky," or "Fight Fire with Fire" when they were still figuring out the chorus. Kirk and Cliff start losing their voices barking out the "Die" part of "Creeping Death" at Kabuki Theatre, before it became an audience screamalong. The box sets uncover a Metallica that comes in sloppy, misses notes, and learns on the job, but already shows a magic that makes it work. There's an almost supernatural ability that will make those stadiums in a few years feel as visceral as the Keystone.

HARDWIRED . . . TO SELF-DESTRUCT (DELUXE EDITION) (2016)

You thought those club shows on the box sets were exhilarating? How about one more show, of all pre–*Master of Puppets* songs, in a small venue . . . only this time, Metallica is one of the world's biggest bands? The boys celebrated the *Kill 'Em All* and *Ride the Lightning* box releases with a Record Store Day show at San Francisco's Rasputin Music, thrashing out an hour of their earliest songs with punk energy and spontaneity (perfectly timed belch on "The Four Horsemen," James), but with a better mix and musicianship. The band channels their *Kill 'Em All* rawness with scary pre-cision, even dropping Diamond Head's "Helpless" and a "Metal up your ass" chant, but still sound like metal survivors, dedicating "Fade to Black" to Cliff and speculating on the late Paul Baloff (James: "This place would be a disaster area"). It's enough to make you wish they played more shows like this, once you've collected yourself from the final blasts of "Metal Militia." The disc ends with the live debut of "Hardwired" at U.S. Bank Stadium in Minneapolis, and Metallica is still thrashing at their hardest.

HELPING HANDS . . . LIVE & ACOUSTIC AT THE MASONIC (2019)

Metallica's first annual All Within My Hands show plays like a culmina-tion of the chops they developed for Pegi and Neil Young's Bridge School Benefit shows, with ten of twelve songs here originally performed at their

Bridge School appearances. The result is the *Metallica Unplugged* record you didn't know you wanted, with surprise covers (Nazareth's "Please Don't Judas Me," Blue Öyster Cult's "Veteran of the Psychic Wars"), originals reworked with acoustics and pedal steels ("The Unforgiven," "Bleeding Me"), and, best of all, thrashers that get revamped into sweeping folk-metal epics, unrecognizable until the words start ("Disposable Heroes," "The Four Horsemen," and even "Enter Sandman"). The show raised $1.3 million for Metallica's nonprofit All Within My Hands, in addition to all record sales proceeds, as if there weren't enough reasons to do this again. Maybe next time with more of Metallica's Bridge School covers, like "Clampdown," "Only Happy When It Rains," "Brothers in Arms," or—what the fuck—"I Just Want to Celebrate"?

S&M2 (2020)

The twentieth anniversary of one of Metallica's best-known shows is a gift to fans who have been tracking the band over the past two decades. Metallica is now old enough to play with a San Francisco Symphony made up of several musicians who grew up with *Master of Puppets* and the Black Album, in an era where, thanks in part to the original *S&M*, metal and classical are more connected. While *S&M2* doesn't top its predecessor, it reveals a pathos in songs you may have thought you didn't like. The gorgeous, slowed first release "All Within My Hands" sounds like no other Metallica single, and "Unforgiven III" gets a beautiful reading from James, sung alone with the orchestra weeks before he headed back to rehab. But by far the best moment comes from Symphony bassist Scott Pingel, who creates a Baroque-sounding solo when Metallica leaves the stage, leaving the Metallica audience as hushed as it ever will be. The cheers break in a little over one minute into Pingel's piece when the crowd recognizes it—he's playing Cliff's "(Anesthesia)—Pulling Teeth."

11

OPPOSITION, CONTRADICTION, PREMONITION

. . . And Justice for All

"Lyrically, we were really into social things, watching CNN and the news all the time, and realizing that other people really do kinda control your life. . . . We discovered how much money influences certain things, and discovered how things work in the United States."

—James Hetfield

One of the only consistencies in Metallica's unparalleled career is their insistence, usually Hetfield's or Ulrich's, that they are not a political band. (Lars: "There are very few people I respect as much as Tom Morello or Bono. But it doesn't mean that I want to use Metallica in the same way.") This is bullshit, and a fine example of why artists aren't always the best interpreters of their art. "All good art is political," Toni Morrison stated in a 2008 profile. "There is none that isn't. And the ones that try hard not to be political are political by saying, 'We love the status quo.'"

On . . . *And Justice for All*, Metallica is at war. It's their most combative album, even if it isn't as fast as *Kill 'Em All*, as heavy as *Master of Puppets*, or as violent as *St. Anger*. Metallica attacks mutually assured destruction, the justice system, oppression, censorship, military corruption, blacklisting, religious abuse, familial abuse, discrimination, social injustice,

warmongering, contaminators, conventional time signatures, song structure, production standards, and the world's notions of what a metal band
could and couldn't do. Songs average over seven minutes, bizarre production mixes out new bassist Jason, and time signatures reach 7 and 9. Songs
cut out and come back on off beats, build without resolving, asking questions without answers in septuple meter. Progressions drop out and return
six minutes later, heavier and more distorted. Tracks like "Blackened" and
"Dyers Eve" rank among Metallica's fastest and heaviest, "To Live Is to
Die" among the gentlest. Typical metal themes were absent from their
lyrics. "We have nothing against sex," Lars told the *Washington Post*'s
Richard Harrington, on behalf of the biggest rock band to never write any
songs about sex (at least until *Lulu*). "It's just another cliché that's easily
avoidable, as is Satanism, religion, drugs, or car songs." Metallica ushered
in the nineties with a heavier, darker, socially conscious form of rock.

"There are all sorts of stereotypes: speedcore, thrash, or fuckin'-death-
super-Satan metal," James stated in 1989. "I don't see us fitting into any
of that shit."

Much can be argued about Metallica, but the most irrefutable point this
book can make is that Metallica, especially on records like . . . *And Justice
for All*, make great art, thus political art. Politicians, generals, and academics could give speech related to some of *Justice*'s ideas, but they would
not be as effective without Metallica's music. By not being as blunt as their
peers, Metallica made their political songs timeless. There's no Metallica
equivalent to Jello Biafra updating the Dead Kennedys' anti–Jerry Brown
"California Über Alles" for Ronald Reagan and later Arnold Schwarzenegger. On *Justice*, Metallica are even timeless in addressing the Dead Kennedys, who in 1986 were charged with distributing harmful material to
minors, and faced a lawsuit over their album *Frankenchrist* that included
artist H. R. Giger's aptly titled *Penis Landscape* in the liner notes. The case
ended in a mistrial, but *Frankenchrist* was pulled from many stores and the
Dead Kennedys broke up within the year. Metallica, sometimes playing a
variation of the Kennedys' "Holiday in Cambodia" on the *Master of Puppets* tour, responded to this on . . . *And Justice for All*, testifying for freedom of speech with "Eye of the Beholder." It was the least Metallica could
do for Jello Biafra, who in 1986 defended *Master of Puppets* and "Fade to
Black" in an *Oprah* debate with the PMRC's Tipper Gore. "I think it's

damaging, both to a parent and to a kid, to twist the lyrics of a Metallica song like that out of context, to try and tell a parent what that song is about when that may not be what the song is about," asserted Biafra. "I know Metallica, they're brighter people than that. . . . It takes a real chicken parent to blame the suicide of their child on a musician."

Metallica have been coy about their politics in interviews. They don't want to be defined, musically or ideologically. "We're real serious about the words," James remarked in his first *New York Times* interview, in 1988. "But we're not trying to push any subject across or do any dictating how people should live. We're just stating an opinion." James has stated both liberal and conservative values, on record as both pro-choice and pro–death penalty, and stopped short of Lars' condemnation of the CIA's use of Metallica songs to torture prisoners. (James: "We've tortured people with it for a long time. A lot longer than the CIA.") Lars and Kirk have occasionally slammed Republican presidents in the press, making blunt (Kirk in *A Year and a Half in the Life of Metallica*) and thoughtful (Kirk's social media page) cases. But over thirty years after its release, . . . *And Justice for All* stands as Metallica's most enduring political statement, the greatest political metal record ever, a fight for civil liberties, the environment, and human rights that gets more critical with time.

"Never being direct by explicitly stating their political beliefs, the band didn't have to offer a direct message to challenge the nationalistic assumption of American Exceptionalism through any means necessary," author Laina Dawes wrote about "One" in *Billboard*. "Hetfield countered the prevailing narratives that assert masculinity while eschewing vulnerability and 'weakness' that no (it was thought) American soldier should ever feel."

"Every song was a riff tape, in itself," James recalled years later. Part of the excitement was that Metallica wasn't stocking up; they were unloading. The band on *Kill 'Em All* five years earlier doesn't sound capable of "The Frayed Ends of Sanity," "Dyers Eve," or "Blackened." Metallica walked the prog line with falling into wankiness, subverting prog-rock and post-punk by bridging them on the title track, the only ten-minute song to ever (as James notes on a box set demo) resemble Killing Joke, even if you forget both those things while it's playing. When punk met polymeters in mathcore bands like the Dillinger Escape Plan, it's no surprise that DEP titled a song "82588," after the release date of frontman Greg Puciato's favorite album.

Inspired by Samson's *Shock Tactics* and Frankfurt's Lady Justice sculpture, James and Lars commissioned an acrylic painting by Stephen Gorman for the cover, dubbed "Doris" in statue form on Metallica's Damaged Justice tour. The album title is tagged on the stone, but Metallica's name is engraved. Justice is temporary, but Metallica is permanent. Metallica's justice is subversive, in graffiti art on the statue, but it's also fragile and removable.

"Blackened," the raging nuclear holocaust tale that kicks off . . . *And Justice for All*, starts with a distant intro, several layers of guitars played backward, somehow sounding like both Jimi Hendrix and an orchestra tuning up. For years fans have tried reversing the song's intro, which Metallica backmasked for dramatic effect on the recorded version. Reversing it uncovers another great progression from an era when Metallica was practically spewing them out. None of the reversals (or the demo version of "Blackened" where Metallica plays it in its original form) sound quite as cool as it does on . . . *And Justice for All*. Nearly any other thrash band would be content to have the original version on a record, but Metallica will play it backward, inside out, or bassless to get the fiercest result. The urgent, air raid siren–esque riff takes off, twisting into a different end each time and the drums gallop in. The waves of riffs part for James' apocalyptic warning, increasingly plausible by the time Metallica released a stripped down, mainly acoustic "Blackened" in 2020, with a gallery view video showing each bandmate's quarantined performance.

Metallica was getting bigger on *Justice*, but they weren't getting friendlier. Kirk's divebombs on "The Shortest Straw" blade the listener, and the machine gun kicks on "One," written before the lyrics, bind us to Joe's crib-like bed. He can't tell if it's true or dream, but we see that he'll never know. Musically inspired in part by playing around with Venom's "Buried Alive," James delved into his own fears for "One," which he recalled years later as "such a scary and dark place. . . . It was easy to write, really was, because it felt very comfortable."

That sense of fear and alienation humanizes . . . *And Justice for All*, even in its most stoic moments. The shaking rhythms of "Harvester of Sorrow" and "The Shortest Straw" convey the instability of their subjects, the latter inspiring Jason to say in an interview with KSDT, "That song, personally, makes me dance. I don't know if any of the rest of you think that's stupid, you can fuck off, it's a bouncy song." Even when his bass is hidden in the mix, Jason's liveliness couldn't be stifled. "Jason came in with a different attitude," James recalled of the sessions. "He reminded me of a basketball. I don't know why but he was always moving, always."

By the paranoid "The Frayed Ends of Sanity," they're crazed enough to start a song with *The Wizard of Oz*'s "March of the Winkies," which may have inspired no less a musicology scholar than Butt-Head to argue to his fellow theorist Beavis that James resembled the Cowardly Lion on *Live Shit: Binge & Purge* (James, a Leo, did a solid on-camera impression of the character on the Damaged Justice tour). It also centered "Frayed Ends" in the great trilogy of late-eighties "March of the Winkies" interpolations, between Prince's "It's Gonna Be a Beautiful Night" in 1987 and LL Cool J's "I'm the Type of Guy" in 1989. Making up placeholder lyrics in the demo version of "The Frayed Ends of Sanity," James sings, "Kill your mom and kill your dad." Until 2014, when Helsinki voted for it on the Metallica by Request tour, "The Frayed Ends of Sanity" was the only song from Metallica's first five records that had never been played live. But on the Worldwired tour, Metallica gave show closer "Enter Sandman" a false ending by tagging the "Frayed Ends" main progression. Lars counts in one more time, the fans screaming on their feet, and the band launches in, a reminder that Metallica still surprises, goes beyond what's expected, and that even the most rarely played deep cut from their first ten years as a band can blow a stadium to pieces.

The funeral mass "To Live Is to Die" is composed of unused Cliff Burton riffs, the strangest and saddest song on the record. Nearly ten minutes in length, it moves from an acoustic medieval melody into prog-metal riffage, over hills and valleys before resting in its original form, picking up a brief spoken word along the way. It's sometimes thought of as *Justice*'s one instrumental, considering the previous three albums each had one, but in honor of Cliff Burton, Metallica break their own rules. In one second, all the instruments cut out, giving way to a movement so delicate it barely registers at first. The guitars and drums take several measures to pick themselves up and work back into the earlier progression. The lyrics are attributed to Burton, but the first half are adapted from the seventeenth-century German poet Paul Gerhardt, coupled with the second set adapted from the 1981 film *Excalibur* (death metal fans: listen for the words "Anaal

Nathrakh" in Merlin's incantation) and the fantasy novelist Stephen Don-aldson's *Lord Foul's Bane*.

It's a difficult song, and Metallica didn't perform it in its entirety until their thirtieth anniversary shows in 2011. But in the Seattle 1989 show on *Live Shit: Binge & Purge*, Jason closes a bass solo with an elegiac move-ment of "To Live Is to Die," leading Kirk and James to join in for the show's most stunning moment. It is perhaps an equally fitting Cliff tribute that James still plays his "EET FUK" Explorer, or that the band rips right into Cliff's favorite, "Master of Puppets," at the end. "To Live Is to Die" is gorgeous and revelatory with Jason's bass, but it never sounds like it should be on *Justice*.

. . . *And Justice for All*'s songs needed to be long. By the Black Album tour, Metallica had compressed some of the record's best movements into a "*Justice* Medley" and a career-spanning "Instrumental Medley" that took the steam out of the songs. They tried medleys again in their *Cun-ning Stunts*–era identity crisis, including "Mastertarium" and "*Kill/Ride* Medley," before more or less giving them up (none of their medleys have been in the setlist for years). People complain about . . . *And Justice for All*'s length and production, but no one, not even Metallica themselves, have improved the songs.

. . . *And Justice for All* closes with its shortest and fastest song, "Dyers Eve," which takes its title from a line in the 1970 Dustin Hoffman film *Little Big Man*. As Kafka's *Letter to His Father* in thrash luaguage, James bluntly lashes out at his parents for the first time on record, furious but dependent on them. Kirk galvanizes on the solo, and Lars' double bass brings the storm. Years later, James would discuss being unable to manage grief, poverty, or confrontation without his parents, telling NPR's Terry Gross he struggled with whether he was still supposed to hate them. Asked whether he was surprised by any Metallica song's popularity, James named "Dyers Eve." "Now that you're gone, I'm out here in the world and lost, and scared," James reflected, admitting that he didn't know or care what his father thought of the song. But Metallica didn't play "Dyers Eve" live until years after Virgil Hetfield's death, on March 5, 2004, in Los Angeles, on the twenty-first anniversary of Cliff Burton's first Metallica show.

Like much of America in 1988, Lars was an *Appetite for Destruction* fanatic, and he sought Guns N' Roses producer Mike Clink for . . . *And*

Justice for All. But when sessions fell through they amicably split, and Metallica returned to Flemming Rasmussen, who initially turned down the record to care for his newborn daughter. Jason spent one day tracking his bass with the assistant engineer, separate from the rest of the band (Rasmussen called Jason's tracks "fucking brilliant" in 2016). But like most Metallica fans, Jason was shocked that his bass barely existed in the final mix.

Reading up on . . . *And Justice for All*'s production, no two participants have the same story. Engineer Steve Thompson recalls being stunned when Lars prompted him to turn down Jason's bass, and galled when Lars asked him what happened to the bass twenty years later. James has connected the mix to everything from hearing loss (being unable to hear high end) to his scooped tone (all lows and highs, no midrange) eating up Jason's frequencies to him and Lars having "the fucking shackles on everybody." "Playing-wise, I mirrored pretty much everything that James played," Jason related. "I was completely influenced by that guy, in all aspects of my life." Whatever the case, mixing out Jason was not a careless decision. *Garage Days Re-Revisited*, released a year earlier and advertised as "Not very produced by Metallica," consciously displays Jason. Cliff was not present for most of the mixing for *Master of Puppets*, but he's still audible. "I don't know if the bass being down was a little subliminal, 'Hey, welcome, motherfucker, you gotta fight for your fader to go up,'" James recalled. "I would say we were still mourning. I was still sad that Cliff was gone, but excited that Jason was there." The lack of bass is Cliff's ghost, but also meant sacrificing Jason.

All four musicians have expressed regret over *Justice*'s production over the years, while praising the riffs and lyrics. "Sometimes when I hear it, I sit there and roll my eyes," Lars stated in 2005. "And other times I think, Jesus, this was the blueprint for a whole generation of music."

"It stands up, over time," Jason concurred in *Loudwire*. "Maybe not the mix, but the songs do, and the impact that it made."

Fans have remixed it to showcase the bass, with titles like . . . *And Justice for Jason* or . . . *And Jason for All*. Some versions implement the available separate bass tracks from *Guitar Hero: Metallica*, or even rerecord it with an idea of how Cliff, one of the most unpredictable bassists outside of free jazz, supposedly would have played it. For years, fans have approached Jason with their own versions of *Justice*, to which Jason has been gracious but firm. "How it's supposed to be is what came out and how it made a mark on the world, but cool." The most recent remastered . . . *And Justice for All*, in 2018, still leaves out the bass, keeping the mystery for fans to explore.

Even devoted metalheads didn't know what to do with the record's production, pacing, lyrics, or rollout. *Kerrang!* gave *Justice* a lukewarm three stars out of five. A former fan saw James at the Stone, and spit at him for making a music video. Listeners conflicted over the antiwar and pro-euthanasia messages in "One," and theorized whether the blacklisting themed "The Shortest Straw" was about Cliff Burton's death. It's the first Metallica record where each part of the percussion is audible, paving the way for more drum-heavy production on great metal records—*Painkiller*, *Rust in Peace*, and *No More Tears* among them. "The drum production was unlike anything that had been heard up until that point and the clarity was unrivaled," stated Lamb of God's Chris Adler. "In fact, I don't think there has really been that much of a revolutionary change in drum sounds since . . . *And Justice for All*." Proto-groove metal first single "Harvester of Sorrow" gets honored lyrically on Machine Head's *Burn My Eyes* and musically in most of Machine Head's career (definitely the best parts). The accelerated prog-metal tempos show up in bands like Between the Buried and Me and Periphery, both of whom have recorded . . . *And Justice for All* songs. *Justice* is audible in metalcore bands like God Forbid, who fused thrash, politics, and crumbling statue art on their fourth album, *IV: Constitution of Treason*. You can hear Revocation in "Dyers Eve," even before they covered it in 2013, Dave Davidson throating like a young Jason Newsted.

It reaches politics, too, topping the Virginia delegate and metal vocalist Danica Roem's favorite metal records (she has also called *S&M* "my most listened-to album"). "I saw a Metallica bio clip with a woman talking about how the band would chat with fans, sign autographs and pose for photos for hours until they talked to every person who wanted to say hello," said Roem in 2018, after a discussion panel in a Virginia high school library. "That's the work ethic I want to emulate."

Metallica added Delaware and Vermont to their Damaged Justice tour itinerary for the sake of playing all fifty states. Touring was taking its toll on the band, with Kirk and Lars getting into cocaine, and James' stomach problems and blackout alcoholism worsening ("People were hating me, and I didn't know why"). Cocaine, phenomenally, made Lars Ulrich even more talkative, which exasperated James, by then a violent drunk who would throw things at Lars. "On the road you get so pampered," Lars acknowledged. "Everybody around you works for you and that's a dangerous environment." But in *Circus* he cited AC/DC as a role model for Metallica's success, predating both Metallica's *Back in Black*–inspired blockbuster and their decision to make AC/DC's "It's a Long Way to the Top (If You Wanna Rock 'n' Roll)" the last song played over the PA before the lights go out at Metallica shows. "They just stuck to it year after year and gradually got bigger, until four or five years down the line they were a major band," noted Lars. "People had changed for them and liked what they were doing, instead of them having to change for some fad that would only last a year or two. And that's what I think we're doing." It was a path to Metallica's success but also a degree of stability. Metallica would almost implode, but unlike quicker (if not overnight) successes Guns N' Roses or Nirvana, they stayed together.

"Our band had a lot of respect for Metallica, for sure, we always did," Dave Grohl stated. "Because it seemed like they had come from the same place. . . . They were the little bad-asses that changed the world one club at a time."

On tour, the *Justice* songs' complexity started draining the band (Lars: "Every night became an exercise in not fucking up") and, by Kirk's account, the audience. "I couldn't stand watching the front row start to yawn by the eight or ninth minute," Kirk recalled, waiting for the exploding and crumbling Doris statue to shake up the crowd. Self-described band "cheerleader" James found trouble getting fans into a ten-minute song, taking progressive Metallica as far as it could go. The "Last Caress" encore was often a relief. Metallica didn't play ". . . And Justice for All" for another nineteen years, until 2008. But if fans were bored, they'd forgotten by the Metallica by Request tour, where it was voted into the setlist for twenty-four of twenty-six shows. It's included in *Metallica Through the Never*, over "Fade to Black," "Seek & Destroy," "Sad but True," or "The Unforgiven."

Astoundingly, Metallica broke through with their strangest, most difficult record to date. "Harvester of Sorrow," built in part around the word "infanticide," was weird enough to chart in the UK, if not the United States. "One," a song which felt, sounded, and (thanks to the video) looked like nothing else in popular music, debuted at number one on *Dial MTV* in 1989 and even put Metallica in *Billboard*'s top 40 singles. . . . *And Justice for All* was the first Metallica record to appear on music critics' *Pazz and Jop* poll (at #39 out of 40). Metallica was named one of *Rolling Stone*'s "Top Ten Bands You Won't Hear on the Radio," while Kirk and Jason mocked tourmates the Scorpions' choreographed stage moves in the publication. Airport security started waving these scruffy longhairs through, and stewardesses on commercial flights started calling them by their first names. Crew members Metallica had counted on working for free were now getting paid. In a *Metal Forces* interview, Lars gets defensive when the journalist indicates that James has been using some of the same banter every night on the Damaged Justice tour. Lars wasn't used to having fans follow them all over the country before.

Metallica were the first metal band to play the Grammys, nominated for the inaugural Best Hard Rock/Metal Performance Vocal or Instrumental award. Kurt Loder covered the show for MTV, announcing the nominees AC/DC, Metallica, Iggy Pop, Jane's Addiction, and . . . Jethro Tull. "No Guns N' Roses," sighed Loder. "Just Jethro Tull." Metallica showed up, told interviewers they expected AC/DC to win, got ragged on by host Billy Crystal, and played "One" in what looks like half of a steel cage. An unassuming James Hetfield tries not to eye the camera and lets out one nervous expletive on TV, years before Metallica became the token metal act at TV awards shows. It's one of Metallica's greatest TV performances, but it's less remembered than prog rock stalwarts Jethro Tull's upset win.

James said the first Grammys show turned them off of TV. "You can't do what you want do. It's all fucking planned out," he stated, years before a dead mic botched Metallica's 2017 Grammy performance of "Moth into Flame" with Lady Gaga. Lars, somewhat presciently, commented, "If we release anything for the rest of the nineties, every year we'll get a Grammy for it, just because they fucked up that first year." He was less than one year from winning Metallica's first Grammy, for "One," although not much had changed with the Recording Academy by 1990. Announcing the award, Robbie Robertson's praise for metal was greeted with silence. Megadeth's name was misspelled and individual songs were thrown into a category with full-length LPs. At least Lars had the graciousness to thank Jethro Tull for not releasing an album that year. As of 2021, Metallica's name is still misspelled on the official Grammys website ("I don't like to be pigeonholed, and I really like that people never really know what's going on with Metllica [*sic*]."—Lars Ulrich). The only "Unforgiven" to get a Grammy nomination is "Unforgiven III," which is the Recording Academy equivalent of nominating *Rocky III* instead of the original. But Metallica thrives without industry appreciation. Losing to Jethro Tull added to Metallica's mystique. By the time the night's Record of the Year award went to Bobby McFerrin's "Don't Worry, Be Happy," Metallica were known for being too cool to win.

The fact that Jethro Tull beat Metallica for a Grammy is now roughly as famous as *Aqualung*. Elektra had already printed up "Grammy Award winners" stickers for . . . *And Justice for All*, which Metallica got to amend with "LOSERS" scribbled over "winners," which looked more badass than the original. Interviewed by Canada's MuchMusic backstage, James laughed off the notion he was bummed about Tull's win. "One step forward, three back," says the reporter.

"Nah," says James. "It's all forward."

Metallica soldiers on. On . . . *And Justice for All* Metallica warred against the world. Musically, they were about to war against . . . *And Justice for All*.

12

DEALING OUT THE
AGONY WITHIN

Kirk Hammett

"I think heavy metal is therapeutic—it's music that blows the tension away. I think that's why people who have had really bad childhoods are attracted to heavy metal. It allows people to release aggression and tension in a nonviolent way. Also, heavy metal has a community feeling—it brings outsiders together. Heavy metal seems to attract all sorts of scruffy, lost animals, strays no one wants."

—Kirk Hammett

On January 13, 2018, Hawaii's Emergency Management Agency (EMA) sent out an urgent message to the state's residents, which appeared on phones, televisions, and radios:

Emergency Alert

BALLISTIC MISSILE THREAT INBOUND TO HAWAII. SEEK IMMEDI-ATE SHELTER. THIS IS NOT A DRILL.

Kirk Hammett, practicing yoga in his Hawaii home, was, in his recollection, "on my back, upside down or something," when one of his sons told him his phone had sent him an emergency alert. Kirk picked himself up and read the message. "There was no jet scrambling, no boats leaving Pearl Harbor," said Kirk, noting the base near his home. "There were no sirens or anything, you know, no air raid sirens. So I thought, 'This has got to be a mistake.' And I just continued doing my yoga."

Kirk was right, and the EMA employee who accidentally sent out the message was quickly fired. But without casting doubt on Kirk's knowledge of America's missile defense system, Kirk is the guy who will practice yoga in the face of an oncoming ballistic missile. From his first few weeks with Metallica, he was already breaking up fistfights between James and Lars while Cliff sat back and smiled. His bandmates call him "the referee," the mediator who sets an example of humility for James and Lars. In true Kirk fashion, he credits Cliff for teaching him this. In James' first six months of rehab, Kirk was the only bandmate he reached out to. "He could understand more than anyone else what was going on and pass on the word in an understanding way," James says in the *Some Kind of Monster* commentary. James first rejoined the band for Kirk's surprise birthday party. Even in the film's most heated moments, from James and Lars' fights to Phil's encroachment (Kirk recalled being furious at the moment where Phil hands James lyrics for *St. Anger*), Kirk doesn't bat an eye. Lars has called Kirk Metallica's most relaxed and least guarded member. To this day, Kirk is reportedly the only Metallica member who has never punched a bandmate.

In a famous *Cliff 'Em All* scene, a Kirk solo at Chicago's Metro drives the crowd wild enough to grab Kirk's Gibson and capture it in a tug of war. Kirk smiles helplessly while a roadie rescues the guitar. It's hard to imagine someone grabbing a young James' or Cliff's instrument without leaving the venue on a stretcher. But to Kirk, unleashing a guitar solo that whips people into violent madness is no big deal.

The angriest Kirk has ever looked is on the *Master of Puppets* back cover, in a photo taken at Donington shortly after someone from the audience had thrown a deviled ham sandwich right into vegetarian Kirk's black Jackson Flying V (he'd dodged a pig's head earlier). In the 1990s, when Kirk enrolled at San Francisco University to study film, Asian arts, and jazz for a semester, Kirk remarked that his classmates seemed surprised at how kind he was, as well as how short. Maybe they'd only seen him on the back of *Master of Puppets*.

"He never complained or got angry," Scott Ian wrote in his autobiography *I'm the Man*. "He was probably the nicest guy I'd ever met, and he never, ever changed, even with all the money and fame. He's still the same sweet kid I met the day after he arrived from SF."

The music is where Kirk gets vicious. He picks heavily, beating up his hands and slamming into his guitar. One of his first moves in Metallica was defying Jonny Z's insistence on playing Dave's solos, choosing instead to base his off the first bars and change them. He astonished Metallica by being Kirk—he didn't imitate Eddie Van Halen's tapping or Yngwie Malmsteen's arpeggios. When more effects and trends, like Dimebag's whammy, Zakk Wylde's pinch harmonics, or Fredrik Thordendal's djent made waves, Kirk didn't imitate those either. "My whole goal, when I play, is to take a listener into a darkness, to a place they've never been," Kirk states in his terrific horror book *It's Alive!* "And whether by route of angels or by route of devils, I'll do anything to get the listener to that zone."

"I THOUGHT I HAD A NORMAL CHILDHOOD UNTIL I SPOKE TO OTHER PEOPLE."

Kirk was born November 18, 1962, in San Francisco and raised by a Filipino mother and Irish dad, government clerk Teofila "Chefela" and naval officer Dennis Hammett. His father was a heavy drinker who frequently beat his wife and son. As a boy, Kirk walked to a strict Catholic school in the Mission District a few blocks from his house. A neighbor started molesting Kirk when he was nine or ten, and even had sex with Kirk's dog, Tippy, in front of him. Kirk remembered the dog still wagging her tail afterward.

At home, he coped with a small collection of horror toys and comics. "All the abuse didn't really start manifesting itself until I was ten or eleven and I have been collecting since I was six or seven," Kirk writes in *Too Much Horror Business.* "In a way it brings me back to a time when I wasn't tainted. Psychologically it helps me, and I find refuge in going into a room with all my stuff around me."

That collection started shortly after a fight with his brother and sister ended with Kirk's sprained arm. Unable to go outside, Kirk's parents sat him in front of the TV just in time for *The Day of the Triffids.* Young Kirk was terrified by the human-eating plants, but spent the rest of the day trying to draw the triffids that scared him so much. By the first grade Kirk was saving his school lunch money to buy *The Fantastic Four*, *Creepy*, *Famous Monsters of Filmland*, and *The Monster Times*, some of which got past 1954 Comics Code censorship rules by marketing themselves as magazines instead of comic books. Chefela didn't mind so much—she encouraged her son's reading, sometimes giving Kirk bedtime stories such as *The Little Prince*. Years later, he'd put out requests to trade comic books and toys with fans in the Metallica fanzine *Metal Militia*, and even appear on a special Halloween episode of the Travel Channel show *Toy Hunter*. *Master of Puppets* would allow him to pick up *Fantastic Four* #1. "To obtain the unobtainable is a real rush in itself," Kirk smiled.

Kirk liked to play the monster in childhood games with his siblings and cousins. He loved Godzilla and King Kong, and was fascinated by Lon Chaney's *The Hunchback of Notre Dame* and *The Phantom of the Opera*, finding a profundity that was missing from the G-rated films his classmates enjoyed. But the first monster Kirk really connected to was in the original Boris Karloff *Frankenstein*. Kirk watched it with his dad, who told him it was a great movie to watch stoned. Kirk was captivated, watching the monster struggling and failing to connect with humans. He also loved watching outcast monsters break free of their chains, cages, or ropes, escaping imprisonment or fighting their oppressors. "It was easy for me to relate to the monster's condition of loneliness and sorrow," Kirk wrote of *Frankenstein*, "and how abandoned he felt in his quest to be understood. . . . I suppose that's how I felt deep down, and these movies were the ones that started to help me, in some way, know it."

Kirk spent much of his boyhood in comic book stores and movie theaters, enjoying three films for a quarter at the Grand Theater on Saturdays and Sundays. Occasionally his father took him, though his older brother took six-year-old Kirk to *Barbarella*. But few of his friends or family could sit through three movies in a row, especially ones with taglines like "It will scare the living *yell* out of you!" (*How to Make a Monster*). So Kirk often went by himself, escaping into worlds of horror, sci-fi, blaxploitation, and kung fu. *The Exorcist* terrified him into sleeping with the lights on, and *The Texas Chainsaw Massacre* gave him nightmares. But no matter how many nights Kirk spent gripping his pillow tight, he kept coming back to movies. In his teens he loved *Eraserhead*, and *Carrie* made him a lifelong Stephen King fan.

Kirk was not a great student. He was more interested in comic books and movies than Catholicism or religion classes. At home he built, painted, and sometimes firecrackered his own rockets and model creatures. He also worried he'd grow up to get bullied like one of the skinny kids in Charles Atlas ads. Home didn't provide much relief. Kirk spent his sixteenth birthday trying to keep his dad from attacking his mom, which led to Dennis smacking his son around. Dennis left Chefela to raise Kirk and his siblings on her own.

"It never really goes away," Kirk said in 2017. "You just learn how to deal with it. For me, that well of anger, I can tap into it at any time in any sort of situation, and it's really helpful when I tap into that anger when I'm playing my guitar."

Kirk's first record was *A Partridge Family Christmas Card*, but his brother got him into Hendrix, Led Zeppelin, and Santana, sending Kirk down an irreversible path. He started going to Day on the Green to see bands like AC/DC and Van Halen. Kirk cast a wide net for noise, growing into the kind of kid who could dress as Ace Frehley for Halloween and love the Sex Pistols. Inspired to pick up a guitar, Kirk traded $10 and a copy of Kiss' *Dressed to Kill* for an old Montgomery Ward catalog special with a shoebox amp. "There was nothing else in my life that had ever inspired me to just like sit down and do one thing, just like guitar had," he'd say in a Guitar Center interview years later.

"I wasn't motivated by a lot of the things that might motivate people—fame, fortune, whatever. I was just motivated by wanting to play the guitar well."

EXODUS

"I was on a pretty bad path when I discovered music, and music kept me from going further down that path," Kirk told San Francisco radio station the Bone in 2017.

The discovery meant taking public transit for an hour to Berkeley to go to Rather Ripped and Rasputin Records, planning his trips around when the metal imports would come in, on Tuesdays and Fridays. He started meeting friends at shows and record stores (including his De Anza High

School classmate Les Claypool, whose future Hammett collabs would include a Kirk appearance in Primus' "John the Fisherman" video and a Tom Waits cover set with Kirk and Gogol Bordello). Kirk also started finding the bands he'd later bond with his Metallica bandmates over. "This was next level, and you needed to concentrate a little bit more and commit yourself a little bit more on first listen to these bands, but once you got it, you really got it," he remembered. He didn't feel protective about it—on the contrary, he made cassettes for his friends.

Kirk upgraded to a Marshall and the Gibson V he'd use on Metallica's first four records, acquired with money from his Burger King job. He cut his teeth in a five-piece called Legend, with Paul Baloff (vocals), Gary Holt (guitar), Geoff Andrews (bass), and Tom Hunting (drums). At Kirk the movie buff's suggestion, Legend changed their name to Exodus, after a 1960 Otto Preminger film written by Metallica's *Johnny Got His Gun* hero, Dalton Trumbo. Holt, who'd been playing guitar for six months when he met Kirk, remembers Hammett teaching him his first chords and some scales, along with Rolling Stones and Judas Priest songs. "It was Kirk's baby when I joined," Holt recalled. "He wrote all the music." Some of that music stayed on Exodus' thrashterpiece debut, *Bonded by Blood*, and others, like "Impaler" and "Die by His Hand," were written into the Metallica songs "Trapped Under Ice" and "Creeping Death," respectively.

Kirk's bandmates were not happy when Metallica recruited him. Baloff poured a beer over Kirk's head. But Kirk stayed friends with Exodus, and the Holt-led version became a great band on their own (Kirk performed with them again at Kirk Von Hammett's Fear FestEvil, Kirk's horror and music convention, which has also hosted Death Angel, Carcass, Meshuggah, High on Fire, and Agnostic Front). "I thought that was my band, but then when I met [Metallica] and started playing with them, I felt more at home than I did in the band that I started," Kirk admitted on *The Howard Stern Show*. "There's a lot of guilt that came along with that, but the second I played with these guys I felt better." All was forgiven by Holt, who once called *Master of Puppets* the all-time greatest metal record and joined Slayer in 2011, in time to jam with Metallica on the Big Four tour.

"We all came from disenfranchised stock, and because of that we played our instruments a certain way," Kirk states in *It's Alive!* "Our music was about confronting subjects that most people feel aren't appropriate to confront, the stuff they're afraid to confront."

"QUIRK HAMMETT"

In a November 1986 interview with the metal journalist Masa Ito on the Japanese TV show *Music Tomato World*, Metallica is asked what they have to say to fans who are on the fence about seeing the band's upcoming show. Kirk tries suppressing a smile. "If you don't go," he starts, ". . . you don't know what you're missing." Kirk tries again. "We see you on the street, we'll, we'll, smash . . ."

Image-conscious Lars jumps in to save the band's reputation. "If you don't go, we'll find you, and I'm sure your parents wouldn't want that."

But Kirk has to be Kirk. On the same tour, he'll tell *The Mercury News* that parents shouldn't worry about their kids seeing his band. "Metallica is a great babysitter," he asserts. "Just remember to bring the ear plugs. Even we wear them."

"Kirk brings kind of a 'not-give-a-fuck' attitude in a different way," James said in *So What!* "Obviously, his attire, his fashion sense, he legitimately and truly does not give a fuck and it's cool. And it's a total metal attitude, which I totally love."

"Quirk Hammett," "Kirk Hamster," Kirk "The Ripper" Hammett is the strangest of Metallica's strange and the coolest of its cool. He's the only member of Metallica who will eat a banana onstage while accepting an MTV award. He's Metallica's resident goth, inviting Cocteau Twins to play Lollapalooza, turning his bandmates onto PJ Harvey and Godflesh, and talking up Bauhaus, Siouxsie and the Banshees, the Birthday Party, Ministry, the Cramps, and the Gun Club in interviews. He's the guy in Metallica who will call Patti Smith "one of my heroes" and tell *So What!* that he loves Captain Beefheart ("Everything & anything!"). Kirk's tastes have no boundaries. He'll co-produce a Death Angel demo, but he'll also lay down guitar tracks for Orbital, Pansy Division, Septic Death, Santana, K'Naan, or Michael Schenker. He names his cats after characters from *River's Edge* and *The Pink Panther*. He might be the only man in the world who practices yoga, Transcendental Meditation, Buddhism, vegetarianism, surfing, and philosophy (*Zen in the Art of Archery* is a Kirk favorite) who is still macabre enough to take a date (his future wife Lani) to watch autopsies being performed. Reader, they're still married with two children.

Kirk brings those ghoulish sensibilities to the stage, where fans might get Gounod's "Funeral March of a Marionette" (the *Alfred Hitchcock Presents* theme), Liszt's "Hungarian Rhapsody No. 2," "The Hearse Song," or even the theme from *The Munsters* in one of his solos. He's also Metallica's funniest, deadpanning a story about Jesus Christ smoking a pipe on *Jon Benjamin Has a Van*, or letting himself get ribbed with James on *Space Ghost Coast to Coast*. And unlike most of his bandmates, Kirk doesn't care who his political beliefs offend, lashing out over the years against the alt-right ("Just another sneaky euphemism for white supremacy"), climate deniers ("The only people who deny climate change are the same people who stand to lose from renewable energy"), and anti-choicers ("A woman should be able to make her own decisions whether or not she should have a baby. She should have control over her body, not the fucking government, congressmen, or whatever"). In a band that often looks like it doesn't care about its image or reputation, Kirk is the least image-conscious.

"The message of our culture is that you have the right to make your own decisions, and do what you want, but as soon as you learn to walk and talk, society bats that down," Kirk stated in 2015.

Musically, ideologically, intellectually, Kirk is as uncontainable as one of the monsters he loves, breaking free of anything trying to hold him down. Meditating on mortality in a review of David Bowie's *Blackstar* in 2016, Kirk wrote about wanting to go out as artistically as his boundary-breaking hero, a goal he aims for in every note he plays with Metallica. "We thrive on spontaneity and we thrive off being challenged," Kirk said in 2018, accepting Metallica's Polar Music Prize. "We thrive off doing things that make people say, 'Oh, you can't do that.' And we're, like, 'Oh, yeah? We'll show you.'" From horror to humor to headbanging, Kirk always does.

13

SO WICKED
AND WORN

Metallica's Fashion

*"When you're fortunate enough to not be part of anything
that's too fashionable, you have the opportunity to stick around
as all the other fashions and things wither away."*

—Lars Ulrich

Combing through scores of early Metallica interviews, it's astonishing how often their wardrobe comes up. (Q. "Why don't you get dressed up for your shows?" James: "We are.") Metal had already established some fashion sense, from Judas Priest's leather and studs to Motörhead's bullet belts to Def Leppard's spandex. The biggest bands wore costumes, but people are curious to see young Metallica in T-shirts, ripped jeans, and sneakers. "We're doing a segment called 'Addicted to Style,'" an MTV interviewer tells Jason Newsted and Lars Ulrich in 1986. "Visually, describe your style." The boys laugh, and Lars says, "Comfortable."

"The only look we had was 'ugly,'" James recalled in 2001.

Several critics, Chuck Eddy and Chuck Klosterman among them, have called Metallica their generation's Led Zeppelin, which ignores that (a) Led Zeppelin is every generation's Zeppelin, just as Metallica is each generation's Metallica, and (b) Metallica in no way entertain the sexy rock star image in Zeppelin's ethos. Other critics, particularly metal-averse ones, like to write about how Metallica brought punk realism to metal on

Kill 'Em All, and there's some truth to that. But in person, they dressed more plainly than punk—no dye, spiked hair, safety pins, or really any look associated with the punk movement. Years before grunge was celebrated for giving rock music a disheveled look, Metallica were changing notions of how rock stars dressed. Only after grunge blew up on the heels of the Black Album, making jeans and flannel the standard rock star look, did Metallica start glamming up with guyliner on *Load*. When nu metal brought baggy jeans and ball caps to MTV, Metallica were donning dress shirts for *S&M*.

Of all the biggest nineties rock music video stars, Metallica might be the only one with no members who could be turned into a recognizable Halloween costume. Nearly everyone has a defined sense of how Axl Rose, Slash, Kurt Cobain, Angus Young, Ozzy Osbourne, Courtney Love, Bono, Trent Reznor, Anthony Kiedis, or Eddie Vedder dress. Not so much James Hetfield or Lars Ulrich. In a 1988 Monsters of Rock documentary, Sammy Hagar marvels at the opening band who just rocked LA so hard that the Memorial Coliseum power had to be shut off while security tackled and arrested fans. "When you see Metallica in the hotel, on the day off, they're dressed exactly like when you see them onstage," quips the Cabo Wabo man. "They're not putting on a show." (Goth Kirk has one of the best lines: "This is the most sun I've gotten in two years.")

But Metallica does put on a show. Dressing more like their fans than other metal bands showed that Metallica had a different sense of who their peers were. Lars' purposely unshaven peach fuzz on the back of *Kill 'Em All* makes him look even younger than his nineteen years, more like someone walking out of the principal's office than a guy whose band is about to play Holland with Twisted Sister. When Lars saw the fan-designed "Alcoholica: Drank 'Em All," shirt, Metallica printed and wore their own. Metallica's 1986 *Spin* profile notes their wardrobe is as important to their image as Angus Young's schoolboy outfit is to AC/DC, described as "the uniform of their average fan, the Teenage American Slob." "Whatever those guys did in front of the camera, me and my friends got it," remembers a young fan in *Back to the Front*. "Whether it was having a laugh or looking hard . . . we felt like these are our friends. 'I know those dudes.'"

"We're doing something people aren't used to, which is to act like real people both onstage and off," Lars told *Metal Muscle* in May 1987. "Metallica is not a band you put on a pedestal."

It's a philosophy that's served Metallica well. Watching Metallica's awards show performances through the years, it's fun to see how dated the younger bands sound and look. When Metallica steps up with "Hit the Lights" at *MTV Icon*, written before some of the show's celebrity guests were born, Metallica sounds more like the future than anything performed in the show's preceding hour. The older men are unaffected by the kids' pop punk and nu metal fashions, although Snoop Dogg looks sharp in a Metallica long sleeve.

In his *It's Electric!* appearance, Billy Corgan remembered young Metallica at the Aragon Ballroom in Chicago. "You guys come out, James is wearing the cut off jean jacket, you guys looked like the guys I went to fuckin' school with. I was like, 'These people understand the world I'm in. . . . Thank God somebody gets it.'"

It didn't come immediately to Metallica. In photos pre–*Kill 'Em All*, Lars can be seeing wearing spandex and James has a bullet belt he took turns sharing with Dave Mustaine. They look more like boys in metal god cosplay than the metal gods they'd become. Even Metallica's infamous demo tape, named for the first lyric of their first song, takes its name from fashion, embodying the trend they were about to demolish. Looking at teenage Metallica is a little like looking at pre-fame photos of the Beatles smoking cigarettes in leather jackets, or the Stones in mop tops and matching blazers, trying to figure out what skin they're most comfortable in. Their eventual look helped make Metallica iconic, giving them a style that's outlasted the fashions of the MTV VJs interviewing them. The fans noticed—in D. A. Pennebaker's *101*, the Depeche Mode doc at the Rose Bowl, a fan traveling with the fashionable band (literally their name—French for "fast fashion") compliments a young Latino's shoes. "Isn't that like the newest trend here?" he asks, snapping a picture. The young man smiles. "Metallica-style," he beams.

"We stay off any image thing—we don't come out with spiked hair, all this makeup or a ton of leather and studs," Lars told *Circus* in January 1987, dismissing punk and metal fashions in one swoop. Metallica created thrash fashion (thrashion?), building the trends that didn't define but distinguished its best bands. Slayer abandoned blood and corpse paint shortly after *Show No Mercy*, looking infinitely scarier on the back of *Reign in Blood*, where it's revealed the most Satanic music is made by guys you might see on the street. Armored Saint's Joey Vera credits Lars with encouraging him to ditch their band costumes. When Dave Mustaine left Metallica for Megadeth, he didn't take the bullet belt with him.

Being Metallica, they also abandoned the trends they created. The *Load*-era Anton Corbijn photoshoots distanced themselves from the bands they inspired, angering some fans as much as "The Unforgiven II." Metallica's bank accounts started showing up in their outfits (Kirk: "If you saw my army of shoes, you'd call me Imelda"), something many *Master of Puppets* fans never forgave them for, even the ones who claim to care exclusively about Metallica's music and not their image. A photograph of James Hetfield in plaid shorts, sunglasses, and flip-flops, carrying his wife's Armani shopping bag while Robert Trujillo looked on went viral in 2008, inspiring memes, parodies, and other derision, and was even used to criticize the band in several major publication *Death Magnetic* reviews (James laughed it off in a *Newsweek* interview). But to paraphrase Lars, Metallica didn't come to fashion, fashion came to them. Metallica made ugly fashionable, to the point where they were invited to be the faces of the Italian luxury menswear line Brioni in 2016, selected for their "rugged, masculine" look. They've since modeled Saint Laurent for a *Clash* magazine feature. They're not pretty, which is part of their brand. If James Hetfield looked like Sebastian Bach, he couldn't be James Hetfield. But Metallica changed conceptions of who could set trends and model fashion.

BUT CAN YOU NAME A SONG?

In a 2016 video for BuzzFeed Mexico, James is shown a series of celebrities wearing Metallica shirts and asked to judge them (James: "What'd you call it? 'Reggaeton'?"). He laughs about their choices and being unable to remember the name Ryan Gosling. But after years of representing outsider status, Metallica shirts are haute couture. Barney's, H&M, and Urban

Outfitters have all sold comically expensive Metallica shirts. Rappers, pop stars, actors, DJs, and reality TV stars can be seen repping the guys who wanted to name their first album *Metal Up Your Ass*. This sometimes causes an internet furor, as it did when a *Real Housewives* star was unable to name a song by the band while wearing a customized . . . *And Justice for All* shirt. But who can blame her? It's a cool shirt. Besides, the man who wrote the albums and designed the logo has no problem with it. "When I see some kid out on the street with his parents and he's got a Metallica shirt on, whether he's heard of us or not, it's a statement, you know?" James said in 2017. "It is a statement, so I love that."

14

SO LET IT BE WRITTEN

A Metallica Reader

"None of the critics are as bad as the critics in our heads."

—Kirk Hammett

More than any other major metal band except maybe Iron Maiden, whose odes to Coleridge, Lord Tennyson, Poe, and others pioneered the idea that great literature deserved operatic screams and a monster mascot, Metallica's music has served as an English Lit 101 for headbangers. At least as far back as *Ride the Lightning*, Metallica has been sending metalheads to the library and bookstore for Ernest Hemingway, H. P. Lovecraft, Stephen King, the Book of Exodus, and, if you were fanatical, John Donne (onstage, James is prone to changing the awesome "For Whom the Bells Tolls" chorus from "time marches on" to Donne's version, "it tolls for thee"). Their breakthrough single adapted a Dalton Trumbo novel, and many of Metallica's best songs create similar moods and wrestle with some of the same ideas as literature's finest. Metallica may not be as poetic as *Devotions upon Emergent Occasions*, and they won't be taught in the same college courses, but at their best Metallica expresses themselves as profoundly as any great novelist.

These days, Metallica are more famous for inspiring books than being inspired by them (an exception being Frank Wedekind's "Lulu" plays). That inspiration, coupled with the fact that many people will buy anything with Metallica's name on it, has led to a flood of Metallica books. There are some fine biographies, authorized tomes, analytical works, at least one children's book, and plenty of cash-ins. Lars has written forewords for books by Ross Halfin, Lonn Friend, Ian Gillan, Brian Slagel, Status Quo, and René Redzepi. But the shrewd reader can find a good armful of books for your Metallica dissertation, book report, or maybe even for fun. In honor of the band that may or may not have inspired the Black Album's cover and title, this list goes to eleven.

SO WHAT!: THE GOOD, THE MAD, AND THE UGLY (METALLICA, 2004)

Metallica's first official book is a collection of back issues of the band's fan newsletter, *So What!* Like the newsletter, *So What!* reads like a scrapbook, something to pick up and flip through in a spare moment—in short, it's the ultimate Metallica bathroom read. Editor Steffan Chirazi doesn't get much out of the band in some roundtable discussions, though as one might expect for a band on their way to group therapy, the men are less guarded in one-on-one interviews. The fans don't get much more in some Q&A sections that usually find the boys in smartass mode (sample: Amanda W. from Marietta, Georgia, asks, "Where in the world do you dudes get your songs from?" James: "Kid Rock." Kirk: "Napster."). Still, the book reads like an all access look at Metallica, in part because it doesn't correct James' spelling errors or edit Lars' responses, which tend to be twice as long as James', Kirk's, Robert's, or Jason's. The pictures are mostly DIY fun, the opposite of the Anton Corbijn's press photos from the same era, and often they're strewn among handwritten lyrics, Metallica memorabilia, and minutiae like Metallica's first-ever print review (Terry Atkinson for the *LA Times* on March 29, 1982, noted that the band opening for Saxon "needs considerable development to overcome a pervasive awkwardness"). Some fans complain that *So What!*, which started in 1993, doesn't cover enough from Metallica's prime songwriting years, but that misses the point of the magazine and this book. The first ten years of *So What!* covered the band's most tumultuous time, from the Napster lawsuit through replacing Jason through band therapy through controversies you forgot mattered to anyone in the 1990s (Lars and Kirk kissing on camera, anyone?). *So What!* is more about the artists than their art, and gives a fascinating look at the Metallica men.

METALLICA: THIS MONSTER LIVES (JOE BERLINGER AND GREG MILNER, 2004)

More than a companion piece to *Some Kind of Monster*, *This Monster Lives* is a story of camaraderie, fandom, filmmaking, and artistry that should strike a chord (hopefully the Devil's Tritone) with anyone who's ever pursued their artistic dreams. Berlinger's book is part memoir, part behind-the-scenes look at *Some Kind of Monster*, from the author's youth working for documentary legends the Maysles Brothers in the 1980s (*Some Kind of Monster* starts in the present as an homage to *Gimme Shelter*, Berlinger's favorite rockumentary) through the release and reception of his Metallica movie. Unlike the corresponding film, *This Monster Lives* makes its filmmakers part of the story. Prepare for tangents defending Berlinger's role working on *Blair Witch 2: Book of Shadows*, which to be fair, sounds like an awful experience. Yet Berlinger makes it work by relating his process with partner Bruce Sinofsky to Metallica themselves—see how the filmmakers divide business and creativity in their projects, or even how they go from piggybacking on Metallica's sessions to ending up in their own therapy sessions together. *This Monster Lives* also includes sometimes excruciating dialogue and stories that were left out of the movie, such as a more complicated look at Jason's ousting and Q Prime's fears that Towle's relationship with the band would turn abusive. Readers won't come away wishing these exchanges had been included in the movie, but some outtakes brought to light in *This Monster Lives* are as revealing as the movie's best moments.

DAMAGE, INCORPORATED: METALLICA AND THE PRODUCTION OF MUSICAL IDENTITY (GLENN T. PILLSBURY, 2006)

Damage, Incorporated is Metallica for musicologists—a scholarly read that examines the cultural and historical importance of the band and its music. If you're ready for thirty-three pages about the significance of

Phrygian mode in "Wherever I May Roam," or a more detailed analysis of the changes in James Hetfield's stage moves than you'd think possible, this is the book for you. Musicology PhD Pillsbury inspects the incalculable amount of math, science, art, and history that goes into writing records like *Master of Puppets* and . . . *And Justice for All*, showing that even if Metallica isn't your band, this is not music for clods. On top of dissecting their songs by scale, timbre, tunings, and time signatures, Pillsbury analyzes Metallica through theories of politics, masculinity, race, otherness, the American concept of "the Road," and more. He also does an elegant, sometimes amusing job of studying the historical context of Metallica's music—note how a look at the complexity of "Master of Puppets" is set next to President Ronald Reagan's 1982 assertion, "Drugs are bad and we're going after them." As with any well-rounded book covering the first twenty years of Metallica's career, *Damage, Incorporated* looks at various "sellout" controversies and the band's place among other metal bands, like the Big Four. But for the avowed Metallica reader, *Damage, Incorporated* is often most exciting for the way it makes dense aspects of music theory accessible through Metallica's music.

METALLICA AND PHILOSOPHY: A CRASH COURSE IN BRAIN SURGERY (EDITED BY WILLIAM IRWIN, 2007)

Metallica and Philosophy gives Metallica the kind of analysis granted to fellow iconoclasts such as Nietzsche, Kierkegaard, Kant, or Socrates. Released as part of the Popular Culture and Philosophy series (other favorites include *The Simpsons and Philosophy: The D'oh! of Homer* and *Star Wars and Philosophy: More Powerful than You Can Possibly Imagine*), *Metallica and Philosophy* explores the band's lyrics, history, musicians, and more in twenty chapters divided into five parts: "On Through the Never," "Existensica: Metallica Meets Existentialism," "Living and Dying, Laughing and Crying," "Metaphysica, Espistomologica, Metallica," and "Fans and the Band." The essayists, an accomplished bunch of professors and academics, connect and contrast Metallica with existentialism, metaphysics, identity, justice, epistemology, and more with enough vigor and curiosity to reward repeated readings. Several writers, including the series editor/Metallica superfan Irwin, write about James' lyrics, including his skepticism and rejection of Christian values ("The God That Failed"), the struggle of morality ("The Unforgiven"), the mind/body relationship ("One"), the search for meaning in life ("Fade to Black"), the search for authenticity ("The Struggle Within"), and nonconformity (see Metallica's career). Other essayists raise questions about Metallica's history (is the band that made *Kill 'Em All* the same band that made *St. Anger*?), the bandmates themselves (What, if anything, do fans and Metallica owe each other?), *Johnny Got His Gun*, and Metallica's gadfly reputation—like Socrates, our heroes have long been accused of corrupting the youth, and as with Socrates, it took years for the masses to realize that Metallica usually had it right. None of the writers are blindly in love with the band, and Napster, *Some Kind of Monster*, and *St. Anger* are all explored with good measure, but that's part of how the book does Metallica justice. No band that confronts the dark underbelly as intensely as Metallica does deserves anything less. Recommended to any reader brave enough to philosophize Metallica and Metallicize philosophy.

THE DAY METALLICA CAME TO CHURCH: SEARCHING FOR THE EVERYWHERE GOD IN EVERYTHING (JOHN VAN SLOTEN, 2010)

Get over your fear of reading the words "Metallica" and "church" together, in a book written by a pastor. Van Sloten offers a thoughtful, empathetic look at Metallica and Christianity that's never preachy or sanctimonious, and metalheads should approach his book with the intellectual curiosity he shows in finding God in Metallica, Van Gogh, the Coen Brothers, Ray Charles, the Calgary Flames, and more. It's easy to see why Metallica gets the title of his book—they're the basis of his best-known sermon, both because they're hugely popular and because they give Van Sloten's sermons more novelty value than the other artists he discusses (I'm guessing Van Gogh has already appeared in plenty of sermons). The title sermon stems from a conversation with a teen congregant, who approached Van Sloten after a sermon about U2 to ask him to preach Metallica. After an impressive bout of prayer, soul-searching, and research, including reading through every Metallica lyric online and attending their May 6, 2004, show in Calgary, Van Sloten is unexpectedly wowed by the band. He connects them to church and Christianity in some surprising ways, sympathizing with Hetfield's anger at God and religion in songs like "The God That Failed," while preaching through science, parables, theologians (St. Augustine and John Calvin are among his most quoted), and more. This is a long, long way from religious fundamentalism. As one might guess, Van Sloten gets some angry calls from churchgoers who weren't ready to accept "Creeping Death" in Psalm 78:49–50, ". . . And Justice for All" in Amos 5:7, or "Holier Than Thou" in Matthew 23:34, but the pastor listens to the complaints and works to get closer to a God he believes loves Metallica. The Metallica story is almost entirely in the first chapter, but its introductory themes are all over the rest of the book, exhibiting the kind of searching and awareness that finds God in Metallica's lives and thoughts, and in songs such as "Dirty Window," "The Unforgiven," "Fade to Black," and "Fixxxer." When Van Sloten stands among 17,000 metalheads swaying to "Nothing Else Matters," he gives the show the highest praise he can come up with—"This feels like church."

THE ULTIMATE METALLICA (ROSS HALFIN, 2010)

Ross Halfin, the primary Metallica photographer for the majority of their career (Peter Mensch called him to shoot Metallica in November 1984, when Halfin was photographing Queensrÿche in Seattle), is famous for his uncompromising rock photographs. Thus, it's only fair for Metallica to give Halfin an uncompromising book, a candid look at the band and the man photographing them. *The Ultimate Metallica* features a foreword by Lars Ulrich and an afterword by Kirk, but its main attraction is the pictures—glorious photographs of Metallica, on- and offstage throughout their career, in black-and-white and in color, across numerous countries. Looking through Halfin's photos, one can almost smell the band's sweat, or feel the heat from their pyro. Halfin himself provides commentary, photography tips, and entertaining backstage stories that may or may not be true, but which usually present Halfin as just the kind of eccentric, high maintenance pro you'd expect to meet at the top of metal photojournalism (and don't you dare, as Lars allegedly did, imply Halfin ever imitated Anton Corbijn). Under Halfin's eye, Metallica are sometimes dudes, sometimes metal gods, and always a compelling subject. *The Ultimate Metallica* argues that Halfin's photographs show the band at their best, but it also reveals that Metallica captures Halfin at his best.

TOO MUCH HORROR BUSINESS (KIRK HAMMETT WITH STEFAN CHIRAZI, 2012)

Delve into any Kirk Hammett interview and you'll likely learn he's a horror buff (check out the band's first *Howard Stern Show* appearance, wherein Kirk informs Howard that his signature *White Zombie* ESP guitar is repping Bela Lugosi's movie and not Rob Zombie's band). *Too Much Horror Business*, which takes its name from a Misfits lyric referencing Chuck Berry, displays a colorful array of over 300 horror and sci-fi artifacts from the Hammett home, ranging from classics like *Night of the Living Dead* to a film that's really called *The Beast with 1,000,000 Eyes*. Hammett starts in an era before radio, TV, and internet ads, when filmmakers relied primarily on posters to promote their work, hiring top illustration artists to put extra work into the imminent monsters and their victims, while showing how the monster craze changed with the arrival of mass merchandising, historical events, and more. The films, TV, and comics vary by genre, era, and quality, with memorabilia from *Hellraiser* just pages away from *Groovie Goolies*, all connected by eye-catching art and Hammett's loving, enthusiastic, knowledgeable, and entertaining captions (sample Kirk: "Why do these monsters always know where all the hot women are?"). Readers will learn Kirk's favorite horror actors (Bela Lugosi and Boris Karloff, with Kirk contrasting which was a better actor and which had a more interesting career), his favorite *Famous Monsters of Filmland* artist (Basil Gogos), and even his first crush (Frank Frazetta's Vampirella), as well as a touching personal history from a boy who went from going to two or three movies a day by himself to owning one of the world's most enviable horror collections. Near the end of the book, Hammett mentions his hopes to display his horror collection someday, which in 2017 resulted in *It's Alive! Classic Horror and Sci-Fi Art from the Kirk Hammett Collection*, an exhibit curated by the guitarist at the Peabody Essex Museum in Salem, Massachusetts. The exhibit has since moved, but its gems can be enjoyed in an excellent art book that coincided with the show, also titled *It's Alive!* To be read with your movie queue at hand.

METALLICA: 30 YEARS OF THE WORLD'S GREATEST HEAVY METAL BAND (EDITED BY *GUITAR WORLD*'S EDITORS, 2013)

You don't need to be a guitar nerd or music theorist to get caught up in *30 Years of the World's Greatest Heavy Metal Band*, an anthology of the popular guitar magazine's best Metallica articles. It's the only Metallica book so far to focus primarily on Kirk, who stars in several interviews that emphasize technique, musicianship, and influences (musical, spiritual, visual, habitual) over road stories. Kirk comes across as Metallica's George Harrison, a quiet, thoughtful guy who loves music, never says a word too many, stays in touch with his former guitar teacher (Joe Satriani, although the book is too diplomatic to say whether the lessons ended because Satriani's fusion career took off or because Kirk proved himself a better axeman than his teacher), and defers to James Hetfield when he worries he's getting too much attention. Along the way, we also get James' first-ever encounter with Tony Iommi, in which the mighty Het fanboys out and nudges the riff master into telling the story about the time he set Bill Ward on fire. A few pages later we're treated to Tool's Adam Jones dorking out in conversation with his hero/peer Kirk Hammett, mentioning an upcoming Tool record that won't come out for another eleven years. Long-defunct adversaries from the PMRC to the first Bush administration (clamping down on Body Count's "Cop Killer") are discussed by a band that has outlived them. With interviews from all over Metallica's career, *30 Years of the World's Greatest Heavy Metal Band* offers an outstanding oral history of the band, as well as a nerd-baiting list of Metallica's 100 best songs, including a #1 pick that—spoiler alert—is not "Enter Sandman," "One," or "Master of Puppets."

METALLICA'S METALLICA (DAVID MASCIOTRA, 2015)

Bloomsbury's 33⅓ series has released nearly 200 paperbacks about individual albums, varying wildly in genre and format—the books can be analytical, historical, personal, or some combination of the three, but each is a pocket-sized book about a specific record. The series is generally scant on metal, although its editions on *Master of Reality*, *Reign in Blood*, and *I Get Wet* are terrific. Add to those standouts David Masciotra's *Metallica's* Metallica, a mostly historical and analytical book on the record everybody else calls the Black Album. Masciotra is an enthusiastic fan, who doesn't always check his facts (he's not the first metalhead to believe 1991's "The Unforgiven" was inspired by the 1992 Clint Eastwood film *Unforgiven*, but perhaps the first one to get that myth past a publisher), and his song analysis should be enjoyed more for the ideas Masciotra raises about Metallica's music than any definitive answers. But what makes *Metallica's* Metallica a stellar part of the Metallica canon is the interviews. Masciotra gets access to James, Kirk, Lars, Jason, and Bob Rock, and questions them like a guy who keeps stacks of metal mags at home and wants something different. James gives some of his most openhearted answers in print, exploring the feelings that inspired "Sad but True" and "The Unforgiven" and how centering the Black Album's songs around his vocals changed the music. Kirk traces his metal rebelliousness to being a child fascinated with the 1960s Civil Rights and antiwar movements, getting reprimanded by his parents but recognizing kindred rebel spirits in his metal heroes. Jason, removed enough from Metallica to no longer be angry about it, sounds like the fan he was in the 1980s but with insider perspective, pinpointing the cerebral role each musician plays in the band and even making a case for the Black Album following in the footsteps of the cult blues hero R. L. Burnside. Masciotra shows awareness of his subjectivity in the book's introduction, quoting Lars, "If you line up twenty different Metallica fans against the wall, you are going to get twenty different responses about what it means."

TO LIVE IS TO DIE: THE LIFE AND DEATH OF METALLICA'S CLIFF BURTON (JOEL MCIVER, 2016)

English author Joel McIver is one of metal's most accomplished writers, and any serious metal reader has probably read some of his books. Subjects of his biographies have included Black Sabbath, Motörhead, and Rage Against the Machine, plus autobiography cowrites with Max Cavalera,

Cannibal Corpse, Glenn Hughes, and more. Unsurprisingly, McIver's best-selling book is *Justice for All: The Truth About Metallica*, an informative, entertainingly opinionated take on the world's greatest metal band. But McIver's best book is *To Live Is to Die*, which will probably remain the most comprehensive Cliff Burton biography fans are going to get. Culling from interviews with Cliff's family, friends, bandmates, and fans, *To Live Is to Die* creates a portrait of a bookish kid who loved music, quickly outgrew his boyhood bass teachers, and changed the course of metal over just three albums in four years. Unlike most rock biographers, McIver has a sense of musicianship that he can articulate without going over anyone's head, describing Cliff's pedal innovations and chord sequences in a way that's more primal than technical. But McIver knows nobody picks up *To Live Is to Die* to read about arpeggios, and the book's selling point is the Cliff stories. Nobody seems to have a bad word to say about the bassist, perhaps still missing him too much to reflect on his debauchery, but Cliff's acquaintances remember him as the eccentric, megatalented metal sage he's often idealized as. Some of this can be found near the end of the book, where McIver compiles tributes from Opeth's Mikael Åkerfeldt, Morbid Angel's David Vincent, Queens of the Stone Age's Nick Oliveri, and more. Some readers complain about McIver's decision to spend so much of the book on the other members of Metallica, including the post-Cliff years and interviews already covered in *Justice for All*. But entwining their stories helps to convey how rooted Cliff was in Metallica, and how much he looms over them. In McIver's world, Cliff *is* Metallica. Be sure to pick up the revised 2016 edition, with a foreword by Kirk Hammett and an afterword by Anthrax bassist Frank Bello.

METALLICA: BACK TO THE FRONT (MATT TAYLOR, 2016)

Part oral history, part yearbook, part 33⅓ book imagined as a coffee table tome, *Back to the Front* is the definitive *Master of Puppets* read, packed with stories, photographs, memorabilia, interviews, and some wisdom (particularly in Ray Burton's touching afterword)—really, almost everything anybody could want from *Master of Puppets* that isn't the album itself. While Metallica's first authorized book, *So What!*, was a hodgepodge of Metallica items, *Back to the Front* is crafted with meticulous care, packing a wealth of information into the kind of organization we'd later see on Metallica's box set reissues. The surviving bandmates are fully involved in telling the story in both past and present—check out a letter from Lars insisting that although Slayer have been talking shit about his band in metal mags, it turns out they're "allright [*sic*] drunken idiots like us. Ha! (And quite friendly, too!)" But it's often the accounts from fans and other associates that best capture the excitement of *Master*-era Metallica. After all, James, Lars, Kirk, and Cliff have scores of stories like this, but for the fans who got to talk comic books with Kirk or smoke a bowl with Lars, it's a once-in-a-lifetime experience, accomplished in the last days of an era in which Metallica was still fringe enough to frequently chat with their fans (yes, that's future Andrew W. K. guitarist Jimmy Coup recapping a surprise encounter with Cliff Burton). The book explores the social, logistical, and financial struggles of a band that's scraping by but starting to get recognized in public on a major scale, big enough to get a tour with Ozzy while juvenile enough to get into skateboard accidents and sneak into hospitals, all while exuding the brotherhood only known by four boys touring and recording in a band together, except these boys are making *Master of Puppets*. As *Through the Never* did for concert films and *Some Kind of Monster* did for rockumentaries, *Back to the Front* blows away expectations for authorized band books, credit due Metallica but also Taylor, hand-picked by the band for his equally comprehensive film book *Jaws: Memories from Martha's Vineyard*. *Back to the Front* is the book *Master of Puppets* and Metallica deserve, although you'd read a tome this great about *Reload*.

15

MY FRIEND
OF MISERY

Jason Newsted

*"Loud equals free. It represents rebellion, and not being afraid
to scream and make yourself heard. You have to do it loud to
do it right."*

—Jason Newsted

For many fans, Jason's story is the hardest. Not because he's the least accessible (if anything, he often seems like the easiest to get along with), and definitely not because he's the least important. He's played on more Metallica records than anyone except James, Kirk, and Lars. He cowrote "Blackened," which is better than anything Dave Mustaine contributed, that incredible main riff that ends differently each time, sparking James into action. He was in Metallica for three times as long as Cliff Burton and performed over 1,030 shows with them, more than any other bassist. But Jason is hard to address because he uncovers the worst in Metallica.

It's a fan's nightmare, to meet your heroes and find out they're a bunch of jerks. But Jason suffered through that more publicly, and more harshly than any other metal musician. Invited to join metal's most exclusive club, one of four guys who could play in the world's greatest band, making classic records and performing for overflowing stadiums, Jason was dealt the harsh reality that the best art isn't made by the best people.

All this abuse, just to appear in the liner notes (and sometimes just that, in the case of getting buried in the mix on . . . *And Justice for All*) of the greatest metal band ever. Metallica fans watching the movie homages in the "I Disappear" video will note that the films cited correspond to the bandmates' personas—cineaste Kirk is in *North by Northwest*, while vintage car buff James is in *Bullitt*. Jason, who said this was the Metallica video he was most involved in, reenacts Robert DeNiro in *Brazil* and gets disappeared into a crowd. It was his last music video with Metallica, and the last song he recorded with them.

Three years later, James would tell MTV his band grieved Cliff through bullying Jason, taking out their survivor guilt on the new bassist. "We were brutal with him. And it never ended, really."

"GO-GETTEDNESS"

Jason Curtis Newsted grew up on a farm in Battle Creek, Michigan, with two older brothers and one younger sister. "It's where I learned about life—seeing a baby cow born right in front of your eyes when you're eight years old is pretty intense," he'd recall. "I was from a very strong family and I was raised to be a strong, pure Americana farm boy." That meant feeding the animals at 6:30 a.m. before the school bus arrived, plus strict adherence to Christianity. Jason didn't like going to church on Sundays, but credited his regimental parents for, in his words, the "go-gettedness" that helped make him Jason Newsted. It probably didn't hurt to have a father who was a documents manager for an equipment company and a mother who worked at a hearing aid center.

Jason started playing guitar in church at age nine and moved to saxophone in junior high, inspired by his brothers' Jackson 5 records. But like many kids in the 1970s, Jason was bowled over by the party-loving rock superheroes who called themselves Kiss. Captivated by the flying, fire-breathing demon of a bassist on *Dressed to Kill*, Jason removed the middle tuners on each side of his acoustic to make it more like a bass and co-formed a band called Diamond. Geddy Lee's agility and Lemmy's distortion also caught his ear, but soon his favorite band and bassist were Black Sabbath and Geezer Butler.

The Newsteds moved to a Kalamazoo horse farm to raise stallions when Jason was fourteen, but Jason didn't like his new high school and dreamed of leaving rural life. As an adult, he'd tell *So What!* he wished he learned more about science, the Renaissance, and the Civil Rights movement in school. He ended up quitting at eighteen, three months before gradua- tion, to join Gangster, a band of twentysomethings who played Kiss and AC/DC covers, and were moving west to be rock stars. His parents freaked, but Jason sold much of his record collection, packed a suitcase, and moved to Phoenix, keeping himself fed by working restaurant jobs. He learned a thriftiness he maintained in Metallica, seen in *A Year and a Half in the Life of Metallica*, where he takes backstage catering to the hotel instead of ordering room service. He agrees with a roadie who calls him a cheapskate. "We'll see who's laughing last."

Gangster didn't work out, but in 1982 Jason saw an ad from Kelly Smith in a Phoenix music store that cited Iron Maiden and Rush, and ended up joining a band called Paradox. They soon renamed themselves Dogz, but didn't settle on a name until a term from J. R. R. Tolkien's *The Two Tow- ers* stuck.

FLOTSAM AND JETSAM

Jason was the Lars of Flotsam and Jetsam, the band's managerial go-getter. He'd later be wowed to see Lars handle Metallica's business on a much bigger level, reading and answering dozens of messages within minutes (Jason: "Every spare minute of his time is taken up with other business and band-related shit"), but also annoyed when it made his boss late for practice. Jason's songwriting and business smarts would later help him get his most famous gig, but for now he was like any other devoted metalhead in 1983, obsessed with a new record called *Kill 'Em All*. "This was other- worldly," he recalled. "We were instant fans." Jason bought *Kill 'Em All* in its first week of release at Zia Records and learned "Whiplash" to cover for Flotsam and Jetsam encores, when he would take over vocals. He was enthralled with "(Anesthesia)—Pulling Teeth," which Jason described as "Cliff opening up the sky for young aspiring bassists to venture out past the edges of where bass lived previously."

Flotsam and Jetsam were moving fast and had potential. In summer 1986 *Kerrang!* gave Flotsam's first record *Doomsday for the Deceiver*, which thanks Metallica in the liner notes and has a song called "Fade to Black," six stars out of five. He'd later insist he would not have left Flotsam and Jetsam for any other band ("Not even Slayer!"), except one.

Metal Blade founder Brian Slagel recommended Jason to Metallica, despite Flotsam and Jetsam being on Slagel's own label. Jason's bandmates were mad at him, but tensions cooled when Flotsam and Jetsam got a deal with Elektra in 1987, as well as an opening spot for Megadeth on the Wake Up Dead tour, interest newly prompted by their Metallica association. Jason played his last Flotsam and Jetsam gig on Halloween night, 1986.

"JASON NEWKID"

Jason's auditions are on the *Master of Puppets* box set, perfectly high in the mix for a band that was looking into every last detail. He sounds awesome. In his first audition he smokes "Master of Puppets" and "Battery," next time he nails "Seek & Destroy," "Creeping Death," and "Fight Fire with Fire," locking Metallica's sloppiness outside the room. Newsted beat out about forty bassists, including Primus' Les Claypool and Testament's Greg Christian. An anonymous musician who showed up with a bass autographed by Quiet Riot was told to leave.

Jason showed up for his audition early, before any other bassist and even before the band themselves. He had stayed up for days practicing Metallica songs, blistering his fingers to the point where he could feel the nerves. He borrowed money from several friends, scraping together $140 for a plane ticket to San Francisco. When James asked him what Metallica songs he could play, Jason said all of them. "Jason had this incredibly useful positive energy and was like a fireball," Lars remembered years later.

On October 28, the fifth anniversary of Metallica's first rehearsal, the band leaders took Jason to Tommy's Joynt in San Francisco. James and Lars went to the bathroom to make their decision and returned with an offer. James remembers Jason jumping off the table and doing backflips. "He was so fucking excited to be in the band it was almost embarrassing."

"He was the kind of guy that you could tell, 'Okay Jason, you'll get the gig in Metallica on one condition. You have to go lay in the street and get run over by a truck,'" Lars states in *Louder Than Hell*. "I mean, he would have done that."

Metallica broke in Jason with a secret show November 8, 1986, opening for Metal Church in Reseda's Country Club. "Jason Newsted, we fuckin' love him man, so make him feel at home, alright?" James yells before "For Whom the Bell Tolls." The next night, at Jezebel's in Anaheim, Jason took charge when the power went out during "Master of Puppets," killing all the electricity except the bass amp. The kids screamed along with Jason's bass and Lars' drums. Days later, Metallica were on their first-ever tour of Japan. Fans didn't recognize Jason yet and assumed he was a roadie, but nothing could kill Jason's buzz. Torben Ulrich and the Burton family welcomed him to the band. Fans brought homemade signs with messages like "WELCOME JASON, CLIFF REST IN PEACE" to the audience.

"The vibe this time is so much more urgent, especially with this guy," Lars told *Sounds*. "I think, with this firecracker in the band, the eagerness and excitement has spilled over on everyone else."

"I would have done it for a sandwich," Jason said in *Hired Gun*. "I would have paid you guys [Metallica] five bucks to let me go!"

"IF THEY TRY TO CHARGE MORE, STEAL IT!"

Metallica went back to the garage, square one after Cliff's death, with *The $5.98 E.P.—Garage Days Re-Revisited*, so named to keep stores from overcharging (some editions included a sticker reading "If they try to charge more, STEAL IT!"). Jason was unfamiliar with most of the songs Metallica chose to cover but stepped up, both with his experienced carpentry skills in making Lars' garage into a rehearsal space (credited "under the direction of building master J. Newkid") and his performance, best showcased on "Crash Course in Brain Surgery." Jason scraped together $4,000 and enlisted friends to make a rehearsal space, sound-proofing the walls with old beer-stained carpet scraps from his apartment building, giving the room a rock 'n' roll stench that no amount of AC could clear up. The record was mixed and recorded in six days at Conway studios (Ted Nugent is thanked in the liner notes for giving Metallica studio time), and

Garage Days Re-Revisited assured fans that weird, raw Metallica wasn't going away on a major label, holding on to their roots while reaching new heights. It's now widely known as metal's greatest EP and one of the best metal covers albums, arguably matched only by its more complete but less consistent 1998 companion.

"THE WORST THING YOU CAN DO"

"Looking down on people who look up to you is the worst thing you can do," Jason told *Loudwire*. "Especially in this business."

He spoke from experience. Sadly, Jason joined Metallica on their way to their egotistical worst. He suffered through years of hazing that started as a joke but didn't end. Some of it was lighthearted, like crossing out the "b" on Jason's "bass face" signature at fan signings, or announcing his birthday to an arena crowd and pieing him in front of the fans. But much of it was not. On tour, Metallica welcomed their new bassist by drunkenly bursting into his hotel room in the early morning, wrecking the furniture and throwing it out the door. They charged massive hotel bar bills to his room, told him the minibar was free, and watched him eat hot wasabi after they'd told him it was a mint sauce. They took cabs and went drinking without him, and told interviewers he was gay. In the 1990s, Jason objected to Metallica's homoerotic indulgences, including Kirk and Lars' PDA and the semen on the cover of *Load*. He'd later say his words were misconstrued, but knowing Jason's Metallica history one sees him overcompensating.

"They're crazy like that, they're children," Michael Alago remembered. "And Jason turned into a very, very strong individual. He just stood up to all the pressure that the boys in the band heaped upon him and now he really is one of the guys."

For years Jason put on a good public face, telling *Metal Forces* the hazing lasted only six weeks. "These guys have made it ultra-comfortable for me, more than I ever expected, really," he says in a TV interview on the *Master of Puppets* box set. "At first it was really harsh, but now it's all right." When he says his bandmates can give but not take hazing, Lars proves his point by looking aggravated.

"You have to understand that it didn't really have anything to do with Jason," Lars told *Revolver* in 2018. "Obviously, Jason was awesome, and he stood his ground."

More hurtful than the hazing, Jason would state, was Metallica turning down his bass and rejecting his ideas. He got a total of three studio cowrites, "Blackened," "My Friend of Misery," and "Where the Wild Things Are," two of which were never performed in full while Jason was in the band. Counting live releases gives him credits on "Bass/Guitar Solo" (*Live Shit: Binge & Purge*) and "Bass/Guitar Doodle" (*Cunning Stunts*), but nothing else. Kirk, James, and Lars noted Jason's frustrations in interviews, but not much seemed to come with it. James told interviewers that Metallica hired Jason in part because he could write, but still didn't let him do much of it. Watching Jason as a musician, writer, professional, ally, businessman, and performer, it's clear that Metallica could not have found a better bassist. But they stifled him.

"Part of loving him means that he has to accept us for who we are," says Lars in a Black Album–era video interview, fake crying. "Which is not easy," Jason grumbles.

But not even Metallica could hold Jason back in the place where he, and they, were at their best. "Jason's nuts on stage, he shines there," James has said, proudly, and he's right. Jason bounds around, whipping his hair and engaging the crowd. He's relentless, and when a glass bottle thrown from the crowd hits his head at the Gorge, he's right back—after receiving medical attention. When James injures his back during 2000's Summer Sanitarium tour, Jason steps up and sings lead.

"Jason tried to balance things out by kind of, like, really being prominent on those songs when they were played live," Kirk recalled in 2018. "You can tell that he was giving it his all. And I think some of that was because he was trying to compensate for not being heard on the album."

"THE NEVER-ENDING CONNECTION WITH THE FANS"

Noting how he fit in with James the songwriter, Lars the businessman, and Kirk the artist, Jason self-identified as "the people person." Or as James described him, "He is the never-ending connection with the fans."

Jason is the only member of Metallica who felt like a fan tagging along with his heroes (Trujillo was already famous when he joined in 2003). Knowing what it was like to worship Metallica gave him an appreciation his bandmates sometimes lacked. In separate interviews, both James and Lars singled Jason out as the member who was most dedicated to signing autographs for fans, no matter how long the line or how bad the weather. (His bandmates also called Jason Metallica's "most stable" member, perhaps a harbinger of Jason turning down band therapy.) Jason gave by far the most time in the Metallica episode of VH1's *FanClub* (directed by *Some Kind of Monster*'s Joe Berlinger and Bruce Sinofsky), and even around Metallica's Black Album peak he could be seen playing basketball with neighborhood kids in the East Bay. In several pictures and videos, *Cunning Stunts* included, he's the only bandmate wearing a Metallica shirt, or getting close enough to the fans to let them touch him. He wrote thoughtful, detailed pieces in the *So What!* fanzine about his favorite blues artists (Charley Patton, Son House, Leadbelly, and Robert Johnson among them) and recommended non-metal classics such as John Coltrane's *Giant Steps* and Bob Marley and the Wailers' *Kaya*. When a fan wrote in to *So What!* asking whether anyone in Metallica had ever jammed with someone who inspired them to become a musician, Kirk named Carlos Santana. James named Ozzy. Jason named Metallica.

"He gave 100 percent all the time and he would meet and greet every last fan that he could," stated *Murder in the Front Row* director Adam Dubin.

Looking through Jason interviews, one sees an uncompromised love and awe for his bandmates, particularly James. Jason seems most at home looking hammered on *Rage* with James introducing Motörhead and PJ Harvey videos, or trading music recs in *So What!* (Jason likes Bill Withers and James suggests Los Lobos). He'd remember his taciturn boss as "the most honest person I've ever known," not the most welcoming position for someone whose music ideas were constantly being rejected. "As an instrumentalist in heavy music he's the best," Jason told *Expressen* in 2002. "I've always felt that way about it and I will always feel that way about it. He taught me a lot of shit and helped me develop my playing style and become who I am as a musician."

Joining Metallica as a fan in 1986, Jason knew he had what it took to keep the band together. Leaving Metallica in January 2001, he showed that he was a big enough fan to maybe save the band in the process.

THE *PLAYBOY* DISASTER

Metallica had slowed down from touring and recording when Jason met his future Echobrain bandmates at a Super Bowl party in 1995. Needing a release for his boundless energy, Jason had to write and record music with Echobrain, as well as thrash project IR8, nu-Sepultura's *Against*, and even British trip-hoppers Unkle's acclaimed debut *Psyence Fiction*. But James was enraged, and told Jason the Echobrain tapes couldn't be released.

"I would try to grip harder to keep the family together, that no one would leave—for fear that they might find something better and somewhere else, when initially all he had to do was go jam with some other band and find out that, you know, Metallica is home," James told *Metal Hammer*, acknowledging it as one of many reasons Jason left. "And we're all hoping that he finds it."

But in the late 1990s, Jason was hostage to Metallica, and to James' full-blown alcoholism. Band tensions spilled over in a 2001 *Playboy* interview, the most infamous sit-down Metallica has had outside of *Some Kind of Monster*. Interviewed separately but printed together, the *Playboy* interview shows a band worlds apart, not addressing each other's concerns. Jason releases his frustrations about the hazing and complains, reasonably, that James could appear on other records—he'd anonymously played guitar on Primus' "Eclectic Electric" and sung backup on Corrosion of Conformity's "Man or Ash"—but Jason could not. James insists he didn't want Jason to start touring or selling T-shirts with Echobrain, comparing it to cheating on one's wife (James was doing just that in the late nineties). Both Jason and James, even without each other present, have to change the subject when Echobrain comes up, and Lars says he has bigger things to worry about than his bandmates' feud. Only Kirk shows any respect or understanding of Jason's needs. Kirk, Lars, and James call the then-unreleased Echobrain record "great," "nice," and "respectable," respectively. "I would like [James] to see that this music is truly a part of me, like his child is a part of him," says Jason, feeling confined when the band takes a break for their wives and kids. He's the only member of Metallica who has neither.

JASON LEAVES

"The Metallica guys, they just became distracted by other things, families and stuff like that," Jason reflected. "Now, I've learned my work ethic from Metallica, so don't get that wrong. But that was then. So now there's other things they want to spend their time on and they don't have time to give me eighteen hours anymore."

Metallica performed "Fade to Black" at a VH1 awards show on November 30, 2000, overcoming their ongoing Napster ignominy to be voted "Best Stage Spectacle" for S&M. Jason took the stage separately from his bandmates and didn't give a speech, though it would've been hard to follow Lars, wearing sunglasses indoors, thanking a different metal bassist, Twiggy Ramirez, for letting Lars ralph in his bathroom. Kirk hugged Jason for a long time at the podium.

Less than two months later, having been told he could not take a year off from the band, Jason quits. He ditched them in the most Metallica way possible, without telling the band he was thinking about it. He didn't offer his alcoholic bandmate a chance to make amends, just as Metallica hadn't when they dropped Dave Mustaine off at Port Authority. No second chance. Kirk admitting crying at his decision. "We're brothers, and I was struggling so hard. . . . 'I love you!'" James described the meeting, making a choking motion with his hands. "That's how I was taught to control things. Through intimidation and rage."

Each member released a statement, with Jason calling it the most difficult decision of his life and his bandmates articulating the love and respect he was denied for years. Metallica weren't examining their own lives and thus it got examined for them, Jason's misery forcing them to address their own. Within months, James was in rehab and the band was in therapy. There might not be a Metallica today if Jason hadn't scared them into acting up. Kirk would describe Jason as a sacrifice for Metallica's spiritual, mental, and creative growth. "It just breaks my heart that he can't experience this," Kirk says in *This Monster Lives*, his band is in a happier place. "He was part of the making of it."

In the same book, James notes how poorly he'd treated Jason and describes reconnecting with him. "He said he was happy, and he wanted me to come see Echobrain. There was nothing that hinted he wanted to come back at all."

"Jason Newsted's model for what he wanted Metallica to be is basically the Metallica that exists now," stated Lars in 2003.

FLYING THE FLAG

Jason, for his part, ached over the decision, which he described in *Expressen* as "at least three months of just solid depression, not wanting to eat, sleep, and sometimes not even wanting to listen to music, which is really fucked up for me. You can just imagine, it's like getting divorced from three wives at once. Not just that, you're getting divorced from yourself in a way, too."

In an early sign that he couldn't escape his old band's shadow, one of Jason's first post-Metallica projects was playing bass on the Gov't Mule song "Trying Not to Fall," on a record that also featured James Hetfield (singing "Drivin' Rain"). Almost immediately, Jason was more musically active than his bandmates, joining Echobrain, Canadian metal vets Voivod, and even Ozzy Osbourne (Jason: "It was an honor to be with a great teacher like that"), trading places with Robert Trujillo before Metallica even released *St. Anger*. He sent a few barbs in the press, deriding Metallica's therapy, new music, and the nu metal lineup for Summer Sanitarium (so did fans, who booed Limp Bizkit off the stage in Chicago). But for the most part Jason showed no grudge, even commenting for Metallica's *MTV Icon* appearance. "We need to root for Metallica. I cannot wait to see Metallica live. I'm going to be right there, cheering them on."

Despite opening for Neil Young and getting guest appearances from Kirk Hammett and Jim Martin, Jason left Echobrain in 2002 and the band broke up shortly afterward. None of Jason's subsequent bands—Papa

Wheelie, Newsted, Jason Newsted and the Chophouse Band, and a mediocre charity supergroup with Tony Iommi and Ian Gillan among them—have come close to the impact he made with Metallica. Jason joined Little Kids Rock as an official supporter and was game for an appearance on the CBS reality show *Rock Star: Supernova* in 2006, resulting in a terrible album with Gilby Clarke and Tommy Lee (Jason, who doesn't get a single writing credit, gives it better than it deserves). He performs less frequently, having worn down his vertebrae padding from years of headbanging and getting injured by a falling bass amp in 2006. But his artistic sensibilities and work ethic never wither. Finding inspiration in Picasso, Dubuffet, de Kooning, and Basquiat, Jason took up painting and earned gallery shows in New York City, Miami, San Francisco, and Basel. His more recent bandmates see the same tireless Jason. "He was footing the bill for everything," Newsted guitarist Mike Mushok stated in 2019. "We would practice ten hours, he'd record the whole thing, and when we were done, he wouldn't walk out of the control—he'd sit there and listen to it. . . . This guy was next level."

One other thing hasn't changed. Jason loves Metallica. He stays in touch with his old bandmates and praises newer records like *Hardwired . . . to Self-Destruct*. He downplays the hazing, telling *Rolling Stone* in a 2018 interview that the bad stories were sensationalized and that he remembers much more happiness, brotherhood, and camaraderie. He smiles, reflecting on it all in *Who the Fuck Is That Guy? The Fabulous Journey of Michael Alago*. "I'm still by far the happiest guy in the world."

"I'll always fly the flag of Metallica," Jason said in 2015. "I'm never going to create negative energy about the people who gave me the opportunity and space to realize my dream."

Lars, Cliff, and
James backstage at
Aardshock, 1984.
PETE CRONIN / REDFERNS /
GETTY IMAGES

The Big Four before their first show at
Sonisphere in Poland, 2010.
METAL HAMMER MAGAZINE / FUTURE /
GETTY IMAGES ENTERTAINMENT

At the Freddie Mercury Tribute Concert,
1992. MICK HUTSON / REDFERNS / GETTY IMAGES

Metallica printed negative *Garage Inc.*
reviews on their "Whiskey in the Jar"
single cover.

On tour, February 1984. DPA PICTURE ALLIANCE / ALAMY STOCK PHOTO

Onstage, 1992.
MICHEL LINSSEN / REDFERNS / GETTY IMAGES

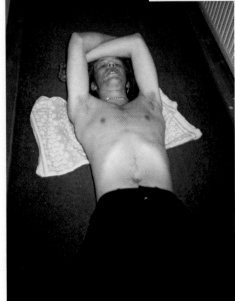

James touring *Kill 'Em All*, 1984.
DPA PICTURE ALLIANCE / ALAMY STOCK PHOTO

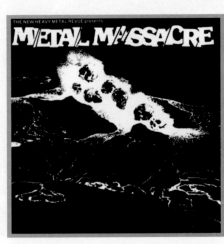

The first officially released Metallica song appeared on *Metal Massacre*, 1982.

Robert played "(Anesthesia) - Pulling Teeth" on the *Worldwired* tour.
PHOTO COURTESY STEVEN THRASHER

Lars signing for fans in Landover, Maryland, 1989. PAUL READ / MICHAEL OCHS ARCHIVE / GETTY IMAGE

Lars at the Rock and Roll Hall of Fame, 2009.
NEILSON BARNARD / GETTY IMAGES ENTERTAINMENT

Taking *Ride the Lightning* to the UK, 1985.
FIN COSTELLO / REDFERNS / GETTY IMAGES

Starting to smile, 1986.
KRASNER/TREBITZ / REDFERNS / GETTY IMAGES

Metallica with Phil Towle in *Some Kind of Monster*. IFC FILMS/PHOTOFEST

Ray Burton talks with fans at Orion Fest, 2012. PHOTO COURTESY LUPE LOZANO

Cliff at the Royal Oak Music Theatre in Michigan, 1985.
ICON AND IMAGE / MICHAEL OCHS ARCHIVES / GETTY IMAGES

Germany, 1984.
DPA PICTURE ALLIANCE / ALAMY STOCK PHOTO

James and Kirk, onstage.
PETE CRONIN / REDFERNS / GETTY IMAGES

Supporting *Master of Puppets* in Chicago. PAUL NATKIN / WIRE IMAGE / GETTY IMAGES

Not even on the ticket yet, opening for Van Halen's Monsters of Rock.
PHOTO COURTESY TIM FORD

With Michael Kamen, 1999.
FEATUREFLASH ARCHIVE / ALAMY
STOCK PHOTO

Program for the Metallica and San Francisco Symphony shows recorded for *S&M.*
PHOTO COURTESY
BRYAN STEELE

On the *Damaged Justice* tour, 1989.
EBET ROBERTS / REDFERNS / GETTY IMAGES

Pamplona, 1988.
DPA PICTURE
ALLIANCE / ALAMY
STOCK PHOTO

Monsters of Rock,
1988. PHOTO COURTESY
TIM FORD

Metallica's new guitarist, 1984.
DPA PICTURE ALLIANCE / ALAMY STOCK PHOTO

Taking the stage at Comic-Con
in San Diego, 2013.
MICHAEL KOVAC / GETTY IMAGES ENTERTAINMENT

Early photo of Metallica with Jason, 1986.
ELEKTRA/PHOTOFEST

Kirk "the Ripper" Hammett.
PHOTO COURTESY STEVEN THRASHER

At the *Through the
Never* premiere
in Toronto, 2013.
PICTURE ALLIANCE /
GETTY IMAGES

Some Kind of Monster poster, 2004.
PHOTO COURTESY NICK MONTELEONE

Jason meeting fans outside
Maryland's Capital Centre, 1989.
PAUL READ / MICHAEL OCHS ARCHIVE / GETTY IMAGES

Ticket for a 1992 show
with Guns N' Roses.
PHOTO COURTESY TIM FORD

Picking up an American Music Award in 1993.
BARRY KING / ALAMY STOCK PHOTO

James' burned guitar from the Montreal incident, on display at 2012 Orion Music + More. PHOTO COURTESY NICK MONTELEONE

Kirk with a fan at the Peabody Essex Museum in Salem, which hosted *It's Alive!* PHOTO COURTESY ANDREW BUONFIGLIO

Lars and James, 2018. ALESSANDRO BOSIO/ALAMY LIVE NEWS

James and Lars onstage in the Netherlands, 1984. PETE CRONIN / REDFERNS / GETTY IMAGES

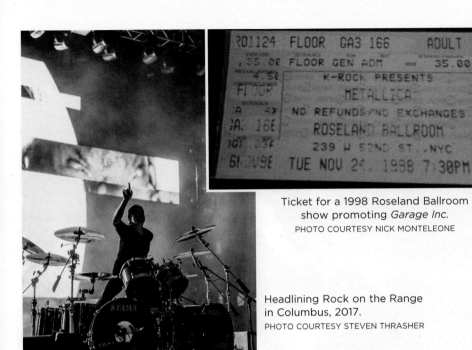

Ticket for a 1998 Roseland Ballroom
show promoting *Garage Inc.*
PHOTO COURTESY NICK MONTELEONE

Headlining Rock on the Range
in Columbus, 2017.
PHOTO COURTESY STEVEN THRASHER

Berlin, 1999.
DPA PICTURE ALLIANCE /
ALAMY STOCK PHOTO

Lars discussing Napster at the Senate Judiciary
Hearings, 2000. GETTY IMAGES / HULTON ARCHIVE

Robert with Metallica in Las Vegas, 2009. ETHAN MILLER / GETTY IMAGES ENTERTAINMENT

Promoting *St. Anger*, 2003. ABC/PHOTOFEST

James in his natural habitat, 2017.
PHOTO COURTESY STEVEN THRASHER

Memorial stone for Cliff Burton in Dörarp, unveiled in 2006. FRUGGO/WIKIMEDIA COMMONS

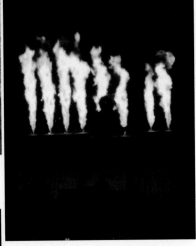

James on the World Magnetic tour, 2009. RICHARD CONTRERAS

James and Kirk, 2008.
PHOTO COURTESY BRYAN STEELE

Fans.
PHOTO COURTESY STEVEN THRASHER

Kirk and Jason with fans, 1989.
PHOTO COURTESY TIM FORD

Email to Lou Reed detailing
31 of his songs sent to Metallica.
AUTHOR'S COLLECTION

Dear Lou,

Here is the list of the 28 songs we sent to Metallica. Now we are also sending the three new ones--
Brandenburg Gate, Iced Honey and Junior Dad.

Can you take a look at this list and reduce this list to 10 to 15 songs?

TOM

Rock N Roll
Vicious
Walk On The Wildside
Sad Song
Kill Your Sons
Charley's Girl
Rock N Roll Heart
Coney Island Baby
Leave Me Alone
Dirt
I Wanna Boogie With You
Waves Of Fear
Standing On Ceremony
Underneath The Bottle
Last Shot
I Wanna Be Black
Betrayed
Busload Of Faith
Temporary Thing
Finish Line
My Old Man
The Gun
Sex With Your Parents
Warrior King
Spit It Out
Ecstasy
Rock Minuet
Who Am I?

Tom Sarig
President Talent & Brand Management, Esther Creative Group

With Lou Reed at a *Lulu* listening party in New York City, 2011.
KEVIN MAZUR / WIREIMAGE / GETTY IMAGES

World Magnetic tour, 2009.
PHOTO COURTESY BRYAN STEELE

James in San Francisco, 2008.
PHOTO COURTESY BRYAN STEELE

Lars at work.
PHOTO COURTESY STEVEN THRASHER

Kirk and Lars onstage, 2017.
PHOTO COURTESY STEVEN THRASHER

Robert in the fire, 2017.
PHOTO COURTESY STEVEN THRASHER

James onstage, 2017.
PHOTO COURTESY STEVEN THRASHER

Pick commemorating Metallica's
2013 Antarctica show.
PHOTO COURTESY NICK MONTELEONE

Closing Outside
Lands in San
Francisco, 2017. JEFF
KRAVITZ / FILMMAGIC /
GETTY IMAGES

16

AND I'LL REDEFINE ANYWHERE

The Black Album

"I can appreciate the people who want us to only go fast. If you dig those bands, please buy their records and see their shows so we can keep it alive—but don't disrespect the people who paved the way and broke down the doors for so many of the groups you enjoy now. . . . I'll go up against any death metal band—pound for pound, hour for hour, we'll crush 'em. I have great respect for them, but those are the facts."

—Jason Newsted

When you put this book down, ask some of your friends what they think the highest selling album of the SoundScan era is. Most people have a basic idea of Nielsen SoundScan, which started tracking music sales weekly in 1991. It's the largest source of record sales figures, displacing *Billboard*'s method of calling up stores for guesstimates. But ask the average music fan about the highest selling record since the nineties and you'll get a slew of answers, ranging from Alanis Morissette's *Jagged Little Pill* to Shania Twain's *Come on Over* to whichever boy band left the biggest dent in their consciousness. You usually won't get the correct answer, which is Metallica's Black Album.

Why is this? Is Metallica underrated? Is their impact so ubiquitous that it's taken for granted? We're living in the world Metallica revolutionized, and there's no greater example of Metallica demolishing and rewriting norms than the Black Album. Few recordings are both as canonized and as controversial. It's Metallica's star-making turn, getting weirder and more accessible in the same songs, the moment where people who took pride in enjoying aggressive music were mortified, and the rest of the world wondered what it had been missing in the past eight years.

By 1990 James and Lars were discussing writing shorter, simpler songs for their next record, with the Misfits, the Rolling Stones, and AC/DC in mind. Lars was drawn to Charlie Watts' drumming and developed a stronger affinity for the way Phil Rudd's swagger supports Angus and Malcolm Young's riffs, more than, in his words, the "progressive Peartian paradiddles" he'd previously favored. Lars' AC/DC obsession led to him listening to them every day around the Black Album's recording, distinguishing his own band against another whose best-known record had an all-black cover. AC/DC and Metallica are forever linked as the two bands on Beavis and Butt-Head's shirts, as well as being the two biggest artists to never release a greatest hits album. But that influence would show up clearest in the Black Album.

BOB ROCK

Metallica reached out to Canadian producer/engineer Bob Rock, who'd gotten his start with Vancouver's Subhumans before more famously working on Bon Jovi's *Slippery When Wet*, the Cult's *Sonic Temple*, and Mötley Crüe's *Dr. Feelgood*. As one might infer from his resume, Rock was not a Metallica buff. He was unimpressed by . . . *And Justice for All* ("I just didn't get it") although he admittedly enjoyed seeing Metallica live, watching them trample the Cult as headliners in 1989. Bob was on vacation in Arizona, making plans to produce his friend Richie Sambora's upcoming solo record (in a 1989 *Rolling Stone* interview, Sambora defended his band by protesting that he wasn't trying to make the guys in Metallica happy). But on his travels, Rock would recall seeing an American Indian kid in a Metallica shirt and hearing . . . *And Justice for All* in a gas station he'd pulled into. He started wondering whether the coincidences were something more.

Not being a thrash fan, Bob did not get starstruck. He wanted to produce the record, not mix it, and didn't want to leave his native Vancouver—people came to him. Metallica ended up recording in Los Angeles and Vancouver, the first time Bob left home to make a record. They decked out Hollywood's One on One studios with billiards, arcade games, basketball hoops, photos of penises (Metallica hazing Bob), and, perhaps most important, a punching bag. Since James liked working during the day while Lars worked at night, Rock ended up spending all hours at One on One. Los Angeles was glam metal territory, but Metallica found a more direct adversary in the studio. Lars was annoyed with Bob's insistence that Metallica hadn't brought their live energy to a record yet, and hated being dragged into upward of forty takes for each song. Metallica had hoped they could make the record they wanted while Bob gave it production like that of *Dr. Feelgood*, but found themselves bossed around in the studio. Lars started to enjoy having a designated villain—he wouldn't tell James himself to rewrite "Enter Sandman," but Bob Rock could. "We've always done things in whatever direction our heads have taken us, but our heads have never taken us in the direction of letting someone else into that inner circle to throw stuff at us when we were making records," Lars told *Faces Rocks*.

James was furious at being told his lyrics weren't up to par, to the point where Rock called him "Dr. No" in the studio. But James worked to write better lyrics. "Before, we didn't even want to hear it," James described working with Bob. "Now we'll hear it. Then we'll say, 'Fuck you.'"

Bob suggested Metallica's first-ever strings, getting cellos for "The Unforgiven" and an orchestra for "Nothing Else Matters," both of which Metallica buried in the mix against Bob's wishes (the full orchestra can be heard on a "Sad but True" B-side, although its arranger, Michael Kamen, got more Metallica leverage as the composer and conductor on *S&M*). But Lars remembered Bob having an "incredible ear for attitude and feeling," which is audible in the band's performances. Bob hurt Kirk's feelings by telling him his planned "The Unforgiven" solo wasn't good enough, and goaded him into a dirtier, heavier, bluesier vibe that helped unleash the solo that Kirk would later say was his most satisfying. The blistering, percussive solo, fingerpicked by Kirk for the first time, is one of metal's most electrifying passages.

By the end of recording, Lars wasn't on speaking terms with Bob. Being Metallica, they still invited him back to produce their records for the next twelve years. "I could never make them do anything they didn't want to do," Bob stated in 2015. "I just tried to help them make the best record they could make."

The conflict surrounding the Black Album wasn't confined to the studio. Metallica lost three marriages in the process—Jason's to Judy, Lars' to Debbie, and Kirk's to Rebecca. Lars has joked that the Black Album's working title was *Married to Metal*, but it does seem that Metallica were more committed to their music than anything else. The Black Album was Metallica's family and their personal life, at others' expense. "I was trying to take those feelings of guilt and failure and channel them into the music, to get something positive out of it," said Kirk, describing himself as "an emotional wreck" during the recording process. "Jason and Lars were, too, and I think that has a lot to do with why the Black Album sounds the way it does."

"I hear the hours and the time and the conflict," Bob reflected years later. "You just can't argue with the songs."

Purists love complaining that Bob Rock turned Metallica into a radio-friendly band. Older fans say the eighties records were better, and younger listeners can't imagine a world where mainstream rock sounds nothing like the Black Album. But Metallica made violent, imaginative music for Rock's production, giving his sonics and engineering a frightening new soundscape that brought out the most in his skills. Metallica didn't need songs like "Nothing Else Matters" for success; they already were one of the world's most popular metal bands. The songs were written pre-production, but Bob built up the performances by provoking Metallica into different keys, lyrics, solos, and drum fills, subverting . . . *And Justice for All* with Metallica's heaviest bass sound to date and rhythms written with Kirk and Jason.

Songs were recorded live in the studio, bringing Metallica's wild stage energy to the record. After their biggest, most constructed tour yet with Doris on Damaged Justice, Metallica were now performing without so much as a backdrop. Lars described the new record as "more emotional" than *Justice*: "When it's angry, it's more angry. When it's subtle, it's more subtle." He also noted Metallica coming back from touring five continents with a reinforced unity and patriotism. "You know, no matter how fucked or corrupt our administration may be, or how many dirty deeds go on that we know nothing about, America, for us, is still the most pleasant, comfortable and exciting place in the world," he noted.

"Writing shit from within is a lot harder than writing the political shit, but once it's out it feels a lot easier to put your weight behind, especially live," James stated, adding that writing political songs had gotten "too easy."

"I've always put taste, phrasing, tone, melody, and hookiness before speed and pure technicality," Kirk told *Guitar World*, describing the process behind his riff architecture. "It's as if there's a big crack in the ground and this big hairy paw hands you this heavy guitar riff."

Metallica were breaking out of themselves on the Black Album. They'd created a formula—a fast, heavy opener with a quiet intro ("Fight Fire with Fire," "Battery," "Blackened") leading into a title track epic ("Ride the Lightning," "Master of Puppets," ". . . And Justice for All") before slowing into a powerful groove ("For Whom the Bell Tolls," "The Thing That Should Not Be," "Eye of the Beholder"), reinventing the ballad in thrash form ("Fade to Black," "Welcome Home (Sanitarium)," "One") with at least one instrumental or spoken word near the end—until the Black Album's focus on vocals. On their first four records, Lars wanted show off Metallica's compositional chops by printing each song length on the back, but did no such thing on the Black Album. Metallica weren't giving hints on the record sleeve anymore. "There is something wrong, innately, with the box," James said told David Masciotra. "It doesn't protect. It confines."

THE NEW BLACK

After creating four of the most recognized and referenced metal images on the covers of *Kill 'Em All*, *Ride the Lightning*, *Master of Puppets*, and *. . . And Justice for All*, Metallica stripped themselves of imagery with an all-black cover. Like everything Metallica, a closer look shows something different, and we can see Metallica's name and a snake faded into the black. People who notice the snake often assume it's the Gadsden flag rattlesnake, with its coiled, striking position (and because the Black Album has a song called "Don't Tread on Me"). But a closer look reveals the supposed Gadsden snake is stripped of its rattle. Metallica removes the snake's identity, just as they shed their own on the Black Album. Just as important, Metallica removes the snake's warning. Metallica is a beast that doesn't tell you it's about to strike.

A black snake, of course, birthed rock 'n' roll as we know it. In Blind Lemon Jefferon's "Black Snake Moan," the lyric "That's all right mama, that's all right for you" was written into "That's All Right" by bluesman Arthur Crudup before being fashioned into Elvis Presley's immortal debut single. In Jefferson's and in Metallica's hands, the black snake marks an evolutionary shift that will unfold over time.

Blackness is a theme, in darkness ("Enter Sandman," "Sad but True," "The Unforgiven," "My Friend of Misery," "The Struggle Within") and in emptiness ("Through the Never," "The God That Failed"), the deepest dive yet into a color as ubiquitous in metal as "blue" is in jazz (*Black Sabbath, Back in Black, Black Metal* for starters). There's barely any cover art or an official title, removing Metallica from the reputation they created for themselves. Technically the album is called *Metallica*. Eponymous records usually suggest a first album, and here in Metallica's rebirth it still kind of is. The Black Album is millions of fans' first Metallica record and first metal record. It's also appropriate for such a deeply Metallica record to be named for themselves, even if nobody calls it *Metallica* any more than they'd call the White Album *The Beatles*. The album's most popular name isn't its official title, but what the fans call it. Like Sergio Leone's Man with No Name in *The Good, the Bad and the Ugly*, Metallica left the title blank so you could use your own.

The titles and cover art are audacious homages to three well-known precursors. Metallica honors the Beatles and inverts them, claiming their place as the biggest band in rock on their own terms, living impervious to trends and creating new ones. There's Metallica's aforementioned fascination with *Back in Black*, a straightforward reinvention of rock music loaded with hits. Metallica responded to the biggest hard rock record of all time with the biggest metal record of all time. Somehow, the Black Album manages to reflect both the Beatles' sprawl over an array of moods and ideas, and the succinct AC/DC over twelve forthright songs, three songs more than . . . *And Justice for All* and still three minutes shorter. Finally, the

Black Album is the brethren of Spinal Tap's all-black *Smell the Glove* cover in *This Is Spinal Tap* (Nigel Tufnel: "There is something about this, that's so black, it's like, 'How much more black could this be?' and the answer is 'None,' none more black"), saluting metal's fine line between stupid and clever.

Metallica premiered the record with a free listening party at Madison Square Garden on August 3, 1991, James' birthday and the anniversary of the Roseland show that got them signed. It was the only album to do so until 2016 when Kanye West, who's been known to wear Metallica shirts and base some of his own *Yeezus* gear on Metallica's famous logo, debuted *The Life of Pablo* at the Garden, breaking streaming and download records in the process the way Metallica broke SoundScan records with the Black Album. Unlike most listening parties, the Black Album debut invited fans, not just exclusively music industry names, allowing an anxious James and Lars to find out metalheads really could connect with "Nothing Else Matters." The band surprised fans by showing up and tapping random shoulders from behind, but had to leave when crowds started catching on.

WE HUNGER TO BE ALIVE

Inspired by Soundgarden's "Flower" and *Louder than Love*, Kirk put the heavy, rocking riff that would turn into "Enter Sandman" on a tape around 2 a.m., driving it into an intro that built every few measures like a nightmare that couldn't be fought off. The riff before the break was inspired by Ice-T's "Personal," which samples "Magic Man" by future James Hetfield collaborators Heart. The lyrics were originally about crib death ("Off to Never Never Land" was "Disrupt the perfect family"), but James would recall the lyrics not being mysterious enough. It ended up being the last Black Album song James completed lyrics for, after explaining the Sandman myth to Lars (who apparently never listened to the Chordettes). The dreamlike lyrics, multiple voices, and stage directions in the chorus blur whether any of this is really happening. Is the father, the Sandman, or one of the terrors speaking? Who is whispering along with the chorus? But one of the most effective things about

"Enter Sandman" is how it reveals the terrors behind comforting tropes like Neverland, being told to "say your prayers," or reciting "Now I Lay Me Down to Sleep." Metallica doesn't need to turn these tropes into horror scenarios because they're already scary. Singing the "Enter Sandman" chorus to the tune of "Edelweiss" makes for a compelling lullaby, but in Metallica's hands it's a nightmare. The "Now I Lay Me Down to Sleep" bridge may or may not have inspired Snoop Dogg to use the same trick in 1993's "Murder Was the Case," ten years before Snoop covered "Sad but True" for an MTV special.

Many songs, like "Sad but True," were based on vocal lines, on the first Metallica record where the vocals were as high in the mix as the guitars and drums. James blew out his voice in the studio, developing vocal cord nodes recording "So What," and eventually took singing lessons from a cantor, which resulted in his more forceful and melodic tone on the album. "It was a process, him learning to say what he wanted but in a more poetic and open sort of way," Bob stated in 2011. James took vocal cues from Chris Isaak songs and worked with Rock to double and build the vocals in the mix, apt for a record where he was embodying multiple characters, sometimes in the same song. The situations were getting more vague and connecting with broader audiences. James' characters weren't getting strapped to an electric chair or chopping their breakfast on a mirror anymore, but the anger, aggression, and fear were stronger than ever in the whipping boys and scapegoats that reached millions.

James described the lyrics of "Sad but True" as "battling yourself, your own addictions, your own temptations." The inner voice in the dream, eyes, and pain of its narrator marked a transformation for Metallica. "I" started showing up in their lyrics more and staying. Musically, "Sad but True" drops enough riffs to become a Metallica standard, one of their most-performed songs, covered by artists as varied as Flipper and the Hu, and hooky enough for a sample to carry Kid Rock's "American Bad Ass" into one of his biggest hits. Along with Snoop's 2003 version and various Jay-Z mashups that appeared online after Jay-Z released his own *The Black Album* in 2004, "Sad but True" shows Metallica writing music that was beat-driven enough to rap over, persuasively or not, and that their heaviest riffs could shine boundless rhythms.

Bob Rock wanted "Holier Than Thou" to the be first single (while worrying it was written about him), something Lars didn't let him live down once "Enter Sandman" smashed. Bob might've been drawn to Metallica's first-ever talk box in the intro, although the effect is far removed from the celebratory hooks it gave "Kickstart My Heart" and "Livin' on a Prayer," forcing out a blare that sounds more like a chicken getting strangled under the heavy riffs and drumming as Metallica conquer radio metal on its own turf, infiltrating the system to change it in their own name.

The Black Album is a James-driven record, and in *Absent* he named "The Unforgiven" as his most personal song. If Metallica fucked with the idea of ballads on "Fade to Black," "Welcome Home (Sanitarium)" and "One," "The Unforgiven" fucks with the idea of Metallica ballads, dealing an angry, heavy verse with a softer, despondent chorus. "It's a showdown with myself," James has said of "The Unforgiven," maybe consciously referencing "The Showdown," Ennio Morricone's *For a Few Dollars More* piece a few Metallica fans have heard in the "Unforgiven" intro. "At the end of the day, it's up to me to forgive so I can move on and live the life I need to live." The melody and pained resentment stayed with him long enough to unwind into two more songs, but none of them hold the weight of the aching, original "The Unforgiven." And in maybe the best sequencing on any Metallica record, the sad kids who skip ahead to "The Unforgiven" get Metallica's most liberating, self-empowering anthem next.

Like the Beatles and Led Zeppelin five or so records into their career, Metallica tinged their sound with the influence of Middle Eastern music ("Sad but True," the first demo given to Bob Rock, was originally slowed down with Zeppelin's "Kashmir" in mind). "Wherever I May Roam" depicts a vagabond unbound by commitment, material possessions, authority, or even a chartered road ("dust in throat"). It's "Invictus" as a headbanger, maybe the most Metallica-worthy song on the Black Album by being the most different. Enlisting an electric sitar sound and a twelve-string bass, Metallica dropped six minutes of metal power without so much as a scream but some of the weirdest, tightest one-man vocal harmonies this side of Prince on rock radio, proving that changing their music without conforming to anyone's standards would only make them bigger. Metallica complemented the loner's narration with music every bit as adventurous as the story, even if a lyric or two had been passed down for generations (see the Temptations' "Papa Was a Rollin' Stone").

The Black Album is Metallica's most cinematic release, from echoing Morricone in "The Unforgiven" to quoting measures from *West Side Story*'s "America" in the intro to "Don't Tread on Me." James described the latter as an appreciation developed from touring ("You find out what you like about certain places and you find out why you live in America, even with all the bad fucked-up shit"), apt for a composer as multifaceted as James and a song that interpolates a Leonard Bernstein and Stephen Sondheim composition about immigrants arguing over the good and bad in the United States. Lyrically it's a patchwork quilt of American proverbs, taking its title from the Culpeper Minutemen, paraphrasing Ben Franklin ("She never begins an attack, nor, when once engaged, ever surrenders . . . she never wounds 'till she has generously given notice, even to her enemy, and cautioned him against the danger of treading on her") and Patrick Henry ("Give me liberty or give me death") and depicting America as through the Gadsden flag (hanging on a wall at One on One studio). "To secure peace is to prepare for war" paraphrases *De Re Militari*, a fourth-century Latin text by Vegetius.

Upon its release, "Don't Tread on Me" faced backlash for its staccato, two-note riffing and middle school history paper's view of patriotism. *Rolling Stone*'s Robert Palmer singled it out as the album's one bad song, disappointed to hear the band of . . . *And Justice for All* turn jingoistic (Kirk: "That was definitely a word we had to look up"). Some listeners heard a meditation on the Gulf War despite the song having been written in August 1990, and growing popularity of "Don't tread on me" as a nationalist slogan in the 2000s kept Metallica from playing the song live until the Black Album's anniversary shows in 2012. Still, "Don't Tread on Me" is one of the Black Album's most invigorating deep cuts, and rock radio stations, desperate for more Metallica, have played Black Album non-singles like "Don't Tread on Me" and "Holier Than Thou" since the nineties. "If we worried about the shit that people were going to throw at us, then it would be a very different Metallica," stated Lars.

Like "Holier Than Thou" or "The Struggle Within," "Through the Never" is among Metallica's fastest, although Lars' midtempo drumming on the Black Album songs gave them a swing their thrashier songs lacked. "The two most underrated drummers in rock, to me, are the Rolling Stones' Charlie Watts and AC/DC's Phil Rudd," Lars said in 2020. "In terms of 'air-drumming moments,' you know, there are so many incredible ones from both of those guys." Even the faster Black Album songs felt like an insult to some fans, as if Metallica could still thrash but chose not to (or maybe the songs really are heavy, and people just hate that they're popular). "Through the Never" kicks off the Black Album's Side B in a furor, armed with lyrics that paraphrase both Carl Sagan's *Cosmos: A Personal Voyage* and Jimi Hendrix's *Are You Experienced*.

James wrote "Nothing Else Matters" for himself in a hotel room on tour, not suspecting he had one of Metallica's biggest songs in his hands and was, in his words, "afraid" to show it to his bandmates. Never opening himself this way is a big pledge from the guy who wrote "Fade to Black," but it might be even more impressive that he next tweaks a lyric from his most-hated song, "Escape," in the next line—"Life's for my own to live my own way" evolved into "Life is ours, we live it our way." James has said that writing about love or sex was "taboo" in Metallica, something that had been done to death by the bands they didn't want to be like. But with "Nothing Else Matters," Metallica wrote the go-to metalhead wedding song, took down hard rock's macho posturing, and elevated any absolute beginner who could pick up a guitar to be able to play Metallica for a few measures, although it won't match versions by Macy Gray, Bif Naked, Doro, Lissie, Lucie Silvas, or best of all Shakira, a wolf-obsessive like James who reimagined "Nothing Else Matters" as a flamenco waltz, graced with triplets between verses of one of her originals, "La Despedida."

On "Of Wolf and Man," James voices a night prowler who pulses with the earth, evolving into his surroundings. Evoking his predatory instincts, and perhaps reconnecting with his estranged father, James becomes increasingly feral in the verses after howling out each call-and-response chorus. Shapeshifting from the familiar into something new is a Black Album theme, as is breaking from repressed instincts, and the humanity in basing a song around vocal line (Kirk developed "Of Wolf and Man" by singing lines and adapting his vocal melodies for guitar). "The hair stands on the back of my neck," James intones in the bridge, but it's a few more measures before you realize what really just happened to him.

Denying nature returns in "The God That Failed," one of Metallica's most harrowing tracks. James attacks religion through his cancer-ravaged mother's faith, spitting some of his best-ever lyrics over a hypnotic rhythm section and an anguished Kirk solo. "It will take me back there as much as I want it to," James told *The Village Voice* in 2012, adding that he'd made some peace with his family and religion since "The God That Failed," while acknowledging the song's power. "I've arrived. Move over, Bob Dylan," he joked in the interview. "It sounded pretty grown-up coming from someone so angry."

Written around a bassline from Jason's demos, "My Friend of Misery" was originally instrumental, still the penultimate song in the place Cliff-based songs "Orion" and "To Live Is to Die" had been on previous records. The band builds "My Friend of Misery" with Kirk and James trading solos, but it's still Jason's song, his stirring intro channeling the jukebox-ready basslines of the Funk Brothers' James Jamerson while still being heavy enough for Dark Tranquility to cover it for their *Decibel* Hall of Famer *The Gallery* in 1995. Closer "The Struggle Within" was never played live until Metallica's Black Album anniversary shows, but in that context, where Metallica played the album back to front (better to end with "Sad but True" and "Enter Sandman"), "The Struggle Within" lives as a new beginning. Introducing the Black Album set with Lars' military drum cadence and James' thrash riffing, "The Struggle Within" now sounds like a rebirth at the end of the Black Album, Metallica already moving on to another world at the record's end.

On the Black Album, Metallica rebelled against the rebels. Like folk enthusiasts hearing Dylan go electric on *Bringing It All Back Home*, much of the metal community rejected the Black Album as a sellout, horrified that their underground metal heroes had gone for the airwaves (Dave Lombardo claimed to have thrown his copy out). Also like Dylan, Metallica brought it back home on the Black Album, jumping over their NWOBHM influences into stadiums with a sound that paved the way for Pantera's

"Pure Against the Grain American Metal," Lamb of God's *New American Gospel*, and an entire 1990s–2000s genre often called the NWOAHM, crafting metal that celebrated and raged against the United States the way previous metal bands examined Hell. It's a heavy, strange album, that puts metal in the mainstream without watering it down. "I think most of our real fans know that we want to play many different styles of music and that's something that we started doing on the *Ride the Lightning* album," said Lars, modestly avoiding the fact that his band was already doing this on *Kill 'Em All*.

The Black Album is a psychologically diverse album that can soundtrack an individual's darkest, most emotionally wrecked moments as well as it blasts Yankee Stadium for Mariano Rivera's walk-up music or serves as Rachel Maddow's ringtone. James has said that he wanted the songs to be both "more inward and more universal," and reflected that the lyrics were personal enough for fans to think they knew him through the words, adding, "Of course they don't know you, and probably never will." But it's the unknowable parts of Metallica and the Black Album that keep fans coming back. Metallica dropped a permanent puzzle, intriguing without being exhausting, which is part of why it's been the gateway metal record for countless listeners ever since its release.

Def Leppard's Joe Elliott, who knows a thing or ten about diamond-selling records, called the Black Album the "metal *Thriller*," and to this day the Black Album still sells four to five thousand records a week, with more weeks on the *Billboard 200* than any studio album not named *The Dark Side of the Moon*. But more than its sales, what makes the Black Album one of the most important albums ever is the release it gives its fans, something for alienated listeners to feed their demons to on a greater scale than any other metal record while still feeling personal.

"I remember in 1991 all of these homeless kids in LA, their anthem was Metallica's 'Enter Sandman,'" *A Brief History of Seven Killings* author Marlon James said in 2015. "And when asked, 'That's a song about a kid being killed in his sleep. Your life is so horrible, why would you like this song?' They would say there is a warmth in coming across something darker than what you live in and there's a kind of thrill in knowing that there's an outcome that's even darker than yours."

FREE TO SPEAK MY MIND ANYWHERE

Metallica played some of their last non-headlining shows in 1991, playing second to AC/DC for the Monsters of Rock show that would become AC/DC's *Live at Donington* and for an estimated over one millions fans in an incredible post-Soviet coup show filmed as *For Those About to Rock: Monsters in Moscow*, celebrating rage and freedom with AC/DC, Pantera, the Black Crowes, and a dismal local band called E.S.T. A greater challenge came in May 1992, when Metallica announced a co-headlining stadium tour with one of the only bands in the world monstrously successful enough to close a show over Black Album–era Metallica: Guns N' Roses. Kurt Cobain nixed a dream triple bill by turning down the opening spot offered to Nirvana, although the selected openers Faith No More, Body Count, and Motörhead more than delivered.

GNR provided Metallica with something no other heavy band did—a substantive rivalry. Blowing away Dokken was no problem, but this was going to be different. "We were having major problems getting onstage on time, riding that high-low rollercoaster," Slash recalled in his autobiography. "Metallica was not a band to pull that kind of shit at all, so they wisely opted to play first so as to avoid being pulled down by our bullshit." Lars would remember GNR's backstage orgies as "a Caligula kind of outlandishness," and their late start times and tabloid-dominating debauchery earned Guns N' Roses lasting notoriety. Less so Metallica, who didn't publicize their bad behavior but were indulging more than ever before. James griped about GNR's excess in interviews with the self-hatred of a guy who was also drinking, fucking around, and buying million-dollar real estate, enjoying the girls and fast cars he mocked other bands for writing about. Years later, he would admit that watching Guns N' Roses on the verge of their initial breakup made him want to keep his emotions locked up, and even sympathize with GNR's volatile frontman. "He's eccentric, but all artists are," James said of Axl to *Spin* in 2008. "They're either pretending they're not or they're pretending they're an artist."

But the most infamous Metallica/GNR moment came during Metallica's set in Montreal, when pyrotechnics during "Fade to Black" caught James, burning his hands to the bone while guitar strings melted and exploded. Jason remembered James' skin "bubbling like the Toxic Avenger," with second- and third-degree burns covering his face and body. Had James been breathing in at that moment, he would have likely been killed. In a 2009 Metallica guest appearance on the Discovery Channel science show *Time Warp*, James would recall his wood guitar being charred black except for where his hand had been. A pyrotechnics specialist reenacted the accident by burning a ham at 2,000 Fahrenheit, causing third-degree burns in a fraction of a second.

The show was stopped, and James was rushed to the hospital. Guns N' Roses' late start and abbreviated set led to rioters overturning cars and breaking windows. Metallica's then–tour manager Tony Smith recalled James already talking that night in the emergency room about how to continue the tour. Auditioned guitarists included Sepultura's Andreas Kisser ("I knew all the Metallica stuff by heart—that's like my school"), who struggled with the newer Black Album songs but made it to finals before James' 1986 replacement John Marshall scored the gig. Metallica were back on the road seventeen days after the incident.

Metallica supported the Black Album for more than three hundred shows over four years. Music critics started grudgingly taking metal seriously, and the *Washington Post* named Metallica "the only heavy metal band that adults could listen to without feeling their IQ diminishing." Metallica's first *Spin* cover story started, "Metallica has always been eerily popular, but never very good" until their "stunning new album," still shortsighted enough to describe their thrash records as a mix of the worst aspects of punk and metal (it should be noted that the same magazine issue, which Lars surely pored over, raved about Robert Trujillo being Suicidal Tendencies' best-ever bassist).

Music critics often credit *Nevermind* for breaking subversive music onto the charts, banishing glam metal to CD store bargain bins and county fairs in the process. But Metallica, whose barn burner dropped a month before *Nevermind*, obliterated the barrier between metal and mainstream, as seen in the subsequent first-ever *Billboard* top ten debuts of Megadeth (#2, 1992), Nine Inch Nails (#7, 1992), Anthrax (#7, 1993), Pantera (#1, 1994), Slayer (#8, 1994), White Zombie (#6, 1995), Rage Against the Machine (#1, 1996), Tool (#2, 1996), Marilyn Manson (#3, 1996), and Korn (#3, 1996). Thrashers Testament, Exodus, and Kreator all released hard rock–based metal records in 1992, on the heels of the Black Album.

Of all the bands cited in the downfall of glam metal, Metallica may have pulled off the hardest trick. They changed what hit metal records sounded like.

Connecting the Black Album once more to the AC/DC record that inspired it, Lars grasped where the record stood in Metallica's context. "You have a record like *Back in Black*. You have a record like *Synchronicity*. You have a record like *Nevermind*. Or you have a record like the Black Album. But you don't have more than one like that."

17

THROUGH THE MIST
AND THE MADNESS

Great Works That Inspired
Metallica Songs

*"There's music on, always, and it doesn't have to be music
specifically that influences our stuff; it's movies, it's books, the
news, or even my kids telling me stuff. You never know where
the influence is going to come from, and I don't worry too much
about that part, because I know it's going to come to us."*

—James Hetfield

While most of Metallica's clearest influences are in the NWOBHM,
1970s hard rock, and punk, they took metal to more cinematic
and literary heights by adapting some of their favorite films and books
into headbanging masterpieces. They weren't the first hard rock or
metal band to do so—Led Zeppelin famously championed *The Lord of
the Rings*, and Black Sabbath is named for a 1963 Mario Bava horror
film starring Boris Karloff. But more than most of their contemporaries,
Metallica went below the surface, undoing what we think we know about
some texts and introducing us to others. Their songs don't have all the
answers, and neither do the texts they're referencing, but that's part
of why we keep watching, reading, and listening. Here are thirteen of
the best works that inspired James Hetfield—and in one instance, Lou
Reed—to pick up a pen.

THE "LULU" PLAYS, FRANK WEDEKIND (1895 AND 1904)

Wedekind is best-known these days for *Spring Awakening*, his controversial 1891 play about adolescent sexuality, which was rendered unrecognizable in a popular Broadway musical adaptation that shared its name. Prior to that, the German playwright was infamous for his "Lulu" plays, *Earth Spirit* (1895) and *Pandora's Box* (1904), a two-part, pre-Expressionist tragedy usually performed together as *Lulu*. The show follows Lulu, a sexually liberated dancer, as she sleeps with, marries, and kills an array of suitors, leading up to an encounter with Jack the Ripper. Unsurprisingly, the show caused an uproar when it was first staged, and theater scholars have spent years arguing whether the title character is a feminist hero or a product of Wedekind's licentiousness and misogyny. Nevertheless, the Lulu plays continue to wow audiences and inspire adaptations over a century later, most famously G. W. Probst's classic 1929 silent film *Pandora's Box* (starring Louise Brooks), Alban Berg's posthumous 1937 three-act opera *Lulu*, and Lou Reed and Metallica's *Lulu*. *Lulu* fans should also check out *Death and Devil*, Wedekind's 1905 play that is sometimes anthologized as the third Lulu play, despite the character Lulu not appearing in it herself.

JOHNNY GOT HIS GUN, DALTON TRUMBO (1938)

One of the most chilling antiwar novels in American literature, *Johnny Got His Gun* is the account of Joe Bonham, a World War I soldier who wakes up in a hospital after a tracheotomy, having lost his arms, legs, eyes, ears, and mouth from an exploding shell. Throughout the story he reflects on his condition and his life before the war, although even the book's grim plot can't prepare readers for its horrifying conclusion (neither can the "One" video, which doesn't give away the book's ending). Trumbo's story has stayed sadly relevant over subsequent wars—when the "peace sign" hand gesture was adapted for the anti–Vietnam War movement, *Johnny Got His Gun* was reprinted with it on the cover, and more recent editions have included prefaces from the antiwar activists Ron Kovic and Cindy Sheehan. Metalheads will recognize Metallica lyrics throughout the book, including a scene where Joe mulls "There was nothing real but pain," and an attempted self-suffocation that leaves him holding his breath as he wishes for death. In a passage thought to have inspired the song title "One," Joe reflects, "He had lost a million to one shot. Yet if he read about himself in a newspaper he wouldn't be able to believe it even though he knew it was true. And he would never expect it to happen to him. Nobody expected it. But he could believe anything from now on out. A million to one ten million to one there was always the one."

FOR WHOM THE BELL TOLLS, ERNEST HEMINGWAY (1940)

Like Metallica, Hemingway's works get pigeonholed as art for aggro guys (usually by people who haven't read them), and, as with Metallica, he's a much more empathetic artist than his image often suggests. *For Whom the Bell Tolls* is Hemingway's towering epic, proof a short story writer specializing in minimalism could take on the Spanish Civil War. Hemingway writes from his own experience, having worked as a journalist during the War supporting the Republican (anti-Nationalist) side against Francisco Franco, and some of his beliefs spill over into his protagonist, Robert Jordan, a fascist-hating American teacher and soldier with an expertise in explosives. Yet like much of Metallica's music, *For Whom the Bell Tolls* speaks broadly enough to connect with numerous ideologies—in 2008, it was the only book that both presidential candidates Barack Obama and John McCain hailed as a personal favorite. Hetfield's "For a hill, men would kill" and "Men of five, still alive through the raging glow" are taken directly from a scene where five soldiers take a position on a hill in the face of airstrikes, and *Ride the Lightning* fans might also recognize a scene in which Jordan can, in Hemingway's words, "hear the silence where it fell." But read the book before you find out who takes a look to the sky just before he dies.

SUNSET BOULEVARD, DIR. BILLY WILDER (1950)

Marianne Faithfull was anything but a has-been when she played one on "The Memory Remains" in 1997, coming off a successful new record (*20th Century Blues*) and a salacious hit autobiography (*Faithfull*) when she graced the song with her signature croak. Still, James Hetfield, who had initially planned to sing her part, praised Faithfull for giving "The Memory Remains" its aura, singling out her "weathered, smellin'-the-cigarettes-on-the-CD voice" in *CMJ New Music Monthly*, "She was the voice, and she was a very intense character." He could have been referring to Norma Desmond, an already faded prima donna played by Gloria Swanson in the harrowing noir classic *Sunset Boulevard*. When a struggling screenwriter (William Holden) shows up at the mansion of a former silent film star ("I am big. It's the pictures that got small!" is the film's second most famous line), he agrees to help her with a screenplay that will supposedly relaunch her back into stardom. The project is an adaptation of *Salome*, in case you couldn't tell where this is heading. The film gets creepier and Desmond seems to lose more of her mind by the minute, with only her devoted butler Max (Erich von Stroheim) working to keep her from snapping, as Desmond insists that her former director Cecil B. DeMille (played by himself) is interested in her screenplay and demands to see him. The ending is unforgettably dark, and *Sunset Boulevard* remains one of the most highly regarded films in movie history, even being preserved in the Library of Congress, alongside *Master of Puppets*.

THE TEN COMMANDMENTS, DIR. CECIL B. DEMILLE (1956)

Director/producer Cecil B. DeMille made over seventy films, usually distinguished for being lavish, epic, high-budget projects. His most famous and grandiose film, which he also narrated, was also the last one he directed, a retelling of the Book of Exodus that cast Charlton Heston as Moses and Yul Brynner as Rameses II in *The Ten Commandments*. While the screenplay has not aged well, and Heston, for all his movie-star power, gets thoroughly outacted by Brynner (whose "So let it be written, so let it be done" aphorism shows up in "Creeping Death"), *The Ten Commandments* is a stunning piece of filmmaking, with state-of-the-art sets, costumes, and special effects today's CGI can do nothing to diminish. A monster box office and critical success when it hit theaters, *The Ten Commandments* is still one of the highest grossing films of all time, adjusted for inflation, and will likely stay an annual TV staple during Passover and

Easter season for years. James would remember watching the movie with his bandmates, stating, "When it got to the part where the first pharaoh's son is taken and the fog rolls in, Cliff said, 'Look . . . creeping death.' And I was like, 'Whoa, dude, write it down!' Sheer poetry!" James has told this story in several interviews, but never notes that the term "creeping death" also appears twice in "The Lurking Fear," a short horror story published in serial form by "America's zippiest pocket magazine," *Home Brew*, in 1923—written by Cliff Burton's horror hero, H. P. Lovecraft.

ONE FLEW OVER THE CUCKOO'S NEST, DIR. MILOŠ FORMAN (1975)

Rarely does a great book get a worthy film adaptation, but Forman's *One Flew Over the Cuckoo*'s Nest gives Ken Kesey's countercultural novel a vivid interpretation that helped establish both the director and his star, Jack Nicholson, as cinema treasures. Nicholson plays Randle P. McMurphy, an incorrigible convict at a mental institution who mobilizes a motley crew of inmates in trying to thwart the draconian Nurse Ratched (Louise Fletcher) with escape plans and parties. The story is by turns heartbreaking and hilarious, so much so that even Hollywood's old guard at the Academy Awards were inspired to make *One Flew Over the Cuckoo's Nest* the second-ever film to win the top five honors. The patients are enlivened by a first-rate cast, including a pre–*Back to the Future* Christopher Lloyd, pre–*Child's Play* Brad Dourif, and pre-*Taxi* Danny DeVito, but it's Will Sampson as the silent "Chief" who makes the most memorable supporting impression in many of the film's best scenes. James Hetfield watched Nurse Ratched's building fear of what's out there, and told *Back to the Front* he wrote "Welcome Home (Sanitarium)" with *One Flew Over the Cuckoo's Nest* in mind.

THE STAND, STEPHEN KING (1978)

Stephen King's status as a horror legend is indisputable, with *Carrie*, *The Shining* (Kirk Hammett's favorite novel, according to *So What!*), *Pet*

Semetary, *It*, and *Misery* being only a few of the works that have made him horror's most successful author over the past fifty years. For many fans, *The Stand* is his magnum opus, a terrifying, post-apocalyptic nightmare that's been keeping readers up at night since its first printing (the original paperback cover was painted by Don Brautigam, who'd later illustrate the *Master of Puppets* cover). A biological outbreak, accidentally released by the US Army, infects and kills off much of the world's population while the survivors run for shelter and fight for their lives. The descriptions of the illness are enough to send any reader with the smallest case of the sniffles into hysterics, although the supernatural Randall Flagg, a King villain of biblical proportions, may be the book's most notorious creation. *The Stand* has stayed a touchstone of metal culture, perhaps most directly in Anthrax's "Among the Living," but it was a quote in chapter 24—"Why, then you go on to Death Row at state prison and just enjoy all that good food until it's time to ride the lightning"—that made history by catching Kirk Hammett's eye.

MAGIC, DIR. RICHARD ATTENBOROUGH (1978)

In *Too Much Horror Business*, Kirk Hammett admires a poster for the cult horror film *Magic* by noting one of the film's Metallica-worthy themes—the question of who is the master and who is the puppet. "Sad but True" came from Hetfield's affinity for this strange movie about a man and his dummy. William Goldman (*Butch Cassidy and the Sundance Kid*, *The Princess Bride*, *All the President's Men*) adapted his original novel for the screen, with Anthony Hopkins playing Corky, a failed magician who suddenly finds success as a ventriloquist with a sinister dummy named Fats. The line between Corky and Fats evaporates quickly, while a murder cover-up and an affair with Corky's married friend Peggy (Ann-Margret) turn this tense, uncomfortable film into a nail-biter. Try holding on to what's real and what isn't, don't get too caught up wondering why Ann-Margret would be attracted to an unhinged ventriloquist creepy enough to be played by Anthony Hopkins, and enjoy looking for the mind astray and the eyes while you're away. James has been coy about citing *Magic*'s influence on "Sad but True," but noted to *Rolling Stone* that Pushead, whose original album art for "Sad but True" showed two skulls confronting each other, picked up on the song's duality theme on his own.

. . . *AND JUSTICE FOR ALL*, DIR. NORMAN JEWISON (1979)

Perhaps most recognized as the "You're out of order! The whole trial's out of order!" movie that launched numerous references and parodies, . . . *And Justice for All* is a courtroom drama that raises unanswerable questions. Al Pacino leads a superb supporting cast (including Jack Warden, John Forsythe, Lee Strasberg, Craig T. Nelson, and Christine Lahti) as Arthur Kirkland, a troubled Baltimore defense attorney called in to defend a judge accused of rape and battery. This is complicated by Kirkland's history with the judge, which includes a punch-up over the unfair sentencing of one of Kirkland's clients, and the judge's knowledge of an ethics violation that could get Kirkland disbarred. Blackmailed into defending the judge, Kirkland makes a choice that will keep viewers guessing throughout the trial and beyond the climactic finale. The film takes funny and twisted turns, particularly with subplots involving Kirkland's eccentric peers, and has one of Hollywood's earliest sympathetic depictions of a trans character. But it was the courtroom corruption that Metallica found so grim, so true, so real. "It seems like no one is even concerned with finding out the truth anymore," stated Lars. "It's become more and more like a one lawyer versus another–type situation, where the best lawyer can alter justice any way he wants." Seeking no truth, winning is all.

NAMING NAMES, VICTOR S. NAVASKY (1980)

The longtime editor-in-chief of *The Nation*, Victor S. Navasky, won a National Book Award for this informative, heavily researched book on McCarthyism, more specifically the Hollywood blacklist that accused entertainment industry figures of having communist ties, ruining several careers and wrecking lives in the 1950s. Navasky spent eight years combing through letters, transcripts, interviews, and getting into the personal lives of the central figures in the scandal (including *Johnny Got His Gun* author Dalton Trumbo), showing that the damage caused by McCarthyism still can't be calculated today. Navasky delves into the intellectual arguments of the "I was just following orders" crowd who turned in their peers, and uncovers the role of bigotry in the stigmatization of the alleged communists. Cliff Burnstein recommended *Naming Names* to Metallica during the recording of . . . *And Justice for All*, inspiring James' lyrics for "The Shortest Straw," including an allusion to the 1950s right-wing pamphlet *Red Channels*. James described the song as "more political than any of the other songs," and Metallica fans reading *Naming Names* today— particularly the passages citing famous disillusioned communist essay collection *The God That Failed*—might wonder whether it inspired more than one Metallica song.

WOLFEN, DIR. MICHAEL WADLEIGH (1981)

Based on the first novel by the horror master Whitley Strieber, *Wolfen* prowls between scary and campy with a story about an NYPD cop (Albert Finney) and a forensics officer (Diane Venora) investigating some gruesome murders. The culprit is hinted at early on, but the revelation of the lycanthropes' nature, an eerie creature's-eye-view camera that predated *Predator* by six years, and a chilling conclusion help make *Wolfen* an excellent gore and suspense ride. James Hetfield named it as the inspiration behind "Of Wolf and Man" in an issue of *So What!*, and Metallica fans can also enjoy an uncredited cameo (removed from all video and DVD releases due to rights issues, so find another way to see it) from one of James' favorite artists, performing his song "Jitterbug Boy (Sharing a Curbstone with Chuck E. Weiss, Robert Marchese, Paul Body and The Mug and Artie)."

TALES, H. P. LOVECRAFT (2005)

Cliff Burton, Metallica's Lovecraft fanatic in a band full of fans, once told James Hetfield not to read Lovecraft's books because they'd make him crazy. Howard Phillips Lovecraft himself was unfortunately a virulent bigot, but his terrific imagination came up with stories and creatures that will outlive us all, most famously Cthulhu, the tentacled sea beast immortalized in his short story "The Call of Cthulhu," first published in *Weird Tales* magazine in 1928. The story is more famous for its creature than its plot, but the chills are authentic, as seen in the couplet, "That is not dead which can eternal lie. And with strange aeons even death may die," referring to Lovecraft's fictional magic book *Necronomicon* and was later adapted into the verses of "The Thing That Should Not Be" (as well as the cover art for Iron Maiden's *Live After Death*). "The Call of Cthulhu" also inspired Metallica's "The Call of Ktulu" and "Dream No More," and the Cthulhu Mythos inspired "All Nightmare Long" with "The Hounds of Tindalos," a Frank Belknap Long story (also published in *Weird Tales*) about wolflike creatures that hunt their prey through dreams and time-travel, which Lovecraft worked into his 1931 novella *The Whisperer in Darkness*. Lovecraft and *Weird Tales* were often dismissed by critics as sci-fi pulp, but in the twenty-first century he's considered literary enough for the Library of America to give him a prestigious hardcover volume, *Tales*, which includes the aforementioned titles among many others, including Kirk Hammett's two favorite Lovecraft stories, "Rats in the Walls" and "Mountains of Madness."

AMY, DIR. ASIF KAPADIA (2015)

Asif Kapadia's documentary about the late British songwriter Amy Winehouse shows a more complete Amy than the spiraling addict the media painted near the end of her life. *Amy* traces Winehouse from her pre-fame days, with home videos showing an astonishing talent with lovable spunk from an early age, through her sudden stardom and descent into the 27 Club. Winehouse is often funny, even cheerful in interviews and friends' accounts, and fans who come for a glimpse of Winehouse the performer will be awed by her audition for Island Records and studio footage from recording her 2006 neo soul stunner *Back to Black*. But *Amy* is obviously not a happy story, and even fans familiar with her life might be shocked by how much the press, and worse her family and ex-husband, enabled her addiction and demise. James Hetfield saw the amphetamine queen of

"Moth into Flame" in *Amy*, telling *Global News*, "It really hit me in the one part of the movie where she was lost, in her mind, it seemed, and she was just leaving her flat in England to go somewhere, and the press was just hanging out in front her place all the time, you know, just snapping these pictures of her—'Hey Amy, how's it going, how's this?'—talking to her like they know her."

18

TEAR ME OPEN, MAKE YOU GONE

Load

"This record and what we're doing with it—that, to me, is what Metallica are all about: exploring different things. The minute you stop exploring, then just sit down and fucking die."

—Lars Ulrich

It's a long-standing debate among metalheads: Is it better for a band to make similar-sounding records again and again, maintaining predictable but enjoyable consistency, or to take their music to new worlds at the risk of destroying their reputation and infuriating their fans? Is it better for a metal band to be like Metallica or Slayer? Better for hard rock to be like Metallica or AC/DC?

"If I'm in a corner, I like my corner," Kerry King has stated, between twelve albums that are more or less different levels of *Reign in Blood*. "It's the coolest corner I've ever been in."

You don't need to pick Metallica or Slayer. One perk of being a metalhead is that we get both. Part of what makes Metallica exciting is they're constantly trying new things, and one of the biggest thrills about Slayer is their steadfast awesome thrash. If too much of it sounds the same to you, you can always try Metallica. If Metallica gets too weird, dozens of Slayer songs deliver. Metalheads love that *Hardwired . . . to Self Destruct* sounds nothing like *Lulu*, and that AC/DC can endure drastic lineup changes and come back still sounding just like AC/DC. People play the new Slayer or

AC/DC records for the same reason they get their favorite beer at the store. You know what you're getting. Metallica isn't nearly as dependable.

"First and foremost, we're doing this for ourselves," Kirk told *Louder Than Hell* coauthor Katherine Turman. "And if it sells a lot afterwards, you know, that's great. And if it doesn't sell, that's fine, too . . . as long as we're satisfied on a creative viewpoint."

A common misconception about *Load* is that Metallica was jumping onto the alternative bandwagon, trying to stay in the mainstream by pandering to fans of Pearl Jam and the Smashing Pumpkins. While they did headline Lollapalooza that year (which, in true Metallica fashion, pissed a lot of people off), and Anton Corbijn's photos in the *Load* liner notes made them look like Zoo TV–era U2, no one who's listened to the songs thinks this. Musically, *Load* expresses more of a punk-never-happened aesthetic, conveying the seventies hard rock of the bands they'd cover on *Garage Inc.*, such as Thin Lizzy and Blue Öyster Cult. It's the first Metallica record entirely tuned down a half step to E♭, honoring Jimi Hendrix and Thin Lizzy but also extending James' vocal range, bringing out some of his finest singing. The bad times ZZ Top groove "Poor Twisted Me," which inspired the Poor Touring Me and Poor Re-Touring Me tours, could be seen as a droll swipe at alt-rock's (and later nu metal's) self-pitying stars. Even Metallica's alternative influences sound classic rock on *Load*—"Hero of the Day," the first song recorded for the album, was titled "Mouldy" in demo form after Bob Mould, whose Minneapolis punk band Hüsker Dü James had been talking up since the mid-eighties. Metallica honored Mould with the almost power-pop heavy progression that would become "Hero of the Day." But alternative or not, Metallica made a thrashless record, their least heavy or riff-driven music to date, a thorn in their side from the tree they planted.

"Nowadays, I can be just as inspired by George Michael as I can be by a heavy metal band," Lars stated in 1996, perhaps aware that the *Faith* star had followed up one of the best-selling albums in the world with a different style and more somber tone.

By 1996, all four members had cut their hair and had started wearing designer clothes. The haircuts were not a band decision, just something that happened with age, but it caused almost as much of an industry stir as their musical direction (Cliff Burnstein in 1986: "If one of them gets a haircut, I'll kill myself"). Attending Alice in Chains' *Unplugged* taping at the Brooklyn Academy of Music, Metallica watched bassist Mike Inez write "FRIENDS DON'T LET FRIENDS GET *FRIENDS* HAIRCUTS" on his instrument, sparking rumors of a feud (anyone who watched the taping knew it was in jest, especially if you caught AIC riffing on both "Enter Sandman" and "Battery" during the show).

"They need to grow their hair back," a grinning commentator with long blond hair and a hat asserted on VH1's *Least Metal Moments*. "Do another black record and grow that hair back and I think you'll make a lot of people happy."

"It's the same thing that people said about Miles Davis when he started using electronics and electric guitars," the rapper Mos Def told *The Chicago Maroon* in 2001. "It's the same thing they said about Bob Dylan when he went electric at Newport in 1965, it's the same thing they said about Metallica when they started touring stadiums, shit like when they cut their hair, like they're less real now."

The moody first single and video, "Until It Sleeps," showed that Metallica getting sick of their Black Album image didn't make them bored, but restless. They developed a loose recording schedule for *Load*, resulting in their most relaxed music and the band not hating each other as much, despite calling their Sausalito recording studio "Purgatory" in interviews (Kirk: "We're the master procrastinators. We tend to sweat and toil on the beginning of a record, and a lot of that has to do with establishing a stride that works for us."). Kirk remembered watching trends come and go between the Black Album and *Load*, wondering how Metallica fit in. Of course, this was Metallica, they didn't fit in before and weren't going to start fitting in now. Lollapalooza founder Perry Farrell quit in protest over Metallica's headlining that year, perhaps abashed that Lollapalooza, once at the forefront of music and culture, found Metallica after their most cutting-edge days (he came around by 2015, when he endorsed Metallica headlining the festival, although being Metallica they played past curfew and violated Chicago's noise ordinance). Scheduled to play "King Nothing" at MTV Europe Awards, following performances by Simply Red and Kula Shaker, Metallica launched into a baby-killing, goat-fucking medley of "Last Caress" and "So What," live, uncensored, and removed from all future broadcasts.

Playing with artists like Hole and Sonic Youth throughout various *Load* tour dates, Metallica found themselves alone with everybody, outsiders among outsiders. Even if alternative rock wasn't showing up in Metallica's sound, the influence was clear enough for deriders to call *Load* "Alternica." (Kirk: "Soundgarden, they're basically a metal band. . . . Nirvana had fuckin' riffs that could have been on *Master of Reality*! Alternative is just more of a packaging, I would think.") "Until it Sleeps" B-sides included a danceable, industrial tinged remix attributed to "Herman Melville" (actually Richard Melville Hall, newly a critical darling with his electronica album *Everything Is Wrong*), plus a demo version called "F.O.B.D." for sharing a time signature with Soundgarden's "Fell on Black Days." Soundgarden's Sup Pop and SST records gave them alternative cred that made fans overlook their metal instincts, although no one was calling out "Alternica" when Chris Cornell covered "One" in 2015, or when Metallica thrashed two *Ultramega OK* songs at the 2019 Chris Cornell memorial show.

Load is the first Metallica studio album to use a photograph instead of an illustration on its cover. Kirk, who developed a Diane Arbus fixation around *Load*, found the photo in an Andres Serrano collection, *Body and Soul*, which he bought at the San Francisco Museum of Modern Art. The New York artist is best known for his 1987 work *Immersion (Piss Christ)* (yes, metalheads, that's what the song on Fear Factory's *Demanufacture* is named for), which depicted a crucifix in urine and inspired censorship campaigns and protests that went all the way to the US Senate floor. The first lines in *Body and Soul* are from the white supremacist Republican senator Jesse Helms. "I do not know Mr. Andres Serrano. And I hope I never meet him. Because he is not an artist. He is a jerk."

For the *Load* cover, Kirk and Lars picked Serrano's *Semen and Blood III*, a decision that irked Jason and James. The 1990 work, part of a series responding to the AIDS epidemic, was created with Serrano's own semen, cattle blood, and plexiglass in a flamelike design. Fans argued about what it meant—did the seed represent another Metallica rebirth? What about that pool of blood, inspiring comparisons to *Kill 'Em All* and how much they'd changed in this metamorphosis? Was the semen Kirk's? Whose blood was it? What about that logo—on *Load*, Metallica shaved the edges off their iconic font, the new logo literally taking the edge off

Metallica (it wouldn't be back until *Death Magnetic*). They even cropped Serrano's photograph, once more making fans go deeper if they wanted the full picture (Serrano, a Metallica fan, give the alteration his blessing). But as late as 2019 Lars was still calling *Load* and *Reload* his two favorite Metallica album covers.

"I don't want to spend the rest of our careers being associated with some kind of symbol," Lars has said. Despite giving the metal world some if its most iconic imagery, from Doris to the logo font to Pushead's artwork (the artist formerly known as Brian Schroeder met James at a 1985 Venom show and found fame through some of Metallica's best-loved T-shirt art, as well as art for the Misfits, Dr. Dre, Kylesa, and Kool Keith's *Dr. Octagone-cologyst*), Metallica deliberately avoids giving itself a mascot, something like Iron Maiden's Eddie or Motörhead's Snaggletooth to assure fans that they're getting what they want. Metallica doesn't make those promises. Metallica pillars like palm muting and E minor all but vanished on *Load*. Even their blues-based hard rock they were supposedly resorting to sounded different, free of tropes like Bo Diddley beats or twelve-bar blues.

Load also has Metallica's first-ever slide guitar (Kirk was inspired by Duane Allman), pedal steel, fretless bass, and slap bass. It's the first Metallica record where Kirk plays rhythm to James' lead, and the guitars were laid down after the bass and drums. Not only were Metallica writing songs in major, they were releasing them as singles. It's also the first Metallica record to wear thin over its full running time, and the first one that didn't pave the way for the future of metal.

The opening track "Ain't My Bitch" has a heavy, catchy stomp, but got more attention for its title. James has said the "bitch" in the song is a complaint—rural California for "not my problem"—but Metallica aren't dumb. They knew what people would think. Apparently they've stopped caring, since "Ain't My Bitch" hasn't been played since 1998. "2 x 4," so named for its structure as well as James' out-smashing what you can't out-think theme (reflected on in the *Playboy* interview), has to adapt its most memorable lines from *Taxi Driver* and *Sudden Impact* and takes more of its pull from Kirk's Chet Baker–inspired solo. The mass shooting–inspired "Ronnie" has tight harmonies and a good bumper riff for Metallica's *Behind the Music* episode, but not much else. James expressed his band's anxiety with their status on "King Nothing," a subject that weighed enough on them for the song to be originally titled "Load," and "Wasting My Hate," the only song on *Load* or *Reload* under four minutes, gave James a connection to his father by taking inspiration from a Waylon Jennings story about a confrontation.

Virgil Hetfield died in the first winter of 1996. That year, James was telling interviewers his father was his hero, that while getting back in touch with him he'd found they had much in common, and that he was awed by Virgil's resilience in his last days. Jason recalled James smiling and cracking jokes in the aftermath, but *Load* drips with loss, faith, illness, and disbelief. James took some time camping alone in the Wyoming frontier, sans writing materials, to leave Metallica behind and try to put himself at peace with his outdoorsman father. Unable to escape his own mind, he ended up writing new songs with soft-point bullets, using the lead tips to write the lyrics. The first two singles show James delving into his parents' cancer on the brooding "Until It Sleeps" and putting his hopes outside of home on the yearning "Hero of the Day."

James wrote the hushed, "Simple Man"–inspired "Mama Said" without intending it to be a Metallica release, but against Jason's protests that Metallica shouldn't try country, it made the record and even got a single and video. James was getting heavily into country music at the time, in part by reconnecting with his father and by going to country bars where he was less likely to be bothered since people there didn't care who he was. In *A Year and a Half in the Life of Metallica*, James treasures the last grasps of anonymity he can find in an off-night jam, joining a local blues rock band whose bassist wears a "Don't Mess with Texas" shirt and introduces the guest guitarist as "James Hatfield." Thus James told his mama story, donning an apron in her absence, in the tradition of great country men whose mamas tried, or didn't let their babies grow up to be cowboys, although James is too metal to resist telling her he's coming home.

James took the Black Album's internal lyrics further, citing Tom Waits, Leonard Cohen, and especially Nick Cave ("I was turned on by it completely, by the moods he created") in interviews and playing them for his bandmates (Jason's first choice for *Garage Inc.* was Waits' "16 Shells From a Thirty-Ought-Six"). "I think we really wanted these songs to be their own entities . . . to have their own characters," James stated near the record's release. Perhaps defensively, he also started saying the meaning in his lyrics was sometimes less important than the phrasing, sounds, and vowels he used. "I had to kind of go visit some messed up places where I thought 'I'm all better now, I don't have to write that kind of crap anymore," James told MTV's Kurt Loder, describing the record's lyrical themes as "vagueness." James trailed off with a laugh. "But once you're messed up, you know . . ."

James started therapy around the *Load* sessions and took more than a year off from drinking, narrated in the peak deep cut "Bleeding Me." "I was trying to bleed out all bad, get the evil out," James described his therapy sessions in *Playboy*. "I discovered some ugly stuff in there." Between planning his life around the bottle and leeching out pain from the chair, James composed an eight-minute voyage that manifests Metallica's strengths as soundly as some of their thrash heights. Kirk recalled it as one of his proudest moments—"It sums up all my influences, with a good dose of my own style. I'm sweeping my whole lick catalog there."

Metallica sweep through a lot on *Load*'s seventy-nine minutes (it was supposed to be even longer—check out the "Unencumbered" version of the closing epic "The Outlaw Torn" on the "Memory Remains" B-side, which pushes eleven minutes), digging their way to something better and not finding it. Despite selling over five million copies in the United States and earning Metallica their only *Billboard* Hot 100 top ten single to date ("Until It Sleeps," although they don't play it much anymore—Lars think it's too pieced-together), *Load* did not build Metallica's stature or legacy the way their previous five records did. "Metallica's predilection for the rambling, multipart epic, almost charming when their music passed for stoner Stravinsky, seems pretty dumb applied to the sort of side-long boogie jams that went out of fashion before Gregg married Cher," wrote Jonathan Gold in *Spin*, using Metallica's new turn as proof that their earlier critics were right all along. Worse stings came from Metallica's contemporaries. "Admit it, it's good to have us around now that Metallica let us all down," Pantera's Phil Anselmo crowed onstage during Pantera's 1996 tour, just two years after playing a "Pantallica" set that included "Whiplash" and "Seek & Destroy" with special guest Jason Newsted. He later apologized in *Metal Edge* and has since opened for Metallica, but the sentiment was widespread. "The new record is so lame, and I'm not just saying that because of the way they look now," Kerry King told *Kerrang!* "I just

hate the record because it has no attitude, no fire, no nothing. It sucks."
And if I close my mind in fear . . .

"People have come up to me years afterwards and said, 'I never gave the record a fair chance because I couldn't get beyond Jason Newsted wearing eyeliner,'" Lars would recall. Of course, Jason didn't wear eyeliner—he and James protested Lars and Kirk's vision. But Lars would rather blame Jason than admit he fucked up Metallica's reputation. Lars has since defended it, telling *Metal Hammer* he was proud to challenge the metal community. But unlike previous times Metallica challenged the metal community, *Load* didn't change it.

Addendum: In fall 1996, a member of the Scene, an online piracy group known for stealing software and pornography, founded Compress 'Da Audio (CDA), the first group to release pirated songs in a new format called MP3. The format spread quickly, and within weeks thousands of songs were being pirated online through numerous sites. But that story gets traced to August 10, when CDA released what is often credited as the first pirated MP3.

That song? "Until It Sleeps," by Metallica.

19

LIFE IS OURS,
WE LIVE IT OUR WAY

James and Lars' Bogus Journey

"The personalities are so different that it amazes me, and it amazes me that these guys have been able to stick it out this long and not kill each other."

—Robert Trujillo

James Hetfield and Lars Ulrich, what's this strange relationship? They're easily one of the most famous creative partnerships in all of music, yet nobody seems to understand it, least of all the men in the band. Two boys from different countries and social classes, both struggling to impress their fathers, one who didn't care enough for his son's music and one who cared too much.

As with most of rock's greatest songwriting duos, Lennon-McCartney and Jagger-Richards included, one musician tends to get deemed the cool rebel while the other gets pigeonholed as the poseur sellout. As with all these cases, the truth is a lot more complicated—it's not like James didn't write "St. Anger," or Lars didn't book Joan Jett, Ben Weinman, and James Murphy on *It's Electric!* (great interviews, by the way, though one wishes Lars had asked Metallica fan Murphy why his wine bar is named The Four Horsemen). James describes Lars as a charmer and himself as an intimidator in their business, but to read Kirk and Rob's accounts, it's often the opposite, with Lars playing the bad cop to his more understanding partner. (James has praised Rob and Kirk as "great idea people but very good at being okay with someone else doing the driving.")

We can argue for ages over who's coolest or lamest, but there's no way around James and Lars needing each other. After forty years in a band it's almost unfathomable that neither of them have ever gone solo, but at this point it's hard to see either of them making a record without the other. "I don't have the desire to be the Sting, the guy on his own," James has stated. "I enjoy being inspired by the other guys. I enjoy the camaraderie."

James writes music and Lars arranges. Lars likes longer songs and James wants to keep them short. (James: "My body is better at sprinting than marathons . . . Lars? Opposite. He can go on and fucking on.") Lars insists on Diamond Head and Mercyful Fate for *Garage Inc.*, whereas James insists on the Misfits and Nick Cave. Lars writes about mortality for "Frantic" and it comes out sounding like addiction in James' voice. Most people would give up on a partner who roped them into suing Napster, or releasing "The Unforgiven II," but James and Lars aren't most people. A *Rolling Stone* interview revealed that James is the only one who joins Lars on the drum riser because Lars unwittingly spits (Kirk will only get closer for mellower songs like "Nothing Else Matters"). The feeling may be mutual—Bobby Schneider recalls James spitting on Lars when he would get off time in the eighties. But part of James and Lars' closeness means loving each other enough to not mind the occasional expectoration. Like a more agreeable Jack Kirby and Stan Lee, James and Lars designate business and creative duties to get to the top of their game. They're also metal's Strunk and White, influencing the style and language.

"Lars and I have been married for 35 years," James laughed in 2017. "There are times when he'll just do a count in, and we both start playing the same song. And who knows how or why that happens, but there is an energy between us. I know his limitations, he knows mine, and we try to push each other a little bit."

Lars put it more succinctly for MTV. "There's nobody that can push James Hetfield like me. I can piss him off in five seconds flat."

James and Lars met at age seventeen and formed Metallica five months later, October 28, 1981, its only consistent members for four decades and the longest relationship either of them have outside their families. When Lars and James lived in the same room for Metallica's first several years,

Lars admitted he developed codependency, unable to buy furniture for his first apartment on his own without wondering what James would think. When Lars tells James he's too controlling in *Some Kind of Monster*, both inadvertently and on purpose, it's not clear whether this is true, but it is clear James weighs on his mind. Lars also named James as one of his three heroes in 2016, calling his friend "underappreciated" (the other two were Torben Ulrich and Steve Jobs).

Sometimes, Lars speaks of James with a homosocial longing, half-jokingly complaining that James doesn't return his phone calls or even getting more sexually charged than Metallica ever does in song (Lars: "The bottom line is, playing and writing with James still gets my dick as hard now as it did in 1981"). Describing *Some Kind of Monster* to Conan O'Brien, Lars identified himself and James as the bickering "mom and dad" with Kirk as their left-behind child. "I can take you back, when me and him were alone in my room in 1981 listening to new wave of British heavy metal singles—as soon as there was somebody else in the room . . . it just had a very different energy to it," Lars relates in the film. "When James was with Mustaine he became like he never really cared about me. . . . One time during the recording of the *Ride the Lightning* record where me and him went out—forty-two beers later, 'Oh dude, I love you,' but it could never have materialized until it got to that forty-two-beer point and we were alone."

James is rarely so affectionate (search for "James and Lars kiss" for pictures). But speaking publicly, he loves Lars as anyone outside the Hetfield home. He's parodied their relationship in a romantic *St. Anger* instant messenger ad and has gone as far as to get corresponding "F" and "M" tattoos on his hands, for Francesca and Metallica. People remember James making fun of Axl Rose's rider in *A Year and a Half in the Life of Metallica*, but just as revealing is James' unease that Lars is getting spellbound by another frontman. (James: "He likes learning things from people who have that something. Axl had that.") In *Guitar World*, James compares his "opposites attract" relationship with Lars to his own marriage. "I will say one thing, and Lars will be on the other end, saying the exact opposite," James revealed in 1996. "But that's how Metallica have always worked."

BUT THE MEMORY REMAINS

Reload

"The part I like most is we're hated again."

—James Hetfield

Didn't like *Load* much, did you? Have some more. Metallica responded to *Load*'s detractors by giving them the last thing they wanted. Five years after presenting their newest album as a heavier, more precise, and consistent alternative to their tourmates' *Use Your Illusion I* and *II*, Metallica dumped a more erratic two-record set on the world. If *Load* revealed Metallica's fallibility, *Reload* confirmed it by doubling down. Metallica weren't being careless or losing control when they released *Load*. They really were an inconsistent mess. Feed it once and now it stays. It's not an adrenaline rush in "Fuel," but an adrenaline crash.

Load was planned as a double album, but splitting it into two records allowed Metallica to sign on for Lollapalooza, take a touring break and get out of their Elektra contract quicker than a standard double album would have. Hence a thirteen-song companion record, released on Kirk's birthday in 1997. Lars, deceptively, told the press that *Reload* was "more one-dimensional" than *Load*, elaborating, "It'll be ten or twelve five-minute songs that are all fairly heavy. No ten-minute epics, or James going off on his country tangent," managing to throw James under the bus and mislead fans about a record that ran seventy-six minutes and had Metallica's first ever hurdy-gurdy (James' Chieftains-inspired "Low

Man's Lyric," a minor to major waltz that could sit at home with Leonard Cohen).

Metallica returned to Andres Serrano's photography for the cover, this time selecting the artist's *Piss and Blood XXVI*. *Load* was blood and cum, *Reload* was blood and piss. Rebirth and disposal, linked by discharge. The album title on the cover, the hand-scrawled *"Re"* over the printed *"Load,"* depicted a band struggling to maintain their edge, an awkward combination of polish and rawness that showed itself in the titles of their next three records, *Garage Inc.*, *S&M*, and *St. Anger*, one of the strangest runs in metal history. *Load* and *Reload* were the first Metallica records to work as background music, like "King Nothing" and "The Memory Remains" playing in two separate Bada Bing club episodes of *The Sopranos*. The tunes are there, and support dramatic scenes, but don't bustle enough to distract from James Gandolfini.

Over half of *Reload*'s thirteen songs have never been played live by Metallica. Even "Better Than You," a top ten single on the Mainstream Rock charts, which won a Grammy on the sheer force of Metallica's hugeness, never reached the stage. It's not a bad song either, featuring solid riffs and vocals, though a band that already had a song called "Holier Than Thou" should have known better. Don't count on many overlooked gems in *Reload*'s deep cuts. "Bad Seed" plods under a Kyuss riff and "Sweet Leaf" cough, despite invoking numerous Metallica themes, including Kirk's classic horror books and film, James' Nick Cave fandom, and the Matthew parable all three of them were probably forced to learn in religious school. "Prince Charming" nips "The Four Horsemen" for structure and references Prints Charming, a small garment shop that produced hundreds of "Metal Up Your Ass" Metallica shirts in the early eighties. The store's owners had no idea this band of hellions were about to change the world, but if they'd started with "Prince Charming," they might've never had a chance. *Reload* has its surprises, like the captivating "Low Man's Lyric" and the grandiose closer (and Kirk favorite) "Fixxxer," but like its predecessor, *Reload* sees Metallica as a singles band. There aren't a lot of bad songs, but too many are just fine, something nobody wants from a Metallica record.

By far Metallica's most-performed song from *Load* or *Reload* is "Fuel," which sounds written on the fly, although an early version on *Cunning*

Stunts shows some work went into it. "Fuel" is Metallica's "D'yer Mak'er," a monumental band writing a simple, infectious corker that sticks in your head indefinitely. James wrote "Fuel" with Rocket from the Crypt in mind, but the high-speed radio metal production and camp lyrics make it sound more like a preview of Rob Zombie's forthcoming *Hellbilly Deluxe* (Mr. Zombie, who sometimes covers "Enter Sandman" live, enlisted Black Album engineer Scott Humphrey to cowrite and coproduce *Hellbilly*). If Rob Zombie wrote "Fuel" he'd play it every time he tours, and in Metallica's set it's good for about half that.

The other standout is "The Memory Remains," famous for a chanted refrain that Patti Smith, Joni Mitchell, and Courtney Love were all considered for. But James had taken to English femme fatale Marianne Faithfull's *20th Century Blues*, a 1996 live record on which she primarily sings Bertolt Brecht and Kurt Weill songs, including "Pirate Jenny," "Alabama Song," and "Mack the Knife." Lars and James spent a day in Dublin with Marianne, over wine and road stories (she knew Lemmy personally), and she gave the song her indelible voice. Marianne Faithfull chose the lyrics "Say yes. At least say hello" to end the song, taken from the 1961 drama *The Misfits*, famous in part as the last completed screen appearance of both Marilyn Monroe and Clark Gable (yes, the same movie Glenn Danzig got his band's name from). Metallica later took her to New York for their only-ever *Saturday Night Live* performance, hosted by Nathan Lane. "The Memory Remains" gets nuked by an off-key Marianne, who obviously can't hear herself over the band, but "Fuel" thrashes and makes James one of the only people to have said "fuck" uncensored on *SNL*.

Reload's memorable singles end there. One of the nuisances of being a rock radio listener in the nineties was the intro to "The Unforgiven II," which made it unclear for the first few seconds if you were about to hear "The Unforgiven" or its sequel. "The Unforgiven II" shows a rare instance of Metallica ripping off the past, though not in the way most people think— that main progression owes its life to Jimi Hendrix's "1983 . . . (A Merman I Should Turn to Be)." At the time, "The Unforgiven II" was the most successful single from *Reload*, making it to No. 1 on the Mainstream Rock chart and signaling that listeners were more interested in Metallica's past. Like everything else from *Reload* that isn't "Fuel" or "The Memory Remains," it's mostly vanished from Metallica's setlists over the years.

Even Jason Newsted admitted never having listened to *Load* or *Reload* all the way through in one sitting. His Metallica devotion either only went so far, or was being beaten out of him by his bandmates. Jason's only cowrite on either record, the workmanlike "Where the Wild Things Are," was never performed live, and neither was his stated *Load* favorite, the faith-and-forgiveness-themed "Thorn Within." He told interviewers he didn't care, going far enough to state, "I feel more satisfied putting my bass parts on James' cool writing than I would getting five of my songs on the record." But his frustrations were becoming known enough for James, Kirk, and Lars to start answering to it in the press. It could not have been easy for Jason to watch Metallica take even fewer of his song ideas just as their songwriting started to go stale. When a demo tape for IR8, Jason's project with Strapping Young Lad's Devin Townsend and Exodus' Tom Hunting, leaked to radio, James and Lars were furious. "You guys are always getting to be doing your thing. And I always want to back you up," Jason complained in an interview. "But somehow, somewhere, I gotta let my shit out."

Fans were divided about *Reload*, and wrote into *So What!* asking Metallica whether they ever thought they'd be writing songs like "Low Man's Lyric" when the band started. (Lars: "The stuff you'll hear on our records fifteen years from now, I cannot picture writing/playing right now!" That would be *Lulu*.) James has since disdained *Reload*, although admitting he likes it more than *Load*, and even Lars acknowledges *Reload*'s reputation. "I can't sit there and look you in the eye and tell you *Master of Puppets* is a better record than *Reload*," Lars said in a 2017 talk at New York's 92nd St Y. "Maybe to you it is, and I totally, totally, totally respect that, but I can guarantee you that we made *Reload*, or *St. Anger*, or whatever else, with the same vigor, enthusiasm, dedication, belief in what we were doing, belief in ourselves, belief in the material, as we did *Master of Puppets* or the Black Album or the other records."

On *Load* and *Reload*, Metallica entered the internet age with two records that were ideal for downloading services. There's not one Metallica fan who doesn't think *Load* and *Reload* would be better as a single record, with even Lars admitting the records could be cut down by about twelve to fifteen songs. They're the ultimate playlist records, an artistic vision that'd be improved by a fan-made mix tape. Part of the fun of being a Metallica fan is piecing together one good single-disc album from *Load* and *Reload*. Many writers and webzines have tried it, and it's been a go-to activity of metal blogs and forums for almost as long as both records have existed. Maybe your *ReLoad* would have all of their heaviest songs, or all of their singles. Mine wouldn't, but I couldn't imagine it without "Low Man's Lyric." Like the fans who've tried to make a one-disc *Use Your Illusion* or pare down the White Album, it appears that no two listeners would do it the same way.

"Every time that there are natural changes that happen to you, you can mask them and hide them from people or you can just say 'This is what it is, take it or leave it but at least I'm being straight with you,'" stated Lars. "We've always chosen the path of being straight with people."

METALLICA ABIDES

In the 1998 cult classic film *The Big Lebowski*, protagonist Jeffrey "The Dude" Lebowski confides that he roadied for Metallica on the "Speed of Sound" tour. "Bunch of assholes," mutters the Dude. Most of his monologue is based on the life of real-life Lebowski-inspiration Jeff Dowd, who really was a member of the infamous Vietnam War protestors the Seattle Seven, but the Metallica roadie story was made up by the Coen brothers. Purists may insist there was no Speed of Sound tour in Metallica history, but I like to believe the Dude was kvlt enough to work on a Metallica tour that even most of their biggest fans haven't heard of.

21

THE FRAYED ENDS
OF SANITY

Metallica's Tumultuous Years

"I don't think there even was a band for about a year or two."

—Lars Ulrich

Metallica is famous for not compromising or taking any shit. Metalheads love them for it. But what happens when Metallica refuse to take shit from their own fans?

METALLICA VS. NAPSTER, INC.

In a 1999 *So What!* issue, Lars gave his first comments on MP3s. He's open-minded, saying it's too early to have more than a speculative answer. The same year, Metallica even cut an ad for official artist websites with Monty Python's John Cleese. But in 2000, a demo version of "I Disappear," written and recorded for the upcoming *Mission: Impossible 2* soundtrack, leaked to radio stations and was traced to the filesharing service Napster. Metallica's most blatantly commercial song, a single commissioned for a blockbuster Tom Cruise film, started an artist rights lawsuit that became the most infamous moment in Metallica history.

Metallica did not have a lot to lose from Napster. They owned their back catalogue and were more affected by Elektra Records than any downloading service like Napster. Metallica had already successfully sued Elektra in

1994, fending off a countersuit to gain ownership of their master tapes, an increased share of royalties, and a recording/video expenses split with the label. They had also threatened the new tech conglomerate Amazon with legal action for selling bootlegs, years before pirated and unauthorized merch became a major part of Amazon's sales. Financially, it was much more expensive to hire lawyers and a consulting firm to file a copyright infringement suit than it was to lose a few purchases of the "I Disappear" single. But at the music industry's economic peak many fans saw Metallica as being in it for the money. From a PR standpoint, Metallica offending Napster users in 2000 was about as wise as the Dixie Chicks slamming a Republican president in 2003. Like the Chicks, people protested by smashing Metallica records and ridiculing them online, both of which are seen in *Some Kind of Monster*. Not that Lars helped by coming off as a scold in interviews or appearing in an embarrassing anti-Napster ad on MTV, taking turns with Marlon Wayans to see who could be less funny. Maybe fans would be less likely to turn on a band whose last studio release was *Ride the Lightning* and not *Reload*.

"This is not about a lot of money right now," Lars cautioned. "It's about the principle of the thing and it's about what could happen if this kind of thing is allowed to exist and run as rampant and out of control for the next five years as it has been for the last six months. I can guarantee you it's costing us tenfold to fight it in lawyer's fees, in lawyers' compensation, than it is for measly little pennies in royalties. . . . Where it can affect people, where it is about money, is for the band that sells 600 copies of their CD."

Lars' arguments that Napster's founders were in it for the money mostly fell on deaf ears. It looked like a multimillionaire band, already struggling with their anti-establishment image, was suing its own fans, even if those fans were represented by a corporation rich enough to hire lawyer David Boies (*Bush v. Gore, United States v. Microsoft Corp*). "This is not a service they're offering for the good of mankind, to spread love and music. They're doing it for potential IPOs for alignment with a big company where there will be a major cash transfer to the investors," Lars stated. Testifying to the Senate Judiciary Committee, Lars made the case that artists who choose to give away their music for free could do so, but that a corporation that gave it way for free, sans permission, was stealing. "It is clear then that if music is free for downloading, the music industry is not viable. All the jobs that I just talked about will be lost and the diverse voices of the artists will disappear. The argument I hear a lot, that music should be free, must then mean the musicians should work for free. Nobody else works for free, why should musicians?" To many viewers Lars sounded unreasonable. Record sales had their peak year in 1999, selling $40 billion worldwide. How was Napster going to topple that?

No matter how much Metallica assured people that they were suing a major company and not the fans, it felt like a slap in the face to watch the guys who dressed like their fans on *Master of Puppets* shut down what at the time seemed like the new tape-trading. (Lars: "A valid point . . . The bottom line is the size of it . . . When we go in, and check Napster out, we come up with 1.4 million copyright infringements in 48 hours, this is a very different thing than trading cassette tapes with your buddy at school.") Metallica had been laid-back about bootlegging in the past, building their fanbase with a Grateful Dead–like taper's section behind the soundboard during the Wherever We May Roam tour. (Lars: "I've seen lists of like 300 of our gigs that are available on tape. It happens anyway, so why not put 'em in the middle, where at least it will sound better?")

A federal judge ruled in Metallica's favor, and Napster was temporarily shut down. But Metallica's reputation as everyday guys who cared about their fans was tattered. Other artists cared, with Dr. Dre even filing his own lawsuit, but Metallica took the first plunge and the backlash. Lars has since seemed resigned to the industry collapse, telling *Spin* in a 2003 interview ("Lars Attacks!") he was more hurt by the experience than he'd ever let on. Fans who bought *St. Anger* got an access code for free live Metallica downloads, and when *Death Magnetic* leaked ten days in advance, Lars was generous and PR-savvy enough to call "a victory" by 2008 standards.

In some ways Metallica were ahead of their time, years before artists like Prince, Neil Young, and Taylor Swift were praised for taking their music off the internet. The small fraction of one cent that streaming services pay artists today was not on people's minds in 2000. Many of Lars' arguments ("In a couple of years, there will be software where you can download movies, literature, poetry, the whole nine yards") look prescient now. History may prove Lars right, as Mastodon's Brann Dailor argued in 2017.

"Everyone gave him so much shit about it, saying he's just a rich rock star. No, he was trying to protect the little guy that's gonna be coming up. The only way we're putting any food on our tables and our floors for our pets is out there on tour. Where bands would do a couple tours a year, now it's just nonstop touring. That's not healthy, my friend." The Misfits' Doyle Wolfgang von Frankenstein was more blunt in 2019. "Everybody thought [Lars] was a dick. He didn't do it for him. He's got the fucking money. He did it for fucking jerkoffs like me."

The music industry has been almost entirely revamped in Napster's wake. Record labels are folding, signing fewer acts, and dropping artists more than ever before, wrecked by downloading and streaming services. 1999, the year before *Metallica v. Napster, Inc.*, will forever be music sales' most prosperous year, with revenue declining ever since. The crash may have been inevitable, and suing Napster may not have been worth pursuing. But one truth of the music industry crashing is that Metallica has survived. Watching Metallica top streaming and sales charts well into the 2020s, they look poised to outlive it.

TIME AND THE BOTTLE

But Metallica almost didn't survive. Their excess had grown to the point where on 2000's Summer Sanitarium tour James hired someone to collect local dirt for him to stomp around in. At the disastrous Woodstock '99 festival, described by James as the worst show they played all summer, Metallica addressed the abundance of corporate sponsors, the violence-prone audience, and the mostly terrible bill with Anti-Nowhere League's punk novelty "So What," for the second time opening a Woodstock set with an obscure cover. Originally ANL's B-side to their assault on Ralph McTell's "Streets of London," "So What" got more infamous than the A-side when 10,000 copies were seized from retailers and destroyed under the Obscene Publications Act. Their music was appropriately awful for a band of guys with names like Animal and Magoo, but James told *Guitar World* he enjoyed watching the crowd react to his singing "I've even sucked an old man's cock" in Metallica's opening song.

"You continue to try and outdo yourselves for the other bands, the business fucks and backstage poseurs, and, most importantly, yourself," Lars commented on Woodstock '99. "It never ceases to amaze me how easily the hatred comes back, wanting to fucking upstage these other cunts, at least for me."

2001 was the first year since Metallica's start that they didn't play a single show. Tensions that had been brewing for years were spilling out in interviews. Jason was becoming more withdrawn from his bandmates and frustrated in interviews. James grumbled in *So What!* about his band-mates' drug use, annoyed by Metallica losing their drug-free reputation while feeling left out by Lars and Kirk's bond. Kirk told *Playboy* that James was homophobic, and Kirk's kissing buddy Lars suggested that it stemmed from James questioning his own sexuality. In the same interview, James groused about Lars' hygiene, fashion, attitude, drumming, upbringing, and musical taste, revealing that he'd thrown Lars into his drumkit more than once. Lars spent more time defending himself than attacking James, but admitted they'd become more dissimilar with age. Jason, who later called the *Playboy* interview "sensationalism," revealed that anti-drug James sometimes drank too much to show up for rehearsals and photo-shoots. In hindsight, James and Kirk slagging Papa Roach, Limp Bizkit, and Godsmack seems wise, but at the time looked like they were yelling at the kids to get off their lawn, no matter how much James talked up Queens of the Stone Age or Rocket from the Crypt. In some circles Metallica was seen as old guard in the burgeoning nu metal fad, to the point where MTV's claymation show *Celebrity Deathmatch* pitted James against Limp Bizkit's Fred Durst, featuring someone doing an awful James impression before he kills Durst (clay James: "I was expecting to take on Slayer, or even Dokken. What is this Shrimp Bizkit crap?").

"I wasn't able to assert myself to express my feelings," James told *Psychology Today* in 2004. "James was the guy who could take the pain; he could endure anything. So I would build up all this anger and it would pop out as rage or depression—and the way I'd deal with that was drinking, partying, screwing around on the road." A guy who connected with millions of people in songs admittedly couldn't do it in person, still keeping others at bay as a survival technique.

James grew up in fear of drugs with Christian Science, and never tried anything harder than a few cannabis hits with his friends in the Obsession. But alcohol sent James to years of twelve-step meetings, something he still calls part of his "mental or emotional regimen." He'd been a violent drunk for years, letting the occasional interview tidbit slip about getting a bottle cracked over his head in Mexico or getting thrown in a paddy wagon after a Samhain show. But much of his habit was kept under wraps. It took James' wife, Francesca Tomasi, a member of Metallica's security and wardrobe before they married, to send James to rehab. (James: "My wife finally told me, 'Hey! I'm not one of your yes men on the road! Get the fuck out!'") The split was also kept secret in Metallica circles, occurring shortly before the door-slamming scene in *Some Kind of Monster*.

"Finding fault with everything was how Metallica was fueled," James said in 2003. "And not only did I play a part in that, I was buried in that."

Afraid of people knowing who he was, James checked into rehab under a different name. He started his meeting with, "My name is James and I've got a fake tag on," and broke down crying. He used the words "ogre" and "intimidator" to describe the person he'd become and hated, although still music-minded, he compared his habit to a bonus track that was taking over the entire record. Just as he'd found comfort in artists who expressed anger, shame, and despair, James found kinship in meetings. "When I found out there were other people in my situation, with you know, the deepest, darkest, ugliest secrets you have are just poison and they're rotting inside you. No matter what you're hiding, someone else can say they've done that, too."

"You wouldn't really like me if you knew my story, if you knew what horrible things I've done," James stated in a 2015 Road Recovery interview. "I'm coming to grips with that, 'cause I have groups of people that I'm able to share all my horrible stuff with. . . . Shame's a big thing for me. . . . Playing music saves my life. Every day it saves my life."

With Metallica now basically a duo, Lars and Kirk were anxious enough to record "We Did It Again," a *Biker Boyz* soundtrack collab with Swizz Beatz and Ja Rule. The rappers envisioned the song as a Lakers anthem and filmed an entertaining scene cut from *Some Kind of Monster*, but no matter how much they shout Metallica's name over cutting room James vocals it never gels. It wasn't a disaster, but only because Metallica had sunk so low nobody cared. "We Did It Again" may have scared Lars into declining a collaboration with an acclaimed Hollywood director's upcoming *Kill Bill*. Lars would regret turning down Quentin Tarantino, but considering the music Lars was writing at the time, it may have been a good thing.

James was out of rehab by Christmas 2001, reintroducing himself to his family, band, and himself while sending gracious thanks to his fans and Jason in *So What!* messages. Lars would credit the band's survival to the bandmates having kids around the same time. Francesca was pregnant with her and James' third child, and Lars had been raising two kids with his second wife, physician Skylar Satenstein (the inspiration for Minnie Driver's Skylar in the 1998 film *Good Will Hunting*). The kids have inherited some of their parents' belligerence, seen in Lars' boy talking over his father on camera in *Some Kind of Monster*, or an outtake where James' son refuses to wear headphones in the studio. James tries showing him that Dad wears headphones, too, to no avail, but once James puts headphones on the dog, the boy accepts.

"There's still a part of me that doesn't want to give away our innermost fears—our big fear of intimacy," James stated in 2004. "I still struggle with this every day. But I know this has the potential to help other bands and other people." And it does—five years after entering rehab, James won the MusiCares Stevie Ray Vaughan award for helping addicts with recovery.

But the struggle within stays with Metallica and James, who, post-rehab, still used present tense when describing drinking as a part of him, something he'd work on his entire life. On September 27, 2019, nearly eighteen years after first going to rehab and the thirty-third anniversary of Cliff Burton's death, Metallica announced that James, "struggling with addiction on and off for many years," was heading back to a treatment center. All shows for nearly a year were canceled, while metal world names offered support and shared stories about James (Randy Blythe: "James and crew babied me through my first month of sobriety out there on the road—it was a heavy trip. I couldn't have done it without them."). It wasn't until Metallica's killer drive-in theater comeback show in August 2020 ("Pandemica") that James could be seen at his best again. "We're not sure what everyone out there has been doing, but I know they've been listening to music and they've been praying and praying for something live they could grasp onto," James said between songs. "Because music helps us through all things, including this."

This monster lives, in addiction, turmoil, and disasters. But Metallica doesn't stop.

22

POWERHOUSE OF ENERGY

Robert Trujillo

"There's this whole mystique about what they're like, you know, the evil Metallica. I didn't see that. Actually, at first, not seeing the evil Metallica kind of made me uncomfortable."

—Robert Trujillo

The results of Metallica's bassist auditions were known before *Some Kind of Monster*, but it's still a thrill to watch some of America's best bass slingers take their shot at "For Whom the Bell Tolls" and a place in metal immortality. Twiggy Ramirez (Marilyn Manson), Pepper Keenan (Corrosion of Conformity), Danny Lohner (Nine Inch Nails), Eric Avery (Jane's Addiction), Mike Inez (Alice in Chains), Scott Reeder (Kyuss), and Chris Wyse (the Cult) are among the hopefuls, along with some unknowns, all of whom bring some degree of awesomeness to Metallica. But so does Roberto Agustín Miguel Santiago Samuel Trujillo Veracruz.

From a technical standpoint, Robert is the best of the group. He's the only prospective Metallica bassist likely to produce a documentary on the legendary jazz bassist and composer Jaco Pastorius (2015's excellent *Jaco*). His funk metal stylin' was at the forefront of his stint in Suicidal Tendencies, shifting the band's sound from hardcore to thrash. Check out ST's 1987 single "Possessed to Skate" followed by their 1997 rerecording with Trujillo and see how long it takes to realize it's the same song. Lately, Rob's been holding down the low end for the Prince of

Darkness himself, joining Ozzy's band in the late nineties. At the time of his Metallica audition, he's been trying to hide from MTV's cameras for *The Osbournes*, only to run right into Metallica, insisting anyone who auditions has to be filmed for what will turn into *Some Kind of Monster*.

Metallica takes Robert out for lunch, and he makes the final list along with Reeder, Keenan, and Ramirez. Lars is enamored of the rock star stylishness of Ramirez, who went by Jeordie White when he was covering "Trapped Under Ice" with his first high school band, the Ethiopians. James likes his touring and recording buddy Keenan, who matches Hetfield's musical sensibilities but is wary about joining a band with therapist. (Jason, in the press, suggests Armored Saint's Joey Vera and amazingly says Megadeth's Dave Ellefson, loyalist to one of metal's most erratic bandleaders, has the talent for Metallica but couldn't put up with the bosses.) But Robert pulls out a five-string and auditions with "Battery," a song he'd mastered as far back as 2001, when he covered it for the Metallica tribute album *Metallic Assault*. Robert aces "Battery" with the energy of a star and the skill of a pro. He gives the song a funk-based swing that shouldn't work at all and somehow sounds terrific. James, looking dazzled, lets out an enthusiastic laugh and Metallica ends with a flourish, which Robert catches within a blink. Like Cliff Burton, Robert doesn't use a pick, having learned finger-picking from watching his flamenco guitarist father. He's wearing a purple shirt, unwittingly having picked James' favorite color, and imperceptibly suffering from what he'd recall as "literally the worst hangover of my life," on three hours of sleep after Lars took him drinking from 11 p.m. through 5 a.m. the night before. He speaks in the buzzed, good-natured tone of a Tommy Chong character.

James, working through the abandonment issues that helped push Jason out of the band, is initially skeptical of Robert's tendency to leave his bands after a few years. So is Phil Towle, who, in an uncomfortable *Some Kind of Monster* outtake, asks Robert whether he likes having separate projects or wants to really commit to one, to Lars' annoyance. James can take solace in remembering that Rob has already survived a bassist hazing from Metallica, buying Rob shots on the Shit Hits the Sheds tour without taking any for themselves.

For the first time in their auditions, Metallica needed a veteran and not a kid. They were kids when they recruited Dave, Cliff, Kirk, and Jason, but now they need an adult to help take Metallica through middle age. They also need chemistry—Metallica's worst music, like *St. Anger* and the Ramones covers, came from sessions where they didn't have an official bassist, despite Bob Rock's talents. They tell Rob they'll let him know by Thursday. They end up calling him Wednesday to see if he can meet them in the next twenty-four hours. When Robert walks into the room, they all clap.

Metallica take turns praising Rob and give him $1 million plus an advance to join. In one of the film's best scenes, Metallica's lawyer tells the band that Robert is getting five percent ownership in Metallica with a correspondingly small vote on business decisions. James and Lars reject this immediately and insist on Robert getting equality, twenty-five percent for all, and the terms are changed. But the film's best scene comes when Rob does a celebratory dance to "Invisible Kid." He shows the joie de vivre of a kid playing air bass in his room, only this kid has chops and moves (as a boy in West LA, Robert entered pop-locking dance contests with friends). He gives "Invisible Kid" a groove that's almost impossible to hear on *St. Anger* and impossible not to hear after seeing his moves. James cackles at this moment in the *Some Kind of Monster* commentary. "This is my favorite scene, man, this is so great," he laughs. "Awesome."

In the Metallica tradition of hazing bassists, Robert forces himself to listen to and learn *St. Anger*'s songs days before going straight to San Quentin State Prison for his first Metallica gig. His second gig is the next day, at Metallica's *MTV Icon* performance. Rob's third show is for 60,000 people at a stadium in Europe. Perhaps knowing the Jason Newsted story, his friends ask him whether Metallica is treating him right (Ozzy: "I'll kill 'em if they mess with you! I'll kill 'em!").

"Metallica is the most strenuous gig I've ever been involved with," Robert has stated. "I mean that in a good way. The most challenging physically, for sure . . . they want you to cover all angles of the stage." He adapted in part by hiring Kirk's cousin as a full-time chiropractor. But Rob pushes Metallica as much as they push him. Upon joining, he'd say the two songs he most wanted to play were "Dyers Eve" and "The Frayed Ends of Sanity," two of Metallica's most difficult and two of their only originals they'd never played live. When his bandmates struggle to name newer bands they've been enjoying, Rob can talk about Meshuggah, Radiohead, and Candiria. He even gives Metallica shit when they deserve it—promoting the then-untitled follow-up to *St. Anger* in *Rock Hard*, Rob stated, "I would say this album is dynamic, groovin' and you'll probably be excited to know that there will be guitar solos on it! In addition, Lars remembered to tune his snare drum properly this time!" That said, in 2009's *Orgullo, Pasión, y Gloria: Tres Noches en la Ciudad de México*, fans not only hold up *St. Anger* but get carried away enough to shout that's Robert's first record with Metallica (sorry, Bob Rock).

But Rob is best amplifying Metallica in their natural habitat, onstage. During "Seek & Destroy," he swings his bass around in a wild, athletic spin, throwing the instrument back under his arm right in time to boost the final verse. It's not the kind of move anyone could imagine Cliff Burton or Jason Newsted pulling off. That's not a knock on either of those bassists, each the best low ender Metallica could find. But Metallica's bassist has to be a prototype. Paraphrasing Hunter S. Thompson (Rob is a big fan), Rob is a high-powered mutant of some kind never even considered for mass production. Rob knows he's not there to play Cliff or Jason's parts. (Rob: "I have utmost respect for Jason. I don't think of it as me replacing someone. I think of it as a new beginning.") Rob doesn't just complete Metallica, he improves them. He's there to be the grinning, dancing, crab-walking, rambunctious bassist in the greatest band in the world. He's there to be Rob.

LIGHTS . . . CAMERA . . . REVOLUTION!

"A lot of that funk, it's from the earth, it's organic," Robert states in *Rumble: The Indians Who Rocked the World*. "It comes from the war dances. There's something tribal about it."

Born in Santa Monica, Rob's parents split when he was five but passed down a love for music to their son. His carpenter father loved the Stones and Led Zeppelin, while his mother turned him on to Sly and the Family Stone, James Brown, and Marvin Gaye. He grew up with family in rival Culver City and Venice gangs, which made family gatherings complicated. Around age ten he went to the record store for his first LP, deciding between Kool & the Gang's *Spirit of the Boogie* or Santana's *Abraxas*. He went with Santana, turned on by the surreal Mati Klarwein cover art.

Robert wanted to be a drummer, but his family couldn't afford a drum kit (years later, he'd distinguish himself from Jason Newsted by playing more with Metallica's drums than guitar). But in 1978 at Southern California music festival Cal Jam II, thirteen-year-old Rob saw funk rock one-hit-wonders Rubicon ("I'm Gonna Take Care of Everything") on a bill with Aerosmith, Heart, and Foreigner. Rubicon bassist Jack Blades (yes, the future Night Ranger guy) took a solo, and shortly afterward Rob picked up a shabby old hollow body bass from a family friend. It didn't play well, and the action was an inch off the fretboard, but Rob trained all the harder.

He loved hard rock, funk, jazz, and artists like Geddy Lee, John Paul Jones, Chris Squire, and Stanley Clarke. But like all bassists, Robert was blown away by one Jaco Pastorius. "Hearing him was like hearing Eddie Van Halen doing 'Eruption' for the first time," Robert stated. "You thought, 'What instrument is that?' . . . He was funk, he was rock, he was soul. And his whole attitude was punk."

At Culver City High School Rob was a creative kid who loved sports, music, and literature. In his senior yearbook message, he wrote that he planned on studying bass at Musicians Institute and becoming "rich & famous like Led Zeppelin." He also acted, getting a few seconds of screen time in the 1978 Walter Matthau film *House Calls* and the 1980 Gary Coleman TV movie *Scout's Honor*, as well as a small role in a 1982 episode of *CHiPs* called "Rock Devil Rock," about a Kiss-like band (co-starring Elvira, Mistress of the Dark). You can also find him online in a 1989 Yellow Pages commercial looking for a kilt, and appearing with Infectious Grooves in a dance number in the 1992 Brendan Fraser comedy *Encino Man*.

Inevitably, Rob grew into a huge *Ride the Lightning* and *Master of Puppets* fan: "What was so special about Metallica was the creative energy that seemed to flow out of their songs," he'd relate. "They took a genre of music and filled it with a lot of non-pedestrian elements, particularly when it came to what Cliff Burton was doing on the bass."

Rob started playing metal, covering Ozzy and Black Sabbath songs in his high school band Oblivion. But through his Culver City buddy Rocky George he joined punk metal innovators Suicidal Tendencies in 1989, bringing them a funk edge and their biggest commercial success to date on *Lights . . . Camera . . . Revolution!* and *The Art of Rebellion*. Touring and recording was arduous and the band temporarily broke up in 1995, but

Rob, known as "Stymee" ("ST why me?") in the band's liner notes, made himself a metal bass star on songs like "You Can't Bring Me Down," "Send Me Your Money," and "Nobody Hears." He also connected to metal's biggest artists, bringing in Ozzy Osbourne for ST funk metal side band Infectious Grooves' hit "Therapy" and opening for Metallica with Suicidal Tendencies in 1993–94, even performing "So What" with the headliners in Chicago. (James: "I used to think, 'Holy shit, I wouldn't want to get in an alley with them.'") Rob's influence on ST's sound made him an in-demand bassist, and he performed on records by Glenn Tipton, Mass Mental, Jerry Cantrell, Black Label Society, and Ozzy Osbourne before finding his home in Metallica. "He sits down and channels into what goes on in nanoseconds," Lars noted.

"It is nice having another calm person in the camp," James said in a 2003 interview. "He's up for a challenge, all the time. . . . We try and mess with him, 'Hey, you know we're gonna play "Disposable Heroes" you know, ten minutes before we go on.' . . . He'll go learn it! . . . We hope he feels like this is his family for good."

"It's like the best university you could go to," Rob says of Metallica. "This is a smart outfit, and there's a lot of soul in it, too."

In 2017 Robert Trujillo became Metallica's longest-lasting bassist. He seems poised to stay, against the grain until the end.

23

SET MY ANGER FREE

St. Anger

*"We've got something up our asses that makes us want to go,
'We've done that, let's do something else, I'm bored, let's go
somewhere.' We've had that hunger since day one. That, mixed
with total, pure, from-the-heart honesty."*

—James Hetfield

What in the fresh hell is *St. Anger*? Nearly twenty years after its release,
barely anyone wants to reevaluate it or give it contrarian "Why this
album actually rules" takes. Fans who are bold or misanthropic enough
to put on *St. Anger* again still can't make much sense of it, which may be
why *St. Anger* still gets more discourse than some of the better albums that
followed it. But whatever one thinks of *St. Anger*'s music, or its production, or the fact that Metallica thought it was a good idea to release it, it's
an undeniable purge, a catharsis Metallica needed to beat out of themselves whether or not the results were enjoyable for anybody. In *St. Anger*'s
booklet, the record is dedicated to Phil Towle and Bob Rock, two people
Metallica purged along with the songs.

Monsters abound on *St. Anger*. In *Some Kind of Monster*, James refers to
Frankenstein's monster twice, in describing the qualities he'd like to take
from different potential bassists and in discussing putting songs together.
The songs feel more stitched together than organic, like one of Kirk's rean-
imated creatures. "The guy that writes the songs couldn't do it because of

where he was personally," Bob Rock told *Brave Words & Bloody Knuckles*. "So what *St. Anger* became was what the band could do at that point." The title came from Kirk's St. Christopher medallion 'round his neck, a gift from his first wife, featuring a surfer and the words "Come back" on the flip side. "There's a lot of fucking residual anger that came from our childhoods and it's something that fame, money and celebrity is not an antidote for," Kirk told *Classic Rock*. "We were very angry young men and now we're very angry middle-aged men."

"Anger has kinda been this part of me that I've tried to embrace, I've tried to hide, I've tried to do everything with, and it is just a part of me, so I celebrate it," said James in 2017.

It's Metallica's first record where they hit the studio with no riffs, lyrics, or titles, and likely the first-ever album recorded with both a therapist and a film crew. Songs were written and recorded on the spot, played live without overdubs. In Bob's memory, it only took ten minutes to find the drum sound, distinguished by a clanging, jarringly loud snare that made Lars sound like he was banging on trash can lids. (Lars: "It sang back to me in a beautiful way.") It was an unpleasant experience for fans trying to forget Lars' ego, almost as bad as "Shoot Me Again," allegedly inspired by the Napster debacle.

Metallica itself is a stitched together monster on *St. Anger*, a four-headed beast with the engineer sewn over the gaping wound left by the bassist, forcing itself to stay together. Out of over thirty songs considered for the record, only the first four tracks were agreed on by James, Lars, Kirk, and Bob. "In the song 'All Within My Hands' I recognized that I choke the band to death," reflected James. "I had panic attacks that Jason or even Lars would start other projects and like it better than Metallica. To hold the band together I forced Lars, Jason and Kirk to stay and to go on. I love Metallica so much that I almost crushed the band with my love."

As seen in *Some Kind of Monster*, James recorded his vocals in the open instead of in a booth, which adds to the record's raw sound. The Dadaist, cut-up lyrics come from each bandmate contributing for the first time. James has said that it was easier to let go of lyric-writing for *St. Anger* than he thought it'd be, describing the record as "being able to express anger in a healthy way, instead of just shutting up and being intimidating and then raging out on someone when it all builds up" while noting that *Load* and *Reload* had been more of a burden than a release for him. He's called writing his therapy, but on *St. Anger* his therapy was $40,000-a-month performance coaching. Bringing therapy to their music space made it Metallica's primary focus, a bigger part of their lives than the record (and thanks to *Some Kind of Monster*, a bigger part of their legacy). Digging out the personas of James, Kirk, and Lars from the lyrics is an exercise for anyone who can stomach the record. "Frantic" closes its last verse reciting dukkha, which Kirk got from the Four Noble Truths of Buddhism and James got from Samhain's "Macabre." But elsewhere James is reduced to barking out "lifestyle/deathstyle" couplets than would have gotten him laughed out of most high school poetry readings. (James: "That's the line most people talk about. Very cool.") *Some Kind of Monster* reveals that worse lyrics were written out before the record's release, though somehow "madly in anger with you" made the cut.

How did this happen? A Bob Rock production should at least sound great. But if Metallica leapt outside their comfort zone by making *St. Anger*, Bob did the same by ignoring his engineering chops. Recording sessions started in the cold, uncomfortable former US Army barracks at the Presidio in San Francisco, before halting for James' rehab. "There were lots of times where I wanted to sing something over because I knew I could sing it better, but that's not what the part called out for," James remembered. "The part called out for something spontaneous, it called out for the moment." Hearing James close the record by yelling "Kill" until his voice goes out is stirring, even if it might not make you put on the record again.

St. Anger dropped in June 2003 and reviews were positive, including four stars from *Rolling Stone*, 9/10 from *NME*, and an A– from *Spin*. In hindsight, Metallica had gone from being the crossover metal band hipster publications would love to an Emperor's New Clothes–type giant no one wanted to admit was standing naked. Metallica's flop still sold six million copies worldwide, as if no music fan could believe the incredible Metallica could drop such a suckbomb, especially when they'd gotten *Load* and *Reload* out of their system and were returning to thrash. *St. Anger* wasn't the first subpar Metallica record, but it was the first sign that Metallica might be irreparably damaged. Longtime fans had clamored for the raw, heavy songs of old, and as far back as 1999 Lars was telling interviewers he wanted the next record to be "really brutal and harsh and fucked up and ugly," having gotten blues-based riffage out of his system. *St. Anger* was Metallica's most riff-heavy record to date, but it showed Metallica getting savage again only made their music worse.

It's dated not so much for its lack of solos, enforced by James and Lars against Kirk's wishes, but for sounding unlike anything that isn't *St. Anger*. Bob Rock would say the lack of solos was inspired by Iggy and the Stooges' *Raw Power* and San Francisco instrumentalists the Fucking Champs, but by winter 2003 Metallica had given "Dirty Window" a guitar solo live, indicating that they already knew they had fucked up. Metallica's peaks are better than the best metal, but *St. Anger* showed their lows would be worse. "Between Nickelback and whatever else is on US radio these days, obviously it sounds odd and challenging," Lars told MTV. "But look, it's our biggest record in Europe since the Black Album. And in America I'm really digging being the outsiders again 20 years into our career."

Having initially told reporters he loved *St. Anger* so much it was "sickening," James later referred to it as "the low point" and "a purge, just getting that shit out of me as a catalyst for the next chapter." Even touring behind the record, James seemed ready to let it go. "How many of you have brought some anger here with you tonight?" he sometimes asked the crowd. "So have I . . . and I'm leaving it right here tonight."

"It's more of the soundtrack to the movie, in a way," James told Team-Rock in 2016. "Sonically it sounds fragmented, which is exactly where we were at the point. But in that fragmentation it brought us together."

Today, *St. Anger* songs have mostly left the setlist. "St. Anger" was voted for and played again once on the Metallica by Request tour in 2014, and "All Within My Hands" was performed acoustically in 2018. But on May 1, 2019, in Portugal, Metallica played "Frantic." James charges the crowd with a "Hey" and the Lisboners oblige him by singing the riff. It sounds better than any version of "Frantic" you've heard before. The indie folk songwriter Phoebe Bridgers later remembered *St. Anger* making her a

Metallica fan, defending it ("*St. Anger* is a great record") in a 2020 interview with Lars. And in September 2020, the *S&M2* version of "All Within My Hands" made Metallica the first band to have #1 rock songs in four different decades, seventeen years after most people turned off *St. Anger* before even getting to "All Within My Hands." Like the band that made it, *St. Anger* still surprises, and can never be ruled out.

SOME KIND OF MONSTER

Roger Ebert, who understood movies better than just about anyone has ever understood anything, was perplexed by *Some Kind of Monster*. More specifically, he couldn't figure out its characters. He ended his positive review: "What Dr. Phil [Towle] should probably advise Metallica is to call it a day. Why work with people you can't stand, doing work you're sick of, and that may be killing you? Lots of people have jobs like that, but Metallica has a choice."

Roger may be one of the most astute critics to ever type a page, but he got this one wrong. One lesson in *Some Kind of Monster* is that Metallica doesn't have a choice. They're creatively bankrupt and going for each other's throats. They have immeasurable legacies, unimaginable wealth, and loving families. It'd be illogical for Metallica to stay together and make a record, but that's all they can do. It doesn't matter if they're playing with people they hate and releasing their worst ideas. They couldn't stop making music any more than Roger could stop writing about movies. Metallica make music because they can't not do it. "There is this thing in them wound up in them so tight, that they have to let it out, let that thing uncoil. It has to be released," the Red Hot Chili Peppers' Flea marveled while inducting Metallica into the Rock Hall.

"We've all got kids, we've all got other lives, but we can't live without Metallica," James has said.

In *Some Kind of Monster*, Metallica take the Beatles' *Let It Be* film a step further by making the most unguarded documentary of a major rock band, inventing new ways to show anger and vulnerabilities when it can't come out enough in their music. It's called *Some Kind of Monster*, but the more important lyric is the next one, "This monster lives." The monster has not been killed. Metallica has evolved to live with it. Rock theorists from Young to Elliott have proposed that it's better to burn out than fade away, but Metallica forges another road. The posters in the studio are of survivors—Lemmy, *Deliverance*, *Exile on Main St.*, reminding them to plow through the trauma. (There's also briefly a shirtless picture of Godsmack's Sully Erna in the Presidio near Lars' drum kit, but maybe that's serving a purpose like the Kip Winger poster in *A Year and a Half in the Life of Metallica*.) Now the survivors are Metallica, plastered on the walls of innumerable artists as a reminder that they, too, can make it through. Radiohead's Colin Greenwood admitted to watching *Some Kind of Monster* six or seven times. U2 parodied *Some Kind of Monster* in a video for Metallica's thirtieth anniversary, sitting on a couch and agonizing over their inadequacy (The Edge: "Kirk is so fast . . . and that hair!"). "Metallica now owns the 'band in turmoil' zone of the public imagination," Chad Clark of the Washington, DC, band Beauty Pill has said. "If you have a squabble in your band, your friends will say 'Oh man, that sucks.' Pause. 'Kind of like Metallica, right?'"

"I love the fact that bands come up on the road and say 'It's safe. It's safe now for us to be human.' It's okay to be in trouble. It's okay to have fear. It's okay to not know what you're doing. And it's okay to tell that to your brothers in your band," James said in 2014.

Making a documentary as candid as Metallica's music means showing their fans the worst. *Metallica vs. Napster, Inc.* had ended in March 2001, one month before *Some Kind of Monster* started filming, but Metallica included it in the film to show they weren't brushing over something that was still looming over them. At a particularly bleak moment Joe Berlinger comforted James by suggesting there might not be a movie. But this isn't a band that looks for comfort, and James went along with it. Plans to do about four to six weeks of Metallica promo turn into a two- and half-year undertaking. The band approached therapy almost superficially at first, as an afterthought to the new album, but Francesca throwing James out the house underscored the problems' urgency.

"She did the right thing, and she kicked my ass, right the hell out of the house. That scared the shit out of me," James recalled in 2017. "There's no way we're going to let arguments get in the way. We're survivors, and we're going to talk through it."

We see yelling, door-slamming fights that uncover the childish, self-centered worst in James and Lars. (James: "There were a lot of times where I saw myself as I did not want to see myself.") James misses his son's first birthday to go to Siberia for a vodka-fueled bear hunting trip, and Lars is petulant about everything from Jason's new band to Kirk getting more attention at his birthday party. But *Some Kind of Monster* is the fire Metallica walked through to improve themselves and their band, as well as see the difference between the two. Showing the world an insecure Metallica cleared up some of the Napster debacle, either by humanizing them or creating a bigger spectacle for people to poke at. Years later, James would tell *Guitar World* that he gave up hunting after the Siberia trip ("Nowadays it doesn't feel necessary"), replaced in his life by another pastime his father didn't teach him—restoring and customizing cars (James' impressive collection can be seen in the *Reclaimed Rust* exhibit at the Los Angeles' Petersen Automotive Museum, as well as a corresponding book with the same title). After years of changing the world by exploring its darkness, Metallica needed to change themselves the same way.

This came through Phil Towle, who had previously helped the St. Louis Rams on the way to their 2000 Super Bowl championship and had been called in by Q Prime to save Rage Against the Machine in the months leading up to their breakup. Lars had noticed a 1999 MTV special in which frontman Zack de la Rocha had to be interviewed separately from his Rage Against the Machine bandmates, around the time Jason wasn't joining Lars, Kirk, and James in the press room.

Metallica have credited Phil for saving the band, with James going so far as to call Phil "like an angel for me." They have said that the film doesn't give Towle enough credit for keeping the band together. (Lars: "Phil Towle said, when we were nearing the end of *St. Anger*, that everything we went through then would not come to fruition until the next go-round . . . he was really right about that.") But one thing that keeps the film engaging is that nearly everyone involved with the movie could use a therapist. Bob Rock hopes he isn't having too much as Metallica's bassist, telling Metallica he doesn't think they'll ever settle on a permanent bassist and somewhat unconvincingly telling the filmmakers he doesn't want to join the band full-time. Dave Mustaine's insatiable grudge is as penetrating as James and Lars' most personal moments. Berlinger and Sinofsky's relationship was strained enough by *Some Kind of Monster* to send them to group therapy. Even Jason, Metallica's most dedicated supporter, complains about Metallica needing outside help to solve their problems. He's game for an almost unendurable amount of hazing, one of the most strenuous live gigs in music, and hours upon hours of fan inter-action, but therapy was not part of his Metallica experience. Jason called bringing Phil onboard "really fucking lame and weak," incredulous that Metallica couldn't manage their own problems (Lars sounds like he can almost quote Jason's full comment word for word on the *Some Kind of Monster* commentary). An attempt at an on-camera reunion for the movie fell through when Jason thought Peter Mensch had Voivod kicked off a bill (Mensch denies this), leading to an outtake where the band listens to a voicemail where Jason, maybe still smarting from earlier harassment, calls his former bandmates "a bunch of homos." Lars is angered, but James has a more relaxed reaction.

"Maybe the 'homo' thing he's talking about, is this," reflects James. "Get-ting in touch with feelings and stuff. I think he's fearful of this process, and how it's working for us, and how strong it is. . . . Years ago, if I would have heard this stuff, 'What? Just rock, man! Metal's in my veins,' you know? And you know, 'Screw all that feelings stuff!' I can relate to maybe where he's coming from on that."

But a trained psychologist or psychiatrist (Phil is neither) might have the most work with Phil himself, whose attachment to Metallica is already feeling invasive by the time he sells his home in Kansas City and talks about having "performance coach visions for each of you," implying that he's moving to San Francisco to be closer to the band. In outtakes, Phil refers to the band as "we" and even jokes about blaming problems on Lars. In one of the film's most uncomfortable moments, Phil gives James lyrics he's written for the new record. (James: "I kept having flashbacks to that guy who began writing lyrics with Brian Wilson and eventually moved in with him and took over his life.")

Some Kind of Monster shows James learning to create boundaries for himself, and on camera he's unsure this crosses one. But Phil's clinginess leads to James and Lars' ultimate reconciliation: firing Phil. James acknowledges Phil's protests and even his insistence that the sessions aren't finished while putting his foot down, firmly ending the relationship. James later recalled not noticing that Lars was in the same room, either because he was zeroing in on Phil or because Lars having James' back feels natural to him. Metallica is at their best uniting against adversity, even within their inner circle.

"Phil has issues, too," James told the *New York Times*. "Every therapist has issues. We're all just people. We've all got some brokenness inside us. Phil's abandonment issues came up, and he tried to mask them by saying, 'You're mistrusting me.' And it's like, wow—that's a really important point in the movie."

Showing Metallica at their lowest gave them more freedom to be themselves than before. Elektra wanted to promote *St. Anger* and cash in on America's *Osbournes* craze by turning the footage into a reality TV show leading up to the album's release. But Metallica didn't want *Some Kind of Monster* to look staged, or to coincide with *St. Anger*, and ended up bankrolling the film themselves, after giving Berlinger and Sinofsky creative control. While not a box office success, it stands as the biggest part of Metallica's legacy outside the recording studio, the thing most people can name about Metallica besides their music. Lines and moments from the movie are embedded in the metal lexicon, fodder for years of inspiration and derision, sometimes both at the same time. Introducing Lars Ulrich's appearance on *Late Night with Conan O'Brien*, Max Weinberg's house band performed Joni Mitchell's "Twisted" ("My analyst told me that I was straight outta my head"). Animated TV show *Metalocalypse* gave its band Dethklok a therapist in the episode "PerformanceKlok," whose methods and attachment spoofed Phil Towle's. *Some Kind of Monster* gives fans one more thing to argue about, debating whether the movie saved Metallica or ruined them. But like everything Metallica does, *Some Kind of Monster* looks crazy to some people and emboldens others.

"Whether people look at us as a bunch of freaks or a bunch of pioneers doesn't matter that much to me," James stated in 2004. "The fact is that we're doing it and getting a lot better at just letting go of what other people perceive."

"No matter what's going on in your life, no matter how much the resentment you have for somebody, or how much darkness is in your soul, that you think you have, you can get through it," James has described *Some Kind of Monster*'s legacy. "You can overcome it. And you can stand on that stage, or whatever it is, in your life, and let people love you back . . . just for exactly who you are."

HEAVEN YOU WILL MEET

Metallica's Spirituality

"I have bitterness that formed around the religious part of my upbringing, but not the spiritual part."

—James Hetfield

James Hetfield sent the metal community into shockwaves in 2017, when a reporter for the French publication *Clique* asked him whether he believed in God.

"I believe in a higher power, yes," Hetfield responded. "He, she, it . . . I see it everywhere. It is everything to me. And if I choose to see it, it makes me feel better." James continued, "Sometimes I think . . . 'Oh, it's my father coming back to help me,' or my mother, or somebody, or Cliff. . . . It shows up in my wife a lot. She will say, 'What are you doing? Don't do that.' That used to make me angry. 'Don't tell me what to do.' But, okay, I understand that something is here helping me."

Could this be? The skeptic who tore himself from his Christian Science upbringing to write antitheist anthems like "Leper Messiah" and "The God That Failed" believes in God? Internet commenters, some of whom apparently were still recovering from James' 2010 assertion that he was "reborn straight edge" (cemented by his hand-drawn straight edge "X" tattoo, referencing the hardcore punk subculture associated with Minor Threat) or thanking a "higher power" in numerous acceptance speeches, were champing at the bit. A closer look at James reveals many faith-based tattoos, including a higher power eye, an angel coming through fire, "*Donum Dei,*" "Faith," and a prominent St. Michael, famously the leader of God's angels in the fight against Satan in the New Testament and in *Paradise Lost,* two texts with ambiguous sympathies in the struggles between good and evil, God and mankind. (James has a fascination with angels: "My parents leaving this earth earlier than others, having some kind of guide in my life.")

Of course, anyone who read James' response with an ounce of curiosity could learn that the term "higher power" comes from Alcoholics Anonymous co-founder Bill W.'s 1939 book *Alcoholics Anonymous: The Story of How Many Thousands of Men and Women Have Recovered from Alcoholism* (widely known by readers as "The Big Book," which may have resonated with a guy whose biggest-selling record got its popular name from outsiders). The term, used in AA and other recovery programs, is referred to as a belief in something greater that expresses faith in its believer.

Like his hero Nick Cave, Hetfield struggled with a spiritually abusive upbringing, and released the religious imagery and ideology he'd been abused by in his words. Dave White of the San Francisco thrashers Heathen compared young James' stage persona to Linda Blair's Regan MacNeil from *The Exorcist.* "Creeping Death" is close to scripture, and James describes his mother's death in "The God That Failed" as "the healing hand held back by the deepened nail." "Holier Than Thou" interpolates Jesus in in the Gospel of Matthew, throwing Christ's words right back at Christian hypocrites (maybe some of the ones who picket Metallica shows). The body that lies but still roams on "Wherever I May Roam" might be a zombie, or mythology James learned from Jesus and Lazarus. The "four winds" referenced in "The Four Horsemen" show up in Revelations 7:1, preceding the book's Four Horsemen of the Apocalypse, unleashed by the opening of the first four of seven seals. The song's bridge adapts the symbols of each horse—white (Conquest/Pestilence), red (War), black (Famine), and pale (Death)—while James barks out corresponding punishments (yes, it's possible Metallica were mythologizing the four members of their own band). To paraphrase Flannery O'Connor, while Metallica is hardly Christ-centered, it is most certainly Christ-haunted.

"I know there's plenty of people out there that religion works for them," James said on *WTF with Marc Maron.* "I understand the concept of a higher power and it does work for me, but religion itself fucked me up. Especially that one, when I was young."

Metallica is often believed to be sinful or even Satanic by detractors and fans alike (the indie outsider artist Daniel Johnston famously turned down a generous record deal offer from Elektra in fear of Metallica's supposed Satanism, but lesser known is that he was a big fan who owned all their records). But Metallica's antitheism is not a celebration. While other metal bands expressed gleeful Satanism, Metallica poured religious anguish into their songs. "Leper Messiah," inspired by Sunday night TV preachers, plays on words from Ecclesiastes to attack the institution, not the religion. Metallica condemns the congregation flock as "sheep," and their Sunday needs as a "fix," using the same word from "Master of Puppets," skewering evangelism years before Ozzy's "Miracle Man" and Suicidal Tendencies' "Send Me Your Money" (point drilled in by Robert Trujillo, who's been the bassist for all three). When James begs for God's help in the bridge of "Ride the Lighting," it's a desperate last resort. Metallica doesn't preach, but they also don't blaspheme. Their understanding of religion and defiance of its institutions is part of what makes Metallica giants. In Metallica's words, the Four Horsemen and the Ten Plagues are as brutal as anything Stephen King or Clive Barker could dream up.

25

CRAWL FROM
THE WRECKAGE

Death Magnetic

"You can put your heart out there, no matter how black it is, and people can understand it."

—James Hetfield

Yⁿou hear it in the first few minutes of *Death Magnetic*. It's hard to pinpoint where, while the mile-a-minute hooks are throwing you off your rocker, but it's palpable. Metallica is back, Metallica rules, Metallica is the greatest fucking rock band in the world. By the end of *Death Magnetic*, it's a pretty good record. *Death Magnetic* finds Metallica as Batman in Frank Miller's *The Dark Knight Returns*, or Clint Eastwood in *Unforgiven*. The greatest badass is back, missing a step or two from his old self but bringing the toughness and attitude that earned him the reverence of millions. After years out of favor and the public eye, Metallica is going to hunt you down without mercy.

Starting with the distant rhythm of a pulsating heartbeat, *Death Magnetic* comes to life before the instruments even kick in. It might reference the first monster Kirk Hammett watched break free, or the heartbeat intro tape Metallica used at some of their earliest shows. ("Really terrible," James remembered years later. Jonny Z suggested "The Ecstasy of Gold" instead.) Having conquered the metal world, the rock world, and now the music world, Metallica now confronts mortality on songs like "The End of the Line" and "My Apocalypse." Repeating Nietzsche's most overquoted mantra in "Broken, Beat & Scarred," Hetfield sounds like he's chanting the idiom to himself to keep from going over the edge. Appropriately enough, *Rolling Stone*'s Brian Hiatt pointed out the quote is from Nietzsche's *Twilight of the Idols, or, How to Philosophize with a Hammer*.

Reviews comparing *Death Magnetic* to a midlife crisis were not wrong. Metallica thrives in crisis. In this case, that meant leaving the comfort zone they'd developed with Bob Rock, the producer who'd become Metallica family, having helped whip them into transcendence on the Black Album and held them together on *St. Anger* (in *Some Kind of Monster* outtakes, James bosses Bob on basslines to the point where one could forget who the producer is). Rock and Metallica split graciously, with James telling *Guitar World* he missed Bob and felt scared they couldn't make a record without him. "We needed someone to be a pain in the ass," noted Lars, years away from complaining Bob was too big a pain in the ass on the Black Album.

The most obvious thought any metalhead seeking out Rick Rubin could have would be to get the guy behind *Reign in Blood*. But James has said Rubin's *American* series with Johnny Cash drew him to the producer. Ideologically if not sonically, *Death Magnetic* is looking more to old Johnny Cash than young Slayer ("The New Song," one of two new, unreleased songs performed on the Escape from the Studio '06 tour, describes a man in black who comes around). During the sessions, James watched an old Cash interview in which he discusses a near-death experience. "When he came back he had this new love of life, and an intensity around it," James related. "I somewhat connected with that, because of Metallica almost disappearing, or disintegrating . . . death is not a new subject for us, but the way we're writing about it now, or the way I'm perceiving it, is the positive side, maybe . . . or maybe death is not the end."

Rubin gave them an autonomy they'd been lacking, often not showing up to the studio and leaving the band, in James' words, "pretty much on our own." (James: "Bob is involved in every note, every decision, every sound. He has the schedule, he's got the agenda for the day. . . . Rick just wants to hear a good song.") This provoked Metallica to create that structure themselves. After years of warming up separately, they started rehearsing together again, learning the songs by heart to bring the spontaneity of Metallica's live shows to the studio. *Death Magnetic* is the first Metallica record to have all songs credited to all four members of the band (poor Jason).

Rick Rubin advised them to revisit their *Master of Puppets* mindset, but Metallica, thinking ahead, did so by finding the mentality of *Master*'s follow-up, . . . *And Justice for All*. Like *Justice*, *Death Magnetic* takes thrash to prog school, particularly in the ten-minute, hard-grinding instrumental "Suicide & Redemption" and the throbbing, drop D "All Nightmare Long," propelled by a Trujillo bassline but peaking with Kirk's solo fireworks in a top Metallica breakdown. When Metallica relaxes on "The Day That Never Comes," they're gearing up for its piledriving second movement. *Death Magnetic* shows Metallica jumping the trends they invented, taking inspiration from the greatest metal band ever and daring their younger rivals to try.

But if . . . *And Justice for All* rages against the machine, *Death Magnetic* rages against the dying of the light. Metallica recorded it with a picture of the late Layne Staley in studio, whose surviving bandmates James appeared onstage twice with in 2006, and tackled the self-destructive tendencies that had almost torn them apart in songs like the blazing "That Was Just Your Life" and "Cyanide," the latter sporting a riff and drum rejoinder playing the same Morse code "S.O.S." rhythm that fades out "London Calling." The cover showed a coffin in a freshly dug grave, but was abstract enough for fans to speculate—was it really a coffin? A magnetic field? A portal? A door? A sexual organ?—with each page of the liner notes crafted to look like another layer of dirt being thrown on the coffin.

But Metallica was born for dying, and sound most alive withstanding death. Liberated from the asphyxiating, solo-less *St. Anger*, Kirk Hammett unleashes some of his most fluid guitar work to date. His fretboard stunts on *Death Magnetic* leak out in short bursts, epic passages and wah-wah magic in the album's best moments, like the mouth-foaming closer "My Apocalypse," or Kirk's professed favorite "The Judas Kiss" (Nazareth fan James noted that the word "Judas" sang well).

James has said *Death Magnetic* was Metallica's easiest record to make, but that doesn't mean it wasn't work. "All Nightmare Long" was born a lot slower, with its origins heard in a *Some Kind of Monster* Presidio jam, and can be heard with parts of "The End of the Line" in the unreleased "The New Song," but Metallica saved it until they had the song and the bassist it deserved. Robert cemented his role as a Metallica writer, composing the song's intro on a flamenco guitar, hence the demo name "Flamingo." In an online making-of *Death Magnetic* clip, James and Kirk watch Rob work out on an acoustic. Kirk leans over to James: "Maybe you and I should just quit."

Death Magnetic shows James going further into some of his most personal themes. He described first single, "The Day That Never Comes," as "forgiveness and someone doing you wrong . . . being able to see through that in the next situation that might be similar and not take your rage and resentment out on the next person." He fought to get "Unforgiven III" on record, a shanty that bears little resemblance to the earlier Unforgivens (he might've had his preferred trilogy in mind, but even those weren't called *A Fistful of Dollars II* and *III*). "If there was any song that I could listen to a hundred times in a row that would be it," James told interviewers. "I may be sappy, but I like the kinda epic ballad, you know? It was important to make a diverse album this time around." James brought in the piano intro, a first on a Metallica record, with arrangement by David Campbell, known for his work on Carole King's *Tapestry*, Marvin Gaye's *Let's Get It On*, and Leonard Cohen's *The Future*, among many others (not to mention several records by his son, Beck Hansen).

"He sits down, listens to your music and says, 'That's great, that could be better, that doesn't work,'" reflected Lars on Rick Rubin. "What he doesn't do is sit there and go 'Try F-sharp after G and one more dB at 10k.'"

"The recording process becomes more like a gig," Lars elaborated. "Just going in and playing and leaving all the thinking at the door."

Annoyingly, the record could've used more thinking. The worst thing about *Death Magnetic* is how fixable its problems are. Rick Rubin and Metallica should have known to trim *Death Magnetic* to about forty-five minutes and give it a decent mix. The songs are compressed to the point of distortion, so much that a 2008 online petition asking the record to be remastered scored over twenty-two thousand signatures. Perhaps most egregiously, the record got a better mix on *Guitar Hero: Metallica*, which may have been a conscious decision to get fans deeper into the songs, remastering and remixing them from home. As with any old legend coming back, Metallica aren't perfect. To paraphrase one of Lars' favorite *Death Magnetic* songs, Metallica show their scars. But no amount of compression or turned-up drums can drown the potency of "All Nightmare Long."

Death Magnetic has several good songs, and a few great ones. It didn't make Metallica the best metal band in the world again, and most of its songs have since been nudged from Metallica's setlist. But Metallica was back in the ring. For the first time in years, the word on new Metallica music wasn't hoping it didn't suck, but wondering what was next.

"I HOPE THE METALLICAS DON'T PLAY TOO LOUD"

Metallica members have lent their voices to a number of cartoons, including *Dave the Barbarian*, *American Dad!*, and best of all *Metalocalypse*, wherein Kirk and James have voiced some of the show's best first season cameos. James has also narrated for History show *The Hunt*, and Metallica has been cited as a favorite band by characters on *Gilmore Girls*, *Criminal Minds*, *Supernatural*, *House*, and *Barry*. But their best-known TV show appearance came in 2006, when Metallica guested on *The Simpsons* episode "The Mook, the Chef, the Wife and Her Homer." The jokes were typically lame late-period *Simpsons* fare, but internet-savvy Metallifans lifted good GIF from it—*Simpsons* resident metalhead Otto (voiced, naturally, by Harry Shearer, Spīñal Tap's Derek Smalls) holding a lighter and yelling "Metallica ru-u-ules!" Otto had previously placed Metallica's Black Album twice on a list of his must-have CDs for *Entertainment Weekly*, both at #1 ("This is the record I lost my hearing to") and #5 ("Did I say this one already?").

ON YOUR FEET
FOR HONESTY
Metallica Fandom

"All are welcome in the Metallica family. There's no require-
ment, but it helps if you're a fuck up."

—James Hetfield

The *New York Times* podcast *Caliphate* follows the journalist Rukmini Callimachi in her coverage of the terrorist organization ISIS in Iraq. She's helped by a translator and fixer called "Hawk" (not the guy involved in the later *Caliphate* scandal), a Mosul native who lives with terrorist violence and risks his life daily to help this correspondent uncover some of the worst ISIS atrocities, including beheadings, throat-slitting, running tanks over civilians, and throwing LGBTQ people from buildings. On Episode 7 of *Caliphate*, Hawk reveals a secret. He loves Metallica.

Their music is banned in Iraq. The only Mosul record store where Hawk can find them keeps Metallica records hidden. But Hawk risks his life so he can hear their music alone. "The first time I played the tape, I was like 'What the fuck is this?'" Hawk recalls. "Just all noise and chaos. But after, like, two or three times I listened to it, actually, most of his songs are really sincere. It's about armies and wars and 'Why are we dying in vain?' Since I was born, I have seen nothing in this country but wars, and more wars, and more wars. So I made some kind of connection that stood deep with me. And from that minute on, I was like 'That's what I'm looking for.'"

There's no one idea or force that makes Metallica relatable. But listening to and reading over fan accounts, one constantly sees how Metallica helps people process pain. Not by escaping it, although there is an escapism in throwing your horns up and screaming along with "Seek & Destroy." But Metallica fans understand the world through their songs. It's what makes someone like Hawk break the law to find their music. Hawk is not the only one—in the 2007 film *Heavy Metal in Baghdad*, Iraqi band Acrassicauda bond over illegal Metallica records and perform "Fade to Black," years before they moved to America with refugee status (for the best Metallica fan clip available online, watch what happens when Acrassicauda meet James Hetfield backstage in Newark).

"There's you're typical 'Dude!' high fiving guys," James described Metallica's fanbase. "And there's other people . . . 'My Dad struggled with alcohol, and I'm proud of you for doing this.'"

Everyone who loves metal has a mental and emotional attachment to Metallica, whether or not they know it. People from all metal worlds have Metallica stories. The most steadfast obscurists love bands whose lives were changed by Metallica, and the staunchest traditionalists love bands who were amplified by Metallica. No trauma or anxiety is too slight to be addressed in Metallica's music, a judgment-free world in which childhood fears like the beasts under your bed are legitimized as much as adult fears. Even at their most blunt, Metallica channel something personal, a fight that sustains its listeners no matter how removed they may be from Metallica's lives, ideologies, or politics. "The more that people know about my troubles, the easier it'll be to connect with people," James said in a 2004 interview. "I put myself out there, and if people choose to stomp on my heart or to embrace it, that is up to them."

"We're not going to say, 'It means that, it doesn't mean that, you can draw these conclusions, but not those conclusions,'" Kirk told *The Village Voice* in 2012.

In a 2017 interview with Jayson Greene, the acclaimed indie musician Phil Elverum recounted the last days of his wife and collaborator Geneviève's struggle with cancer. Elverum showed Greene his wife's "aspirational book," a homemade children's book started by the late Geneviève chronicling her hospital experience. Looking through the book, Elverum points out a drawing of his wife in a vintage-looking Metallica shirt.

"That was real," Elverum says. "It was her special chemo shirt. One day she just said, 'Phil, buy me a Metallica . . . *And Justice for All* shirt on eBay,' and I instantly did. It was her thing to be the young person in the chemo room, drinking her crazy carrot juice and being so charming to all the nurses."

Metallica might not seem like an obvious source of comfort for chemotherapy, particularly at their most Spartan on . . . *And Justice for All*. But there they are, the freedom and catharsis in their music making the hospital less lonely in the throes of terminal illness.

Metallica can be as fallible as anyone who loves their music. AC/DC isn't going to let you down. Slayer doesn't have a *Load* or a *St. Anger*. Metallica love is a very human, dare I say adult, love. No Metallica fan loves every record they've made (except maybe Dave Grohl), to the point where talking about Metallica's misfires is a popular pastime for metalheads. But through Metallica's embarrassments, we see a band that stays restless and curious, unsatisfied by any amount of success or acceptance. It's why one of the most inclusive bands of all time can still feel private, like your personal band. Even as one the world's biggest acts, they've stayed outsiders in the mainstream. They'd be an unlikely choice to play the Super Bowl or the Academy Awards. Rodrigo y Gabriela could take their Metallica-inspired flamenco all the way to the White House for a state dinner in 2010, but Metallica won't get that invitation. They're the only band big enough to headline Glastonbury and still create controversy for accepting—Metallica sold T-shirts at the 2014 festival featuring disparaging quotes from other performers and publications fuming at the idea of Metallica headlining. (Metallica also filmed a Julien Temple–directed intro video for the show, wherein some fox-hunting Brits were gunned down by rifle-wielding bears. The bears pulled off their heads, revealing themselves to be James, Lars, Kirk, and Robert.) "If Radiohead does it, it's cool," Lars said in 2012, answering questions about Orion fest and *Metallica Through the Never*. "If we do it, it's not."

"They're determined and focused only on what they want to achieve, not what others expect from them," Dimmu Borgir's Silenoz stated in *Justice for All*. "That's why we got the Black Album in the first place. People seem to forget that bit when they bash Metallica."

"Anyone who has ever been to a Metallica show, and banged their head, and thrown up the devil horns, has been a part of something great for humanity," said Flea in 2009. "All those kids at a show rocking so hard to the brutal beat of Metallica have come together for those couple of hours in a way as healthy as any spiritual exercise, any group meditation, any loving anything."

In the Mexico City performance on *Live Shit: Binge & Purge*, Metallica rips through the last few notes of "Blackened," sending the crowd into a unison chant of "México! México!" For another artist, maybe they'd yell "Slayer!" or "Ozzy!" For Metallica, they yell "México!," feeling their own power as forceful as the band's. When we see Metallica, we yell for ourselves.

PSYCHIC SAVAGERY

Lulu

"It'll definitely freak some people out, and that's good."

—Robert Trujillo

Metallica saved one of their strangest setlists for the Rock and Roll Hall of Fame 25th Anniversary concerts in 2009. Even as recent Rock Hall inductees, Metallica look like party-crashers among Stevie Wonder, Bruce Springsteen and the E Street Band, Paul Simon, the Jeff Beck Band, U2, and Aretha Franklin. Metallica are the night's youngest performers to get a top billing, and the youngest to show up at all until the last night, when Tom Morello stops by to rage with Bruce on the "The Ghost of Tom Joad." Metallica play covers for eight of their eleven songs, inviting back the industry suits they scared away with "For Whom the Bell Tolls" and "One." They bring out the Kinks' Ray Davies for "You Really Got Me" and "All Day and All of the Night" (the former shows up in studio form on Davies' unfortunate 2010 collaboration album, *See My Friends*). Less surprisingly, they play Ozzy's two biggest Black Sabbath hits, "Iron Man" and "Paranoid," with the Prince of Darkness himself on lead vocals. But the most consequential team-up of the ceremony comes earlier in Metallica's show. "Please, New York," James announces, "Welcome your own Mr. Lou Reed."

New York's underworld poet straps on a guitar. He plays two of his best Velvet Underground songs, "Sweet Jane" and "White Light/White

Heat," while an image of his young band flashes on the screen behind him. Kirk's solos rip, and James tackles the high harmonies. It's not half bad.

"And then he just yelled down the hallway as we were leaving, 'We should do a record together,'" James laughed in a subsequent interview. "And we thought, 'Yeah, right. Is he talking to us?'"

What to make of *Lulu*? Readers may dismiss this book outright because it doesn't slam *Lulu* as the worst thing Metallica ever laid tracks on. In two of the most unique, iconoclastic discographies in American music, *Lulu* may be the most unique and iconoclastic of either. Long after most of their thrash metal and rock peers settled into careers rehashing their early glories, Metallica and Lou Reed made a record unlike anything attempted in music before. And yet, it's not such a strange pairing, two of music's greatest shapeshifters, moving swift with all senses clean. Metallica had already recorded with another hard-living, proto-alternative icon, Marianne Faithfull, and alluded to "Waves of Fear" on . . . *And Justice for All* only six years after Reed's *The Blue Mask*. Lou Reed made one of his best records, *Berlin*, with Alice Cooper's producer Bob Ezrin, who later recruited Reed to cowrite three songs with Kiss for *Music from "The Elder,"* the *Lulu* of Kiss records. Both were fans of each other's music, with Kirk calling the pairing "just as special as collaborating with Jimi Hendrix" and Reed, perhaps deceptively, claiming "I've loved Metallica since I was a kid" before the record's release.

Most important, Metallica pioneered for heavy metal what Lou Reed pioneered for rock 'n' roll decades earlier, in the Velvet Underground—the idea that the kind of music they were making was high art, something that belonged in libraries and museums. Metallica and Lou Reed didn't write *Master of Puppets* or *The Velvet Underground and Nico* for the National Recording Registry, but they carved room for their music.

"We don't play to the tune of anybody else," Lars told *GQ*, leading up to the record's release. "We're autonomous. We live in our own self-contained musical universe. And we don't have to cater to any fucker. I can't think of anybody that's more suited to each other than these two musical entities."

Reed had been hired by the director Robert Wilson to write songs for a modern theatrical adaptation of Frank Wedekind's "Lulu" plays in Berlin, with a script Reed called "incoherent" and "absolutely impossible" (a look through Reed's archives in New York reveals that he wrote his own *Lulu* script). "My *Lulu* had a head, but she needed a body. It's not a party record," Reed stated. His first idea was to rerecord some of his older songs with Metallica, emailing them over twenty titles, but it's ultimately not in Reed's or Metallica's blood to rehash the past, and the band convened in spring 2011 to record new songs. It was the first time Metallica recorded to the lyrics, with Lou's stanzas coming first, soundtracking his violent, psychosexual depiction of Wedekind's libertine over a two-act, eighty-seven-minute avant-rock drama. Reed described the record as giving rock music "the intelligence that once inhabited novels and film," perhaps indicating such intelligence was never in rock music.

"The hardest power rock you could come up with would have to be Metallica," stated Lou before the album's release. "They live on that planet."

The recording sessions could be as abrasive as the music. Lars recalled Lou challenging him to, in Lars' words, a "street fight," and later told his *It's Electric!* listeners that Lou was the most unfiltered man he'd ever met, an especially big claim from a guy who grew up in Torben Ulrich's house. Unsurprisingly, Lou and Torben hit it off during recording, with Lou calling Mr. Ulrich "one of the greatest fathers you've ever met." But Lou loved Metallica, too, calling them "my metal blood brothers" and "the best group I could possibly find."

"He had a certain type of personality that you could either let it get under your skin, if you wanted to, or you could kinda look at it like, 'Man, this guy is super cool,'" Robert told *Clash*. "He's all about improv and capturing a moment of magic. . . . I know that I learned a lot from him."

And the record does sound improvised, despite Lou forbidding any Kirk solos. It's sometimes atonal, with extended instrumentation supporting Reed's spoken word vocals, a post-rock expressionist theater production conducted by a modernist beat writer and the only band brave enough to imagine it all as a metal show. The first lyric of the opening song "Brandenburg Gate" describes a graphic self-mutilation over acoustic strums, and gets more vicious and excruciating by the second as Metallica kicks in. The long, instrumental passages on "Cheat on Me" veer into art rock, while "Pumping Blood" and "Iced Honey" almost sound like they have distinguishable verse and chorus structures amid the noise and minimalism that make up much of the record. *Lulu*'s loveliest moment is "Junior Dad," a poetic, twenty-minute requiem in complex time signatures that features Robert on upright bass and ends the record with eight minutes of string drones, Reed's and Metallica's instruments evaporating and leaving the moods they created in the previous seventy-nine sinking in. Playback of "Junior Dad" made Kirk and James leave the control room in tears, shaken by Lou's lyrics and the performances he brought out of them (Lou reportedly laughed, "That's a good one, huh?"). It's a gentle but no less strange and experimental coda, two great artists pushing themselves further in their age, still looking for something unheard of, trying something new just because it's the artistic dream.

"I have to have Metallica muscle," Reed stated. "Sixty miles an hour won't do. It's 110 or nothing."

Even at its post-rock best, *Lulu* feels like a collision. James plays hypeman on vocals, Flavor Flav to Lou's Chuck D, jumping in with various quips, asides, and puzzlements, most infamously an impassioned "I am the table!" in "The View" that set off a mound of internet derision and remains a metalhead punchline to this day (it is also the title of a 2008 episode of *Weeds*). It didn't help that "The View" was also *Lulu*'s only single and the most tuneless song on the record (original choice "Iced Honey" would have been better). Solid, heavy Metallica riffs like "Frustration" and the hardcore speed "Mistress Dread" lost their thrash potential under Lou's poetry and song lengths pushing ten minutes. Much of the music was as torturous as the album cover, featuring a broken mannequin with the title written in blood, and whether that was the band's intention it didn't make a lot of people want to listen.

"Nothing we'd ever done prepared us for where this went," James stated. "It's been an authentic, intuitive and impulsive journey. We weren't always sure where it was going, but it sure as fuck was an exciting ride to be on."

"I think the most important thing that any sort of musical artist can do is offer something different to the world," stated Kirk.

Reviews were not forgiving. *The Quietus* called it "quite possibly a candidate for one of the worst albums ever made." *Sound Opinions'* Jim DeRogatis gave it zero stars on WBEZ, dubbing it "horribly, massively, almost inconceivably wrong." Consequence of Sound described "a complete failure on every tangible and intangible level of its existence." The public was about as receptive, picking up approximately 33,000 copies of *Lulu* in its first three years (to be fair, it was Reed's highest charting record in the United States since the 1970s). Dedicated fans of Lou Reed and Metallica could point out that they've both made worse records, and less interesting good ones, but maybe that's beside the point.

Reed and Metallica both brushed off *Lulu* criticism, but plans to tour behind the record were scrapped. Metallica's next release, a fine outtakes EP dropped that December, won better reviews and sales. But ten years later, *Beyond Magnetic* is Metallica fan trivia while *Lulu* stands infamous, debated, mocked, and, yes, belatedly admired. Metallica and Reed performed three songs together at Metallica's thirtieth anniversary shows, and Reed performed *Lulu* songs until his death in 2013, even billing his tour as "From VU to Lulu." He ended his final concert with "Junior Dad" and "White Light/White Heat"; age withered him and changed him. Artist Laurie Anderson, Lou's widow, recalled Lou's friend/rival/collaborator David Bowie telling her, "Listen, this is Lou's greatest work. This is his masterpiece. Just wait, it will be like *Berlin*. It will take everyone a while to catch up." Bowie's response was confirmed by LCD Soundsystem's James Murphy on *The Best Show*, who remembered him stating, "That's some of the best writing Lou's done. People are making a snap judgment and they aren't listening." See if the ice will melt for you.

"I love it. I still listen to it," Kirk said in 2017. "In retrospect, that's one of the most important albums, I think, I've been a part of in my life." One can almost hear Lars imagining the artist he wants to be when he spoke to BBC of working with Lou: "He would just say what he was thinking, and never had to ponder it or be diplomatic or compromising."

Maybe people are starting to catch up. The acclaimed hardcore collective the Armed mysteriously cite *Lulu* as an influence in interviews. "I thought the Lou Reed thing was a great experiment on your guys' part," Howard Stern told Metallica in a 2020 interview, singling out "Junior Dad." "Who's better than fuckin' Lou Reed?" That same year, James Hetfield spent his COVID-19 quarantine time building and raffling off handmade tables for Metallica's All Within My Hands Foundation, citing "I am the table" in the press release. But most of all, *Lulu*'s legacy shines in Metallica's ongoing artistic curiosity. "Love it or hate it, it was definitely something that we enjoyed and that we embraced," Robert stated on the *Rock Talk* podcast. "Lou is a no-holds-barred artist, top to bottom, and he's got a lot of fire in him . . . a wonderful man with a steel armor when it came to rock and roll, and just really edgy and powerful. So I always kind of try to embrace what he had and bring that spirit to life through my music."

Metallica embraces it. They're still collaborating with radical rock heroes like Neil Young (joining for an acoustic "Mr. Soul" in 2016) and Iggy Pop, the sinewy punk godfather whose best-known Stooges song was echoed in the penultimate sentiment on *Kill 'Em All*. For three 2017 Mexico City shows on the Worldwired Tour, Metallica pushed themselves by giving rock's wildest frontman an opening spot, bringing him out the final night for a raging version of Iggy and the Stooges' "T.V. Eye." Iggy lets out a howl and the band strikes, blasting the original's raw power into a night anthem that turns the 26,000-capacity Foro Sol into the world's loudest punk club. James and Iggy make eye contact during the pause, but even mighty James can't contain an exuberant laugh. "Come on, motherfucker!" he yells to the crowd, and the band kicks back in. Iggy sees that cat and James knows who he means. They look extremely happy to be there. All five of them do.

28

I'M YOUR DREAM, MAKE YOU REAL

Metallica's Videos

*"We've always been very adamant about shying away from
the metal clichés—the whole sexist, Satanist crap. . . . Not doing a video and then finally doing 'One' and everybody going,
'Wow!'"*

—Lars Ulrich

66 **A**fter the whole 'One' experience, I just, I feel great about making
videos now," Lars Ulrich states in the short pre-concert movie
seen in the San Diego show on *Live Shit: Binge & Purge.*

The camera cuts to James. "I hate making videos." He laughs. "They're
boring as shit. But in the end run you kind of see why, you know, you had
to stand to there for three hours in the same spot."

For a band that can seemingly do whatever they want artistically,
Metallica's videos often look like they've been made out of obligation.
Lars had been talking about making them as early as July 1985, when
he told *Kick Ass* magazine he had a director lined up for an "Escape"
video, until Cliff Burnstein talked Lars out of it. The next year he told
Metal Forces, "If Metallica finally does one it has to be so much better,
simply because we've said so much shit about videos before." He cited
Mötley Crüe's "Home Sweet Home" video for doing a good job of showing what the band is about. But Metallica's reputation would be more or

less unchanged without all but a few of their videos. On their *MTV Icon* special in 2003, Metallica performed a medley of six songs for the music video channel—only one of which had been filmed for a video. Despite arriving at the dawn of the video era, Metallica didn't release an official music video until their fourth record. Even on the Black Album, three of Metallica's five videos were cobbled together from band footage, which were cool if not artistically inventive. But who doesn't expect Metallica to be inventive? You've heard "Sad but True" and "Nothing Else Matters" hundreds of times—quick, what happens in the videos? Metallica gifted the world some of the most striking, iconic imagery in all of rock music, but for the most part those artistic sensibilities haven't quite crossed over into their videos.

Metallica generally seem less involved in their videos as they get older and richer. Maybe they knew people would watch them no matter what. When Lars Ulrich told *The Straits Times* that Metallica would be filming videos for all twelve tracks on *Hardwired . . . to Self Destruct*, he reasoned, "Now that YouTube is the world's biggest television station, we figured we may as well knock a video out for every song." Much as one can admire his audacity and the urge to keep promoting one of the biggest bands on Earth, one senses he sees videos as more promotional than artistic. Even after telling a reporter he'd wanted the "One" video to be more than a band commercial, he quipped, "We got more publicity from not doing a video than from doing a video."

That said, Lars' businessman sensibilities include quality control, and his band has made a few remarkable videos, several good ones, and at least thirty that are worth watching. Here they are.

"ONE" (1989, DIR. BILL POPE AND MICHAEL SALOMON)

Had Metallica stopped making videos after "One," they'd already have earned an entire music videos chapter in this book. Metallica set their place by making metal stranger, scarier, and more cinematic than before (Lars: "It turned out there were many, many, many disenfranchised kids who wanted their music heavier and darker"). According to Lars,

Trumbo's *Johnny Got His Gun* was given to the band by Cliff Burnstein, and Peter Mensch in turn tracked down a tape of the film, which in 1988 had to be sent from Italy and transferred from European to American format (these days it's readily available, the 2009 DVD release including the "One" video among the film's special features). Metallica bought the rights to the film and hired two directors with no metal video experience, picked over bigger directors whose egos might've tampered with Metallica's vision (Elektra agreed the video wouldn't get released if Metallica didn't like it, and James agreed to not show his "EET FUK" guitar onscreen). The story, intercut with a fierce Metallica performance in an almost empty warehouse, can't be told in seven and a half minutes, but "One" shows just enough dialogue and grainy footage to convey the protagonist's helplessness and confusion. You'll never hear "Keep the Home Fires Burning" the same way. James has said he liked that people didn't know what to say when they saw it, although Kirk was in tune with the media's reaction. "I saw 'One' on MTV at like, 11:30 in the evening," he recalled. "The VJ said 'Wow, that's a real bowl of rainbows!'"

"ENTER SANDMAN" (1991, DIR. WAYNE ISHAM)

Metallica's only video as iconic as "One" was a bigger hit and maybe their only other video as visually innovative. Each member spoke with Isham about their nightmare ideas (James: "There were some pretty wild nightmares that came out that should not ever be seen by anyone") to consolidate into the clip, which sets a series of dream sequences against obscured, flashing shots of Metallica's performance and the most terrifying Sandman since E. T. A. Hoffmann, courtesy of character actor/Sam Peckinpah mainstay R. G. Armstrong. TV static-like sand pours from his hands while a boy falls into snakes, drowning, vertigo, an intruder, and a runaway semi-truck. "Enter Sandman" won 1992's MTV Video Music Award for Best Metal/Hard Rock Video, beating out Def Leppard, Ugly Kid Joe, and even the night's Video of the Year award winner, Van Halen's "Right Now." But its greatest MTV prestige was inspiring a parody on *The Ben Stiller*

Show, casting Stiller as James, Bob Odenkirk as Lars, and Janeane Garofalo as the host of *"Headslammers Ball."*

"THE UNFORGIVEN" (1991, DIR. MATT MAHURIN)

The last of Metallica's transcendent videos, "The Unforgiven" is as vivid as the Morricone score it evokes in its introduction. Like "Enter Sandman," "The Unforgiven" depicts an old man and a boy, only this time they may or may not be the same person. James has revealed that "Yest" being scrawled on the wall is part of "Yesterday," but the video's ambiguities make it effective—is that ink or blood he's writing with? Who's that on the old poster? What's with the keyhole in the foliage? The four members appear almost entirely separate for the first time in a Metallica video, echoing the song's loneliness and perhaps adapting for an era in which all four members were becoming individually recognizable on a major level. Mahurin would keep helping express Metallica's anguish—he illustrated the wretched angel that appears in both the *St. Anger* booklet and the *Some Kind of Monster* cover art. Be sure to also watch the equally haunting eleven and a half minute "theatrical" cut of "The Unforgiven," which introduces more characters, excludes the band, and opens more questions.

"NOTHING ELSE MATTERS" (1992, DIR. ADAM DUBIN)

Adam Dubin, the NYU roommate of future Metallica producer Rick Rubin, helmed this video with footage from *A Year and a Half in the Life of Metallica*, thus we're treated to Metallica's behind-the-scenes goofing, rehearsals, and a clip of Lars Ulrich with a Kip Winger dartboard, which at this point Kip has probably been asked about more than any Winger music. "Nothing Else Matters" is essentially an *A Year and a Half* montage, starting with recording the Black Album before moving into the Wherever We May Roam tour, but it's unclear what else Metallica could have done with this video. James is almost unimaginable as an onscreen leading man, and it's hard to believe anything could have made this song bigger.

"WHEREVER I MAY ROAM" (1992, DIR. WAYNE ISHAM)

"Wherever I May Roam" is the first of several Metallica videos to make use of Metallica's stage power, though unlike the others, "Wherever I May Roam" shows Metallica soundchecking in near-empty theaters, perhaps in honor of the song's solitary themes. We also get some on-the-road camaraderie, like an encouraging handshake from Lars to Jason as they're about to take the stage. Also, cool Sisters of Mercy shirt, Kirk!

"SAD BUT TRUE" (1992, DIR. WAYNE ISHAM)

Not since *Cliff 'Em All* had a video so effectively captured Metallica being the most exciting live band in the world. If showing live Metallica footage in their Black Album videos wasn't the most creative idea, it still depicted the best thing about Metallica. Stage lights illuminate James' face like he's telling horror stories around a campfire, the fans go into hysterics, and the band throws themselves into every second of the song, on the last tour where they'd all have the hair to show it. Keep your eyes peeled for a fan in a sling, banging the arm that doesn't bang.

"UNTIL IT SLEEPS" (1996, DIR. SAMUEL BAYER)

This surreal video was inspired by Hieronymus Bosch paintings, with characters from *Ecce Homo*, *The Garden of Earthly Delights*, and *The Haywain Triptych* all appearing. Director Samuel Bayer had been working with David Bowie and the Smashing Pumpkins, and "Until It Sleeps" matches both artists' decorative extravagance in ways one wouldn't expect the guys who made the Black Album to pull off. Still, the band seems at odds with itself—Kirk and Lars wear makeup, Jason and James do not. Jason is literally "in the dirt," agonizing on the ground while reflecting the exact words he'd use to describe how he felt about . . . *And Justice for All*'s bass mix. Lars looks like he raided U2's *Achtung Baby* photoshoot closet. It's the first Metallica video to cast more actors than musicians. Yet "Until It Sleeps" is potent, thanks to Bayer's Bosch visuals, an emotional James performance, and an *Ecce Homo* Christlike figure whom some viewers believe resembles an iconic bassist, who once came back from New York's Met Museum with a Bosch book for his girlfriend Corrine.

"HERO OF THE DAY" (1996, DIR. ANTON CORBIJN)

A young junkie's TV set shows Metallica in a variety of scenarios—Jason is already separate from the rest of the band, appearing as a game show host for his bandmates, James referees a boxing match between Kirk and Jason, Lars and James advertise a drink called Load, and Kirk looks uncomfortable suited up as a news anchor. There's also a cowboy show, with Lars looking ridiculous dressed as a desperado with a mustache, and it's not clear whether he's taking the piss or stoned enough to think he looks fabulous. The junkie story is generic, save for a startling moment with some mechanical, birdlike bugs. Maybe a reference to William S. Burroughs' iconic junkie novel *Naked Lunch*?

"MAMA SAID" (1996, DIR. ANTON CORBIJN)

James is an unconvincing cowboy in "Mama Said," although it's more the video's fault than the song's. Does any rock star ever look more like a cowboy while wearing a hat? Filmed in London and never aired in the United States, where perhaps someone feared it would alienate metalheads. The video, which cuts the song down to a single edit, shows lonesome cowboy James in a car with a moderately predictable surprise. Watch for cameos from Lars, Kirk, and Jason, none of whom have performed this song live with James, though he's played it solo on rare occasion.

"KING NOTHING" (1997, DIR. MATT MAHURIN)

Filmed in snowy Utah, with the band in full winter gear, "King Nothing" centers Metallica's performance around a paper crown king who looks more like an outlaw country star than a delusional monarch. Some good pyro is the only thing that justifies three-quarters of the band wearing sunglasses at night. Only Jason abstains.

"THE MEMORY REMAINS" (1997, DIR. PAUL ANDRESEN)

Director Paul Andresen would go on to more prestigious work, such as Insane Clown Posse's 2010 straight-to-video prequel *Big Money Rustlas*, but "The Memory Remains" is his peak as a video director. Shot in a Van Nuys Airport hangar, the filmmakers created a stationary room in a two-story spinning box to give the illusion that Metallica themselves were being swung around, presumably controlled by the street organ Marianne Faithfull is playing. Metallica pays Faithfull—"buy the ticket, take the ride"—before jumping onto the platform and menacingly thrashing out the song, though behind the scenes the band was reportedly all on motion sickness drugs. Look for a bear rug on the wall in tribute to Faithfull, who was infamously wearing only a fur rug when the cops found her during a drug raid at Keith Richards' home in 1967.

"THE UNFORGIVEN II" (1998, DIR. MATT MAHURIN)

Metallica bring back "The Unforgiven" director Mahurin for a clip that, predictably, reprises the original black-and-white video, striking a contrast as the song itself flips the original's heavy verse and soft chorus structure. The solitary boy may or may not have turned into the guy we see tied to a spit, trying to unravel a stone that looks like a *Space Odyssey* Monolith and hiding from lightning (flash before my eyes?). James' chorus of turning pages, turning stone shows a guy with his mind in the past, as does the "Unforgiven II" video, though the "turn the pages" lyric might indicate his mind was already moving on to an upcoming single.

"FUEL" (1998, DIR. WAYNE ISHAM)

"Fuel" is a grindhouse-worthy video for a grindhouse-worthy song, as enjoyably dumb as the action-packed movies it pays homage to. White captions flash across the screen ("QUENCH THIRST with gasoline" . . . "on they BURN" . . . "WHITE KNUCKLE TIGHT!" . . . "They live . . . TOO FAST!"). Maybe historians will mark "Fuel" as White Zombie's *La Sexorcisto: Devil Music Volume One* by way of *The Fast and the Furious*, years before Vin Diesel won his first seven-figure check. More likely they'll throw their horns up, bang their heads, and give that man his dabajabaza. Filmed in Tokyo, because of course it was.

"TURN THE PAGE" (1998, DIR. JONAS ÅKERLUND)

"Turn the Page" looks like it will be a rare Metallica foray into sex, with adult film actress Ginger Lynn speaking (to the police? Maybe a judge?) in the intro. It is, and it isn't—Lynn plays a sex worker who lives in a hotel room while her daughter plays with a kitten and tries on her mom's clothes. It's as far removed from "Cherry Pie" as Metallica is from Warrant. Lynn's performance helps make the story of a struggling mom who might be fighting to keep custody of her child as unsettling as it sounds (James has since been known to change the narrator to a "she" in the song's last chorus live). The video's last minute is the hardest moment to watch in any Metallica video, and might've been banned if Metallica weren't huge enough to submit pretty much whatever they wanted to MTV and get airtime. The Lynn footage, with extra narration from her daughter, was later released in 1999 in a fourteen-minute Åkerlund film called *Turn the Page*, featuring an all-Metallica soundtrack.

"WHISKEY IN THE JAR" (1998, DIR. JONAS ÅKERLUND)

Metallica blows any shot at honoring this song's history or lyrics by setting their video at what looks like an all-women college party. Metallica is pretty conspicuously separate from the girl action, preferring to destroy their own room instead. At least the "Breadfan" riff gets played in the intro.

"NO LEAF CLOVER" (1999, DIR. WAYNE ISHAM)

Edited performance footage from *S&M*, for those of us who wanted a glimpse before buying the DVD—the kind of thing that was more valuable in the early days of the internet. Nothing here is superior to the concert film performance, but, man, do Metallica and the San Francisco Symphony look cool playing "No Leaf Clover." Extra points for including James' "Ye-ah!" at the end.

"I DISAPPEAR" (2000, DIR. WAYNE ISHAM)

For their only single that doesn't appear on a Metallica record, the band came up with something appropriately fun but a little out of place. On paper, a monstrously successful rock band should be perfect for a *Mission: Impossible 2* soundtrack video, but Metallica looks awkward in "I Disappear." That might be due to inner turmoil, but also the casting. Kirk, Jason, James, and Lars appear in classic film reenactments *North by Northwest*, *Brazil*, *Bullitt*, and *Die Hard*, respectively, but even as world-famous rock stars in expensive suits, Metallica haven't shaken off enough of their metal grit to be turned into movie stars. Tom Cruise, however, showing off the most famous shot of his movie here (the vertigo-inducing mountain climbing scene), is at his roughest, still too pretty to sell as a Metallica video star. Metallica would've been better off just riffing on Lalo Schifrin's classic *Mission: Impossible* theme, but this being 2000, the film's producers gave that task to Limp Bizkit. Like the film it soundtracks, the "I Disappear" video looks great, delivers action, shows off high budget thrills, and will probably be forgotten by the time the taste of popcorn leaves your mouth. Lars, for what it's worth, in 2019 named it as the Metallica video he's most proud of.

"ST. ANGER" (2003, DIR. THE MALLOYS)

"Welcome to San Quentin," the guard tells the band. "We're all excited you're here, staff and inmates alike. . . . In the unlikely event that you are taken hostage, the state will not negotiate your release in exchange for the release of an inmate." They all sign. One of Metallica's worst singles gets one of their best videos, culling footage from Metallica's 2003 San Quentin performance with some original shots. James has cited Elvis' "Jailhouse Rock" song and video as an early influence in matching rebellion with creativity, but the "St. Anger" video is more like Johnny Cash's live "Folsom Prison Blues," a sea of angry men banging their heads in appreciation of an artist entering a system they'd barely evaded (years earlier James spent a night in jail in London for property damage—he'd drunkenly climbed on top of a movie theater marquee and kicked out the lights). The video ends with the message, "For all the souls impacted by San Quentin, your spirit will forever be a part of Metallica. —James, Lars Kirk and Robert," worded to include victims and families, as well as the prisoners. The video does not mention that Metallica donated $10,000 to the San Quentin Giants, the prison's baseball team, or that they played a full set for the prisoners the day after their "St. Anger" shoot. According to the *Some Kind of Monster* DVD commentary, one of the inmates used to mow Kirk's mother's lawn.

"FRANTIC" (2003, DIR. WAYNE ISHAM)

Once again, Metallica is separate from the action for their video, performing in two scrap yards (James and Kirk are in metal, Lars and Robert are in stone) between shots of a hard-living guy feeding addictions and wrecking his car. On the set of "Frantic," James noted the thing he related to most in the "wasted days" lyric was "mistreating people"; whereas Kirk noted that he didn't believe in wasted days. "As long as I have a book to read during the downtime, I don't mind making music videos."

"THE UNNAMED FEELING" (2003, DIR. THE MALLOYS)

Metallica perform while the walls literally close in on them, intercut with shots of distressed characters looking appropriately asphyxiated for a song Joe Berlinger named as a *St. Anger* favorite. Look for appearances by famed surfer Rob Machado (thanks to Metallica's resident surfers Kirk and Rob) and actor Edward Furlong (*Terminator 2: Judgment Day*, *Detroit Rock City*). "I want to hate it all away," yells James, but the walls keep moving in.

"SOME KIND OF MONSTER" (2004, DIR. ALAN SMITHEE)

Film buffs recognize "Alan Smithee" as a Hollywood pseudonym used by film directors who want to take their name off a project, but the "Some Kind of Monster" Alan Smithee is really Joe Berlinger and Bruce Sinofsky, so we'll infer the nom de plume here is an inside joke. "Some Kind of Monster" comprises scenes from the movie, starting with the journalist who asks if there's any way these guys can retain their *Kill 'Em All* fire after twenty years. Metallica doesn't answer in conversation—the song speaks for them, as always—and the answer is "maybe." Edited down to single format, "Some Kind of Monster" shows off its best power and some of the hookiest *St. Anger* riffs, but most of the band's energy is in the movie, with Lars' "fuck" scene and James' door slam included in the song's audio. Closing out with James' onstage thank-you to the fans makes "Some Kind of Monster" a perfect clip to end *The Videos 1989–2004*.

"THE DAY THAT NEVER COMES" (2008, DIR. THOMAS VINTERBERG)

Lars has said that "The Day That Never Comes" was inspired by a father-son relationship, so it makes sense he and James would hire Dogme 95 co-founder Thomas Vinterberg, director of the traumatic Danish family drama *Festen* (*The Celebration*). But the music video, like the song, hearkens to "One" and picks up in a wartime setting. "The Day That Never Comes" was filmed during America's War in Afghanistan, although James and Lars have both said, in separate MTV interviews, that the song is more about "resentment and forgiveness" and "forgiveness and redemption," respectively. The video's story is vague enough for mass interpretation but too vague to be memorable, although Metallica seem to have intended it that way. "That's the beauty, I think, of writing vague but powerful lyrics," James stated, "that someone like a movie director can interpret it in his own way and obviously, someone creative is able to take the metaphors and apply them to whatever he needs in his own life."

"ALL NIGHTMARE LONG" (2008, DIR. ROBOSHOBO)

Leading up to the release of "All Nightmare Long," Kirk spoke to Metclub.com about buying an animated short film in a Russian flea market for $5, which ended up being the basis for the music video. File this rumor somewhere between "Paul is dead" and "Marilyn Manson got his ribs removed," but watching "All Nightmare Long," one might believe it. Director Roboshobo (the former Robert Schober) filmed the video to look like old documentaries, particularly *Experiments in the Revival of Organisms*, a controversial 1940 short Russian film that purported to show, among other things, a severed dog's head reanimated. Part live action, part animation, all grainy, "All Nightmare Long" imagines *Experiments in the Revival of Organisms* through the 1908 Tunguska event, the biggest recorded impact event in Earth history (generally thought to be a meteor). In Metallica's world, this inspires a zombie apocalypse and an eerie violent takeover of the United States by the Soviet Union. Despite some good visuals, "All Nightmare Long" never takes off as well as the song does. The subtitles are distracting, and they don't correspond to the song—it's lyrically "The Hounds of Tindalos" and visually "Herbert West—Reanimator." "Expectations raised more questions than answers" reads one subtitle. Kind of like Metallica's career.

"BROKEN, BEAT & SCARRED" (2009, DIR. WAYNE ISHAM)

Filmed over two December 2008 California shows on the World Magnetic tour, "Broken, Beat & Scarred" looks more like a highlight reel than a structured music video. The song itself is boosted by added crowd audio and recording the band singing backup in the chorus, which sounds better than the studio version on *Death Magnetic*. We get a great shot of Robert's

"Seek & Destroy" dance, though the high point is a fan sign: "ALL HAIL THE SUPER SAMURAI WHISKEY WARLOARD [*sic*] MOTHER PLUCKER a.k.a. ROBERT AGUSTIN MIGUEL SANTIAGO SAMUEL TRUJILLO VERACRUZ!"

"THE VIEW" (2011, DIR. DARREN ARONOFSKY)

Few Metallica fans defend *Lulu*, and fewer still make a case for Aronofsky's "The View" video. The grainy, blurry performance video won't make you like the song more, but seeing as how this is a collaboration between the guys behind *Metal Machine Music*, *St. Anger*, and *Requiem for a Dream*, maybe that's not the point. Amazingly, "The View" doesn't even make the artists look like a good live band, which anyone who's seen Lou Reed on a good night and Metallica on any night could tell you isn't the case. The final product is a minute and a half shorter than the album version but feels about five minutes longer, even with Lou clapping and yelling "Bravo! Encore! Brilliant!" at the end.

"MASTER OF PUPPETS (LIVE)" (2013, DIR. NIMRÓD ANTAL)

Twenty-seven years after its release, Metallica's masterpiece gets a video. In 1986 it was too hard for a video, but by 2013 "Master of Puppets" was beloved enough to be the promotional video release for Metallica's major motion picture. "Master of Puppets (Live)" is practically an ad for *Metallica Through the Never*, albeit no more so than any music video is an ad for the artist. Like the film it accompanies, "Master of Puppets (Live)" expertly captures the excitement of a Metallica show, along with clips from ". . . And Justice for All," "One," "Ride the Lightning," and "For Whom the Bell Tolls." If you're new to Metallica, this will show you why they matter. If you've seen and heard it before, you'll want to go back— who couldn't be thrilled by "Master of Puppets"? Notice how instead of "Fix me" James yells "Pancakes!" According to Anthrax's Charlie Benante, Cliff Burton misheard the lyric as "pancakes" and mouthed it from the stage to his friends in the audience. Charlie told James this over twenty years later before the first Big Four show in Poland, and James was charmed enough to sing it onstage and onscreen in Metallica's big movie.

"HARDWIRED" (2016, DIR. COLIN HAKES AND THE ARTIST)

Metallica released *Hardwired . . . to Self Destruct* in an era when streaming videos had replaced cassingles, and dropped the "Hardwired" video as a first taste of the record the day the single was released. Playing in darkness with a strobe, Metallica gives a taste of the opening number for the World-wired tour, just a breakneck heavy song with a dizzying spin. Not much by way of bells and whistles, but Metallica doesn't need any.

"MOTH INTO FLAME" (2016, DIR. TOM KIRK)

"Moth into Flame" picks up where "Hardwired" left off, only this time the first video is playing on a TV screen in a moth-ridden room. Cut to Metallica's "Moth into Flame," played in a dark room full of pendant light-bulbs—subtle. To paraphrase an esteemed music critic who also wrote about a lightbulb-filled room, light confirms Metallica's reality and gives birth to their form.

"ATLAS, RISE!" (2016, DIR. CLARK EDDY)

Footage of Metallica recording at their HQ in San Rafael, having the kind of fun you didn't think was possible for them during *Some Kind of Monster*. Fans will enjoy playing *Where's Waldo?* with the Metallica memorabilia spread all over the studio—is that James' "MORE BEER!" Explorer from the Damaged Justice tour on the wall? It's also cool to get a glimpse of the fan-made flags from different countries, like a lucha libra "Mexitallica" or a Brazilian banner emblazoned with Cliff Burton's face. Someone holds up a "Hammit's [*sic*] on FIRE" sign during the solo—as if you couldn't already tell.

"NOW THAT WE'RE DEAD" (2016, DIR. HERRING AND HERRING)

"Now That We're Dead" starts as a performance video before shifting into distorted shots of the band's faces, projected onto each other in different colors, like the *Hardwired . . . to Self Destruct* album art. Lars met directors Herring and Herring when he hired them to shoot his 2015 wedding. They gifted Lars and his wife Jessica with a strange picture of the couple superimposed onto each other, which Lars then showed to James. Take it from there.

"DREAM NO MORE" (2016, DIR. TOM KIRK)

Invisible man–type silhouettes go through their day with a number of visuals haunting them from the inside, including footage of Metallica performing "Dream No More." A tribute to those of us who live with Metallica in our heads all day?

"HALO ON FIRE" (2016, DIR. HERRING AND HERRING)

This black-and-white *Fight Club*–type story follows a young woman stepping into a ring with an opponent who may be an old man, or another young woman, or maybe both? Her challengers get scarier, intercut with shots of Metallica performing in the same crowd cheering on her fights. "Halo on Fire" is best experienced on tour, where clips from the video often make their way into Metallica's LED screens.

"CONFUSION" (2016, DIR. CLAIRE MARIE VOGEL)

A woman in an office imagines herself a soldier in a war zone, or is the soldier imagining herself back at her day job? Metallica's use of war-themed videos was tiring by "The Day That Never Comes" (how could anyone forget or surpass "One"?), but "Confusion" benefits from star Breeda

Wool's unguarded performance, video vet Vogel's (Courtney Barnett, the Regrettes) direction, and a surprise ending.

"MANUNKIND" (2016, DIR. JONAS ÅKERLUND)

Metallica reunited with Bathory drummer-turned-director Jonas Åkerlund for a video that doubled as a preview for *Lords of Chaos*, Åkerlund's film adaptation of the controversial Norwegian black metal book by Michael Moynihan and Didrik Søderlind. It's odd to see actors dressed as the black metal legends Mayhem, complete with corpse paint, a severed pig's head, Petrine Crosses, and even some human gore, playing a midtempo Metallica groove. Kvltists, including (*Lords of Chaos* spoiler alert) surviving members of Mayhem, were not happy about it. Are Metallica honoring black metal in "ManUNkind"? Are they mocking it? Metallica has not commented, but they got people to argue about their music video.

"HERE COMES REVENGE" (2016, DIR. JESSICA COPE)

The inspiration for "Here Comes Revenge" might've been too grim and personal to depict, even in a Metallica video. James told Marky Ramone in a Virgin Radio interview that he'd connected with a couple whose Metallica fanatic daughter had been killed by a drunk driver, provoking him to wonder how people handle a tragedy that horrific. Instead, we get an animated dressed animals story from Cope, whose prog-metal cred includes animated videos for Devin Townsend and Skyharbor. For Metallica, Cope created a wolf and deer tale with an ambiguous revenge near the end.

"AM I SAVAGE?" (2016, DIR. HERRING AND HERRING)

This dreamlike video shows a man who lives and works with people in creepy all-white zentai suits. The protagonist is the only one without a zentai, but he's also the only one—on camera, at least—to succumb to his insane impulses.

"MURDER ONE" (2016, DIR. ROBERT VALLEY)

Like the song itself, the "Murder One" video is a Lemmy tribute that doesn't quite live up to the man. Mediocre animation turns Mr. Kilmister into a cartoon that he never was on record or in person. It's a bad sign that the cartoon has to resort to captions to tell the story, and worse that it has to repeat several of the same shots and images. There wasn't enough to say about the guy who founded fucking Motörhead in one six-minute video?

"SPIT OUT THE BONE" (2016, DIR. PHIL MUCCI)

Metallica's third *Hardwired* video based on a woman kicking enemies' asses looks like a student film, and a pretty campy one at that (is that alien beast thing really flashing metal horns? And now it's singing James' part?). But as far as *War of the Worlds* fan fiction goes, "Spit Out the Bone" is entertaining. It will surprise exactly no one to learn that star Mindy Kelly was a stunt actor for *The Dark Knight Rises* and the *Daredevil* series.

"LORDS OF SUMMER" (2016, DIR. BRETT MURRAY)

In the days leading up to the *Hardwired . . . to Self Destruct*'s release, Metallica debuted videos every couple of hours for each remaining *Hardwired* song and even "Lords of Summer," the 2014 demo digital single/ limited edition vinyl they rerecorded for a *Hardwired* bonus disc. "Lords of Summer" updates their old Black Album video philosophy—Metallica onstage—for the twenty-first century, playing arenas by circumstance and clubs by choice, with fireworks, black beach balls, and Trujillo getting pied for his birthday celebration. More than Metallica's previous videos, we get shots of the crowds jumping in unison and screaming their minds out, a reminder than even a fine song like "Lords of Summer" crushes when James, Lars, Kirk, and Robert bring it. Since "One," Metallica's videos have been a mixed bag, just as their records have. Their live show is not.

29

ALL SINNERS, A FUTURE

Hardwired . . . to Self-Destruct

"I don't really get what people hear about the connection of old stuff to this. It's just us writing the next record, and it feels right . . . We're not interested in redoing what we've done in the past—embracing the past, celebrating it, enjoying that we had done that, but trying to recreate it is not interesting to us."

—James Hetfield

Don't be fooled by the title. If Metallica were facing death on *Death Magnetic*, *Hardwired . . . to Self-Destruct* sees them roaring into life, faster, louder, angrier, weirder, and quoting more Oscar Wilde (*A Woman of No Importance* in "Now That We're Dead") than before. Metallica know we're fucked and shit out of luck, a rhyme that makes James sound like Satan in *Tenacious D in The Pick of Destiny*, but damned if Metallica aren't going to slam right into the abyss with their hardest thrashing. Lars even brought blast beats.

It's Metallica's first studio album for Blackened, their own label they launched in 2012 for ownership of all their masters (its first release was *Quebec Magnetic*). Fittingly, it's the most "Metallica" Metallica record to date, a nearly all-encompassing tribute to their good and bad records with eyes on the future. *Hardwired . . . to Self-Destruct* plays like a Metallica anthology of new songs, from *Kill 'Em All*'s fearless rage through *Master of Puppets'* complexity and the Black Album's arena-crushers. Suggesting they learned nothing from *Lulu*, it's Metallica's second-ever double album of all-new material, despite being short enough, at seventy-seven minutes, to fit on a single disc. Not many bands wait until middle age to release their first studio double album, much less two in a row. James has said this was for sound purposes, Lars says it's for artistic purposes, and fans wonder whether maybe Metallica really did know how much people hated *Lulu* and just didn't care. Would it really be a Metallica record if they didn't figure out new ways to piss people off?

The "Metallica" font on the cover, called the "glitch logo" by T-shirt sellers, shows the name slightly disjointed and torn apart, showing a band fighting to stay on track while any number of adversaries—age, death, accidents, infighting—tries to break it up. Spoiler: Metallica wins.

When thunderous first single "Hardwired," Metallica's shortest new song since *Kill 'Em All*'s "Motorbreath," dropped August 18, 2016, pundits ranging from CNN's W. Kamau Bell ("Finally a song that perfectly describes my mood in these hectic, awful times in which we live. Thank you Metallica!") to MSNBC's Rachel Maddow ("God bless the great Metallica for the new perfect soundtrack for 2016—just in time") chimed in with praises. Like George Romero zombie movies or James Bond films, Metallica records reflect the times they exist in, encapsulating many sentiments but expressing the state of the world and political climate well enough to voice the moods of an era's top pundits. With A Tribe Called Quest's *We Got It from Here . . . Thank You 4 Your Service*, released one week earlier in November 2016, *Hardwired . . . to Self-Destruct* turns on the news, two early 1990s breakthrough artists from opposing coasts, complementing each other with their album titles, making harder music in a harder America.

The easy path would be to build on their *Death Magnetic* comeback and pretend *Lulu* didn't happen, so of course Metallica took the *Lulu* path of jamming songs out in the studio as opposed to writing them beforehand, with rehearsal takes like "Now That We're Dead" and "Dream No More" making the record. When James sings "I don't recognize me anymore" in "Am I Savage?," he knows many of his band's fans don't either. In a Marky Ramone interview, Kirk estimated that 95 percent of his *Hardwired* solos were improvised. *Hardwired* is also the first Metallica record since *Kill 'Em All* on which Kirk didn't have any writing credits, either due to his having lost hundreds of riffs on a phone he left in a cab in Denmark or to James and Lars' stranglehold on the band (Rob gets a sole credit for his finger-picked, Cliff-like intro in "ManUNkind"). Fighting for his place as he did thirty-three years earlier, Kirk makes every second of his leads count, elevating "Moth into Flame" and "Atlas, Rise!" to wah heaven.

The lyrics ain't subtle, "not Shakespeare," as James told *So What!*, before citing the Bard in the same interview to describe "Now That We're Dead," although the song's Romeo and Juliet in eternity themes are more *Agents of Fortune* than Forest of Arden. "Murder One" is a Lemmy tribute for his biggest fans, alluding to Lem's songs, tattoos, autobiography, and gear (his amp names included Hammer, Killer, No Remorse, and Murder One, which was tough enough to blast Lemmy's Rickenbacker for over thirty years before blowing out in 2007) while faltering musically. Metallica would've been better off trying an original song in their honoree's style, as Motörhead did on 1991's standout "R.A.M.O.N.E.S." They celebrate more forebears on "Am I Savage?," nodding to both Diamond Head's "Am I Evil?" and Danzig's "Am I Demon" (which James has sung backup on live), and almost named the album *Inheritance* after a lyric from the song. "My good intention here is to teach you something, and then when you don't want it, I get angry," James described his parenting to Stefan Chirazi. "It's more about me. So from my dad using anger as a big tool in the house to be heard, same with me. That was my inheritance and I started to pass it down to my boy, and I stopped."

Elsewhere Metallica confronts PTSD ("Confusion"), morality ("Halo on Fire"), loss ("Here Comes Revenge," inspired in part by Morgan Harrington, a kidnapped and murdered young Metallica fan whose case Metallica aided with PSAs and a reward for information about the eventually convicted killer), and modern media through a Lovecraftian lens ("Dream No More," the *Godfather Part III* of Metallica Cthulu songs). James got the album title from a recovering addict friend, a detail that gained scrutiny with James' 2019 rehab, but Metallica is always dying to live. No surprise that the record's best tribute is its Amy Winehouse retelling "Moth into

Flame," with soaring, Maiden-esque guitarmonies carrying prime Metallica riffage. In separate interviews, James and Lars both confirmed making sure the record passed the "car test" before release, appropriate for an album that's getting people somewhere.

"We're never satisfied," James stated before the Worldwired tour. "We want it to be the best or we can't stand behind it."

Hardwired . . . to Self-Destruct is not quite the top of the world comeback fans have been hoping for. Like most double records, and every Metallica record since *Load*, it goes on too long. Some listeners would argue that Metallica themselves have gone on too long, something James predicted in 1993 ("There's no doubt Metallica will be around, probably longer than it should be. . . . I don't know what we're gonna do if we're not together. It's a scary thought."). But part of what makes *Hardwired . . . to Self-Destruct* a record only Metallica could make is the way it produces the drama of loving a band as gloriously complicated as Metallica. You don't get "Hardwired" without "Murder One." You don't get that awesome groove on "ManUNkind" without the stupid name James saddled it with. You don't get *Master of Puppets* without *St. Anger* either, or the band that thrived with Robert Trujillo without the band that hazed Jason Newsted. "They have more fun when the idea of things falling apart is in the air," recalled the *Hardwired* producer and *Death Magnetic* engineer Greg Fidelman in *Billboard*, and in Metallica things fall apart often. But millions keep watching and listening.

And on *Hardwired . . . to Self-Destruct*, Metallica remind us why. Right when you're sure they put all the best songs on disc one, James turns a lyric from the British punkers Charged GBH's cannibalism ode "Passenger on the Menu" into "Spit Out the Bone," a two-fisted, multipart adventure with the action and shock of Metallica's best music. Originally ten minutes before the band worked it down to a perfect seven, "Spit Out the Bone" uncovers a strengthened Metallica, with better riffs and composition. A professed favorite of all four members, "Spit Out the Bone" earned internet clamor for a live performance almost immediately upon release (it debuted live almost a year later, in fall 2017), and became Metallica's fifth consecutive *Hardwired* hit, from a band whose previous record had zero. Bookended by Metallica's two best songs of the twenty-first century, including the last song written for the record ("Hardwired" kicked "Lords of Summer" off the final tracklist), Metallica prove themselves stronger than they'd been in years. For all the thrills *Hardwired . . . to Self-Destruct* provides, the most exciting part is that Metallica is still improving.

㉚

WE'LL NEVER STOP, WE'LL NEVER QUIT

The Legacy and Future of Metallica

"I look at someone like Iggy Pop, he's still out there going crazy. It can be done."

—James Hetfield

If you own *Kill 'Em All* (and if you don't, by Lemmy what are you waiting for), you can likely complete the "Whiplash" lyrics in this chapter's title, Metallica's only self-namecheck on record. "We'll never stop, we'll never quit, cause we're Metallica." Or if you've seen them perform, you'd complete it the way James has been singing it for decades—"We'll never stop, we'll never quit . . . cause *you're* Metallica."

Corny? Sure. I can't hear James sing it that way without thinking of Spïñal Tap on *The Simpsons*, trying to tell the crowd that they're the sixth member of the band (yes, Metallica's fan club is even called "Fifth Member"). Metallica's corny sometimes, as well as embarrassing, disappointing, or just downright bad. But they're always Metallica, and they're always real. Whether it's thrash or rock or *Lulu* or a symphony, it's Metallica.

As far as I've found, James has been singing "cause you're Metallica" as far back as October 31, 1983, at Keystone in Palo Alto, another venue Metallica has outlasted, just a few months after *Kill 'Em All*'s release. "Look at all the Kings here," James says, acknowledging several attendees who had the same idea to dress as Mercyful Fate's frontman for tonight's big

Halloween show. James dedicates the first-ever performance of "Creeping Death" to them.

It must have been thrilling to be dressed as a Satanic metal hero, seeing the greatest metal band in the world that night, sharing a room with a bunch of other fans who loved metal enough to know who Metallica were and what King Diamond looked like in 1983. But for Metallica, it's even cooler to be a fan. They didn't dress like King Diamond, they dressed like kids going to see King Diamond. When James introduces another new song at the Keystone show, a fan yells out "Fight Fire!" having either followed Metallica close enough or traded tapes to know the names of songs that won't be released for another few months. It's a touching moment captured on the *Kill 'Em All* box set, a reminder of the kind of devotion Metallica both inspired and exhibited by putting the four most dedicated metalheads in the world on a small stage.

Since *Ride the Lightning*, other metal bands have been marketing themselves as heavier, faster, louder, more metal, or more dangerous than Metallica, which only confirms how much nearly every metal act—really, everyone with the possible exception of Black Sabbath—lives in Metallica's shadow. Any metal band can claim, and many have, to be better or more badass than Metallica. But no metal band touched as many people or offended people as much as Metallica does. Every Satanic black metal band in the world combined can't even come close.

Every time Metallica falls on their gazillionaire asses, we can be thankful they take risks, follow their artistic visions, and don't concern themselves with how they're perceived. If that results in "We Did It Again" sometimes, we can deal. It doesn't diminish their great records at all. Life has given Metallica a profound sense of what is and is not important, which we can see in the fact that they're game for all sorts of silly shit. They'll sing Rihanna's "Diamonds" or "Part of Your World" from *The Little Mermaid* with Billy Eichner on *Carpool Karaoke*, or pretend to be washed up in a *SportsCenter* ad. Fans who hoped James would punch out Mötley Crüe's Nikki Sixx in the eighties can now hear him laughing about his gray hair with Nikki on *Sixx Sense*. Younger bands can mock Metallica for playing "Enter Sandman" with children's instruments on *The Tonight Show* with the Roots and Jimmy Fallon (Vice President Joe Biden, Fallon's guest that night, thanked "my house band, Metallica" on social media). But no one who makes fun of Metallica wrote *Kill 'Em All*, *Ride the Lighting*, *Master of Puppets*, . . . *And Justice for All*, or the Black Album.

They're not impossibly cool, like Motörhead. They're not blessed with the rock god charisma of Ozzy or going to offend your parents as much as Slayer. They're going to embarrass you sometimes, even often. They'll do a Big Four tour in the summer and release *Lulu* in the fall. While writing this book, and probably still while you're reading it, the Wikipedia entry for "Selling out" has a picture of Metallica. But Metallica keeps getting bigger, outlasting trends and staying together longer than almost every other band of their stature. They don't play two nights in a row anymore, not because they're slowing down, but because they're adapting for the long haul ("An investment in our sanity," James says). The famous "Alcoholica: Drank 'Em All" shirt is not available on Metallica's website, but you can get an "M is for Metallica: Spill 'Em All" onesie, a baby bottle with milk replacing the hammer and blood. Old age is always wakeful; as if, the longer linked with life, the less Metallica has to do with aught that looks like death.

They're one of the biggest bands that can still bring spontaneity to a stadium show. On the Worldwired tour, Kirk and Rob play cover songs corresponding to the towns and cities they play, sometimes something goofy like "Take on Me" for Oslo or digging out Donnie Iris and the Cruisers' "Ah! Leah!" to thrill Pittsburgh. They don't care if nobody outside of Sioux Falls, South Dakota, knows about Indigenous' "Things We Do," Metallica will learn it just for that crowd. Like a lot of what Metallica does, it sometimes infuriates internet commentators. "Do You Want to Hear the Worst Prince Cover of All Time?" a *GQ* headline asked after Rob and Kirk bombed "When Doves Cry" in Minneapolis. It's not Metallica's best moment, but everyone in the crowd is cheering.

"I don't know what else to do," James said in an NRK TV interview. "It's like breathing, to me, music itself is like oxygen, I have to hear it, I have to feel it, I have to play it . . . this album's good, the next one's gonna be better. I just know it."

Everybody's Metallica is different. Writing a Metallica book, one learns that a surprising amount of people love Metallica as the band whose fans beat up the boy band in the *Josie and the Pussycats* movie, or can show you the Fountains of Wayne song where Adam Schlesinger daydreams about hanging with James, Jason, Kirk, and Lars. Volunteering with All Within My Hands, one meets college kids who want to know what the World Magnetic tour was like and older fans who swear the Dave Mustaine lineup once crashed on their couch. On the Metallica episode of the *Kids React* web series, a young girl enthuses over "Hardwired" ("It gets you in the zone!"). Years from now, she might remember it the same way some of us remember the first time we heard "Battery." Another fan's book could have entire chapters on Metallica merch, gear, Orion fest, *Guitar Hero: Metallica*, or Blackened Whiskey and Enter Night Pilsner, all integral parts of many people's Metallica stories. Watching someone who doesn't speak a word of English bring down the house for Saturday night karaoke because he knows every syllable of "Enter Sandman," it's clear that no book could begin to summarize all the ways this band does good for people, every single day of its existence.

But if anything can be said about Metallica, it might be that they give their fans a voice. Not a Metallica message to spread through the world, but our own voices, coaxed out and expressed by the power of Metallica's music. Metallica tears down musical, cultural, institutional, regional, and political boundaries, but they also tear down our own.

"When Metallica get together and plug in they just turn into these big teenagers," Robert smiled in 2020. "It feels like there's something new happening."

"It's not just a musical bond, you know," Kirk said after *Some Kind of Monster*. "I really can't picture my life without those guys."

"It's too easy to say something like 'Yeah, we don't care if the album doesn't sell one copy or 10,000 or 10 million,'" Lars stated in *Hit Parader*. "But at the end of the day, the thing that matters is that you make a record that's completely yours from beginning to end, with no sacrifices, no compromises, no corners cut."

"Our philosophy is 'think for yourself' at the end of the day," James told Sweden's SVT Nyheter. "Do what you think feels right. I really believe that humans will survive. I have a lot of faith in mankind that we will overcome and adapt—whatever it is; whether it's man-made or God-made, or Earth/Mother Nature—we have a lot of smart people on this planet that will make something good out of bad."

Forty years after their first rehearsal, Metallica are still looking at the worst of humanity and making something great from it. That's why people love Metallica more than they love making fun of them. It's why their music (and tons of charity work) changes lives daily. It's why their best records are still setting trends, and if their newer ones aren't, they're not chasing anyone else's either. But what do you expect? They're fucking Metallica. On *Kill 'Em All*'s most famous song, Metallica asserted that their murderous instincts wouldn't go away until their dreams were fulfilled. Hundreds of songs, thousands of shows, and millions of fans later, that looks like never.

BIBLIOGRAPHY

BOOKS

Alago, Michael. *I Am Michael Alago: Breathing Music. Signing Metallica. Beating Death*. Backbeat, 2020.

Berlinger, Joe, and Milner, Greg. *Metallica: This Monster Lives: The Inside Story of Some Kind of Monster*. Macmillan, 2004.

Blush, Steven, and Petros, George. *American Hardcore: A Tribal History*. Feral House, 2010.

Brannigan, Paul, and Winwood, Ian. *Birth School Metallica Death, Volume 1: The Biography*. Vol. 1. Constellation, 2013.

Brannigan, Paul, and Winwood, Ian. *Into the Black: The Inside Story of Metallica (1991–2014)*. Da Capo Press, 2014.

Chirazi, Steffan (ed.). *So What!: The Good, the Mad, and the Ugly*. Broadway, 2004.

Christie, Ian. *Sound of the Beast: The Complete Headbanging History of Heavy Metal*. Arcana, 2009.

Crocker, Chris. *Metallica: The Frayed Ends of Metal*. St. Martin's Press, 1993.

Dome, Malcolm, and Wall, Mick. *Metallica: The Music and the Mayhem*. Omnibus, 2011.

Doughton, K. J. *Metallica Unbound*. Hachette UK, 2008.

Eglington, Mark. *So Let It Be Written: The Biography of Metallica's James Hetfield*. Lesser Gods, 2017.

Ellefson, David, and McIver, Joel. *My Life with Deth: Discovering Meaning in a Life of Rock & Roll*. Howard Books, 2014.

Gaines, Donna. *Teenage Wasteland: Suburbia's Dead End Kids*. University of Chicago Press, 1998.

Gilmour, Michael J. (ed.). *Call Me the Seeker: Listening to Religion in Popular Music.* Continuum, 2005.

Guitar World (eds.). *Metallica: 30 Years of the World's Greatest Heavy Metal Band.* Time Home Entertainment, 2013.

Halfin, Ross. *The Ultimate Metallica.* Chronicle Books, 2010.

Hammett, Kirk (ed.). *It's Alive! Classic Horror and Sci-Fi Movie Posters from the Kirk Hammett Collection.* Skira Rizzoli, 2017.

Hammett, Kirk, and Chirazi, Steffan. *Too Much Horror Business.* Harry N. Abrams, 2012.

Hermes, Will, and Michel, Sia (eds.). *Spin: 20 Years of Alternative Music: Original Writing on Rock, Hip-Hop, Techno, and Beyond.* Three Rivers Press, 2005.

Ian, Scott. *I'm the Man: The Story of That Guy from Anthrax.* Da Capo Press, 2014.

Ingham, Chris, and Udo, Tommy. *Metallica: The Stories Behind the Biggest Songs.* Carlton, 2009.

Irwin, William (ed.). *Metallica and Philosophy: A Crash Course in Brain Surgery.* Vol. 71. John Wiley & Sons, 2009.

Kilmister, Lemmy. *White Line Fever: The Autobiography.* Citadel Press, 2004.

Konow, David. *Bang Your Head: The Rise and Fall of Heavy Metal.* Three Rivers Press, 2002.

Kot, Greg. *Ripped: How the Wired Generation Revolutionized Music.* Simon & Schuster, 2009.

Masciotra, David. *Metallica's* Metallica. Bloomsbury Academic, 2015.

McIver, Joel. *Justice for All: The Truth About Metallica.* Omnibus Press, 2014.

McIver, Joel. *The 100 Greatest Metal Guitarists.* Jawbone Press, 2008.

McIver, Joel. *To Live Is to Die: The Life and Death of Metallica's Cliff Burton.* Jawbone Press, 2016.

Mustaine, Dave. *Mustaine: A Life in Metal.* Singapore Books, 2011.

Pillsbury, Glenn T. *Damage, Incorporated: Metallica and the Production of Musical Identity.* Routledge, 2006.

Popoff, Martin. *Metallica: The Complete Illustrated History.* Voyageur Press, 2013.

Putterford, Mark. *Metallica in Their Own Words.* Omnibus Press, 1994.

Rotfeld, Arthur. *The Art of Kirk Hammett.* Cherry Lane Music, 1997.

Stenning, Paul. *Metallica: All That Matters.* Plexus Publishing Limited, 2010.

Taylor, Matt. *Metallica: Back to the Front: A Fully Authorized Visual History of the* Master of Puppets *Album and Tour.* Insight Editions, 2016.

Van Sloten, John. *The Day Metallica Came to Church: Searching for the Everywhere God in Everything.* Square Inch, 2010.

Wall, Mick. *Enter Night: A Biography of Metallica.* St. Martin's Press, 2011.

Walser, Robert. *Running with the Devil: Power, Gender, and Madness in Heavy Metal Music.* Wesleyan University Press, 1993.

Wiederhorn, Jon, and Turman, Katherine. *Louder Than Hell: The Definitive Oral History of Metal.* It Books, 2013.

FILM AND TV

Hired Gun. Dir. Fran Strine. 2016.
Get Thrashed: The Story of Thrash Metal Dir. Rick Ernst. 2016.
Jaco. Dir. Paul Marchand and Stephen Kijak. 2014.
Metallica: In Their Own Words. Dir. Matthew Ginsburg. 2009.
Metallica: The Early Years. Spotify. 2016.
Murder in the Front Row. Dir. Adam Dubin. 2019.
Rumble: The Indians Who Rocked the World. Dir. Catherine Bainbridge. 2017.
VH1 Behind the Music, Megadeth. Prod. George Moll and Paul Gallagher. 2001.
VH1 Behind the Music, Metallica. Dir. Michael McNamara. 1998.
Who the Fuck Is That Guy? The Fabulous Journey of Michael Alago. Dir. Drew Stone. 2017.

WEBSITES

Artist Direct
BBC
Blabbermouth
BuzzFeed
Consequence of Sound
Deezer.com
ExclaimTV
FearFestEvil
Forbes.com
Grammy.com
Guitar Center
HumoNegro.com
Invisible Oranges
Loudersound
Metal Injection
Metallica.com
Metallicaworld.co.uk

MetalSucks
Metclub.com
Metontour.com
Metsanitarium.com
Much.com
MusicVideoWire.com
Noisey
NPR.org
NRK
Pitchfork.com
PsychologyToday.com
RobertChristgau.com
RogerEbert.com
TeamRock.com
TheRinger.com
Vice
YouTube.com

MAGAZINES

Alternative Press
Brave Words & Bloody Knuckles
Circus

Classic Rock
Clique
CMJ New Music Monthly

Creem
Creem Metal
Drum!
Entertainment Weekly
Faces Rocks
GQ
Grinder
Guitar Player
Guitar Sound
Guitar World
Hard N' Heavy
The Headbanger
Hit Parader
Kerrang!
Kick Ass
Loud
Masters of Metal
Maximum Guitar
Melody Maker
Metal Attack
Metal Forces
Metal Hammer
Metal Mania
Metal Maniac
Metal Maniacs
Metal Militia
Metal Muscle
Metal Rules

Metallion
Modern Drummer
Music Connction
Musik
The New Yorker
NME
Planet Rock
Playboy
Q
The Quietus
Raw and Uncut
Revolver
Rhythm
RIP
Rock Hard
Rock Sound
Rolling Stone
So What!
Sounds
Spin
Terrorizer
Thrash Metal
Thrasher
US Rocker
The Village Voice
VirginMega Magazine
Whiplash

NEWSPAPERS

The Chicago Maroon
The Chicago Sun-Times
The Chicago Tribune
Expressen
The Los Angeles Times
The Mercury News
The New York Daily News

The New York Times
The San Diego Union-Tribune
The Straits Times
The Sun
The Toronto Star
USA Today
The Washington Post

INDEX

ABOUT THE AUTHOR

Ben Apatoff is a New York writer and educator whose work has appeared in Metal Injection, MetalSucks, and the Morbid Anatomy Museum. He was born the summer Metallica released *Kill 'Em All*.